# Riding *in the* Shadows *of* Saints

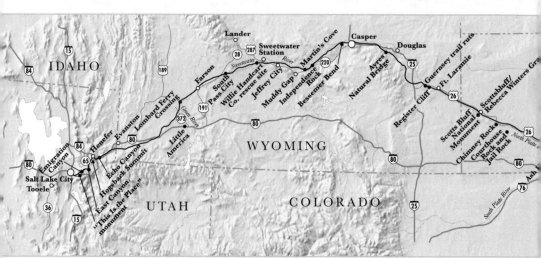

# Riding *in the* Shadows *of* Saints

 CROWN PUBLISHERS   New York

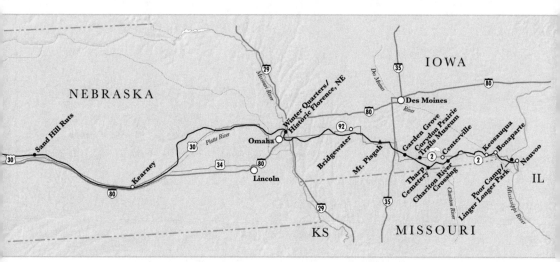

*A Woman's Story of
Motorcycling the Mormon Trail*

JANA RICHMAN

Portions of this work have previously appeared in *Creative Nonfiction*, issue 20;
*Quarterly West*, issue 54; and *In Fact: The Best of Creative Nonfiction*.

Library of Congress Cataloging-in-Publication Data
Richman, Jana, 1956–
Riding in the shadows of Saints : a woman's story of motorcycling
the Mormon Trail / Jana Richman.
1. Richman, Jana, 1956—Travel—West (U.S.)   2. Richman, Jana, 1956—Family.
3. Motorcycling—West (U.S.)   4. Historic sites—West (U.S.)   5. West
(U.S.)—Description and travel.   6. Mormon Pioneer National Historic Trail—
Description and travel.   7. Mormon women—West (U.S.)—History—19th century.
8. Women pioneers—West (U.S.)—History—19th century.   9. Mormons—West
(U.S.)—History—19th century.   10. West (U.S.)—History, Local.   I. Title.
F595.3.R53 2005
917.804'34'092—dc22                                          2004022557

ISBN 1-4000-4542-8

Printed in the United States of America

Design by Karen Minster

Map by Mark Stein Studios

10 9 8 7 6 5 4 3 2 1

First Edition

*For Mom*

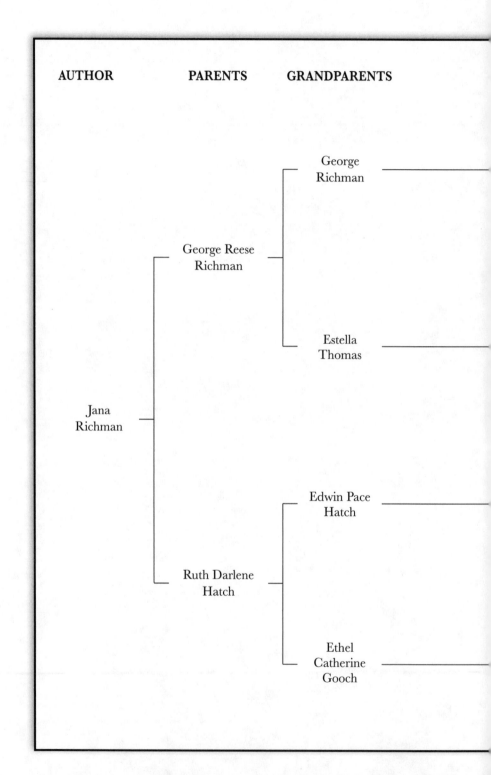

AUTHOR   PARENTS   GRANDPARENTS

George
Richman

George Reese
Richman

Estella
Thomas

Jana
Richman

Edwin Pace
Hatch

Ruth Darlene
Hatch

Ethel
Catherine
Gooch

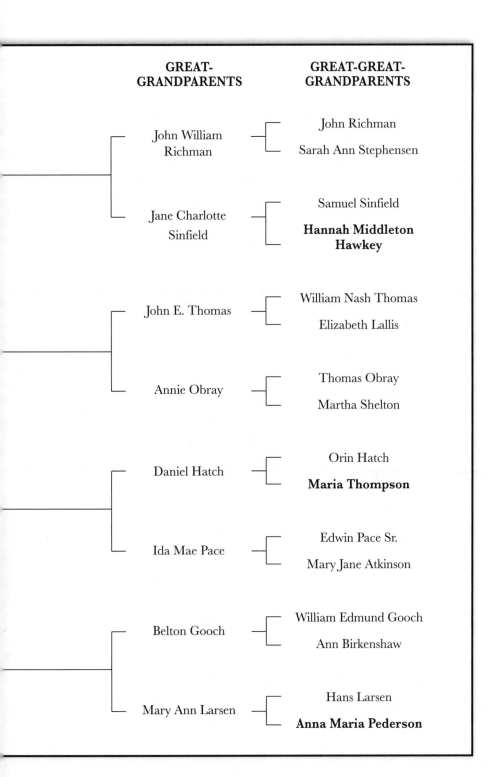

| GREAT-GRANDPARENTS | GREAT-GREAT-GRANDPARENTS |
|---|---|

**GREAT-GRANDPARENTS**

**GREAT-GREAT-GRANDPARENTS**

John William Richman
- John Richman
- Sarah Ann Stephensen

Jane Charlotte Sinfield
- Samuel Sinfield
- **Hannah Middleton Hawkey**

John E. Thomas
- William Nash Thomas
- Elizabeth Lallis

Annie Obray
- Thomas Obray
- Martha Shelton

Daniel Hatch
- Orin Hatch
- **Maria Thompson**

Ida Mae Pace
- Edwin Pace Sr.
- Mary Jane Atkinson

Belton Gooch
- William Edmund Gooch
- Ann Birkenshaw

Mary Ann Larsen
- Hans Larsen
- **Anna Maria Pederson**

# Acknowledgments

PUTTING ONESELF IN A POSITION OF RELYING ON THE generosity of strangers is a humbling experience. On this trip, I carried with me innumerable warnings of dangerous men stalking vulnerable women along highways and at rest stops. I provided the perfect opportunity for such men: a woman traveling alone, small in stature, drawing attention to herself by mode of travel, lingering in parking lots, and preoccupied with pulling on gloves and helmet and strapping down gear.

I could not have made this journey before making the conscious decision beforehand to trust in the goodness of humanity the same way I trusted in the integrity of my tires. Neither let me down.

On September 11, 2001, the shock from a morning of death and chaos on the East Coast quickly spread west throughout the nation, seeping into the homes and consciousness of every American and sending people into a collective state of fear and vulnerability. Prior to this event, my level of fear and vulnerability were already stretched tightly, and after that day I struggled with a high possibility that fear would turn into paralysis.

The kind residents of a small farming community in Iowa kept that from happening. Their small and simple acts of kindness turned out to be gifts of great magnitude.

I thank the folks of Bridgewater for embracing me in the midst of madness as if my story were of great import. In treating it so, they cloaked me in reasonable calm and normalcy, enabling me to function from one day to the next. Those who took part in my rescue were Beverly and Jake Pote, Beth and Wilbur Christensen, Kenny Cousins, Lillian Nichols, and especially Gary Antisdel, who rendered pieces of my story with genuine care and interest as he drove me over the muddy Iowa back roads on September 11, making me feel protected and safe on that dismal day.

All of those kind strangers were brought to me by Dave and Phyllis Nichols, who within five minutes of meeting me turned over the keys to their house and their car, fed me, and gave me safe haven for as long as I needed it. I have nothing to offer them in return except my immense gratitude and a copy of this book, with the inscription to Dave: "To a genuine stud, clear-thinking politically and a dear friend of my liberal-minded father," as instructed and promised.

The day after I left Bridgewater, I made my way to Lincoln, Nebraska, and was taken in by another friend, Pat Emile, allowing me a couple more much-needed days of care and companionship before I struck out alone again for the West.

At the beginning of my journey, Deborah Stoddard and Cindy Lefton put up with a neurotic and frazzled woman functioning only on pure bravado for more days than they had originally agreed to, all the while convincing me it brought them great pleasure to do so. Debbie carries a big, generous heart, and I've been the lucky recipient of it more times than I can count.

Also in St. Louis, a nod of thanks to the folks at BMW Motorrad for responding immediately to my calls for help and getting me on the road as quickly as possible, and at the other end of the trail, the folks at the Mormon Church archives for their assistance with finding historical information.

Prior to the trip, several people read my work and encouraged the project, never exhibiting a glimmer of doubt in either my riding or writing abilities. Gregory McNamee, Fenton Johnson, and Alison Hawthorne Deming have all offered a steady source of advice and encouragement over the years.

My dear friend and brilliant poet and essayist Donna Steiner offered support in innumerable ways, including sending daily pithy e-mails, reading drafts of the manuscript, and offering to slap me whenever I slogged into a state of inertia and self-pity.

Someone once gave me the very sound advice that I should find an agent who believes deeply in my work and is passionate about his own. I've never doubted those qualities in Doug Stewart. He has been a reassuring friend to me every step of the way, taking the worry out of the business of publishing and allowing me to concentrate on the writing. He's a pure joy to work with.

Emily Loose embraced the vision from the beginning and offered great insight during the short time we worked together. Caroline Sincerbeaux picked up where Emily left off, producing a painless transition and making those horror stories of switching editors mid-process untrue. I thank them both for their knowledge and professionalism.

My immeasurable gratitude goes to the people who create and support places like Norcroft, Hedgebrook, and the Millay Colony for the Arts, all of which gave me essential time, space, food, and solitude. My thanks also to the community at Pecos Benedictine Monastery for always welcoming me back. Ken Foster and Lynette Cook Francis, two of the greatest bosses a working girl could ever ask for, always made sure I had the time and flexibility needed to flee to such retreats.

The spirits of my female ancestors—especially Maria Thompson, Hannah Middleton Hawkey, and Anna Maria Larsen—gently guided me on this journey with their persistence, their grit, and most notably with their faith. I thank my cousin Kaylene Allen Griffin for the hundreds of hours she's spent pulling together the records and the writings of the Hatch family.

My father, Reese Richman, has probably influenced me more than I'm willing to admit. He was a dreamer who entertained no hindrance in pursuit of the dream. I am much the same.

Toward the end of the writing of this book, Steve Defa recognized in me the coalescence of my journey, my history, and my geography, and he took me home to live in the shadows of the Wasatch Mountains where I belong. I am humbled by the depth of his love and by his steady trust in the flow.

There are no words that can possibly carry the enormity of my indebtedness to two people: Darlene Richman and Will Rivera. My mother's love for me is unshakable, tried and true. Whatever combination of strength and softness I carry, whatever compassion I possess, comes from that love. She carries within her the spirit of the pioneering women of her family and does them proud, and through the quiet practice of faith, she has passed the legacy on to me.

Will has stood by my side through the wild and sometimes unpleasant exploration into my Mormon trappings and through all my confused attempts at defining myself leading up to it. I've unwittingly demanded sacrifices on his part, and he has given them in heroic silence. Simply said, he's a good guy. We philosophically differ in our approaches to life and now find ourselves on divergent paths. As always, he encourages me to continue down mine, knowing there's no other way for me, and I leave him in peace. All my love, my friend.

# Riding *in the* Shadows *of* Saints

# 1

THE MOTORCYCLE STALLS THEN LUNGES IN THE FAR right lane of Interstate 44 in St. Louis. I hold the grips tightly and give the throttle an angry twist with each cough of the engine, moving down the road in a series of violent jerks and thrusts, as if the bike and I are mad at each other and exchanging strikes. Jerk. Twist. Jerk. Twist. The toes of my right foot rest lightly on the back brake pedal to engage the flashing brake light. Still, several cars approach the rear tire with far too much speed before they dart into the next lane to avoid me. Sweat seeps out of my skin sucking the cotton of my long-sleeved T-shirt to my arms and torso under the heavy motorcycle jacket lined with "armor" around my shoulders, back, and elbows—the places most likely to hit pavement if I go down. None of that will make much difference if I'm hit from behind and catapulted through the air. Or worse yet, dragged under a semi and bounced between the underside of the truck and the road for a while before a tire finally tears me free and expels me off to the shoulder like a worn tire tread. I normally don't allow myself such images when I'm riding, but under the current circumstances, they seem impossible to avoid.

The bike has no intention of delivering me to my desired destination, so I surrender. I signal to my friend Debbie, who drives a lead car while looking anxiously in her rearview mirror and occasionally flashing a hopeful thumbs-up, eager to receive the same back from me. Instead I wave at her frantically and point to the next exit. She unnerves me by driving past the exit and pulling onto the shoulder of the freeway. I'm lost without her guidance, so I reluctantly pass the exit also and pull up behind her. The bike falls silent. She jumps out of her car and walks toward me.

"Get me the hell off this freeway!" I scream.

I can't imagine she can hear me through a full-face motorcycle helmet over the shriek of passing cars, but my message apparently gets through. The look on her face is one of sheer terror. She turns quickly and runs back to her car as if time were a factor in my safety. I flip up my face shield and yell at her, "I'm not gonna die!" She doesn't hear me, and I'd have a hard time convincing her anyway. As my father says, motorcycles are dangerous; any damn fool knows that.

"I'm not gonna die," I say quietly as I slap at my shield, which settles back over my face with a clack. Thankfully, the bike starts again, and I give the throttle four or five ambitious twists before putting it in gear and pulling back into freeway traffic.


DURING THE WEEKS before my trip, my mother called often, her voice always vibrating with false bravery and cheerfulness.

"All ready to go?" she asked during one call.

"Almost," I replied, trying to conjure up a strong, confident voice.

"What's Will going to do without you for so long?" she joked, not knowing what else to say.

"I don't know. He'll probably be happy to get rid of me for a while."

She started to reply, but her voice disintegrated and she began to cry, quietly at first, then gasping sobs. I pushed my fist into my stomach and curled into my reading chair. I hate doing this to her. She loves me so fiercely and dreads life without me so powerfully I am forever causing her anguish with my refusal to live a more *normal* life.

At one time I tried to give her that. I married my first husband right out of high school, and we bought a house less than a mile from my childhood home. My mother wasn't as happy about my marriage as I expected her to be, but I was wrapped up in the excitement of an adult life and never paused long enough to understand her hesitancy. I fully expected to drop into the life most rebellious Mormon kids follow: a few years of coffee and beer drinking before settling into marital bliss at the far edge of the teen years, followed in short order by a pregnancy sparking a tentative return to the Church, then another pregnancy triggering a temple marriage representing a full-blown return to the Church, then possibly another pregnancy. I had seen variations of this design numerous times and have since seen it work for most of my high school friends. Some take longer than others—two of my friends just married in the temple twenty-five years after I attended their civil marriage ceremony—but the pattern holds steady.

We referred to those who didn't follow this system as our town's oldest teenagers—still guzzling beer and dragging Main Street well into their thirties. Marriage and Mormonism seemed a better way than dragging Main to spend a life, and those were the only two options apparent to me in Tooele,

Utah, in 1974. A month before my nineteenth birthday I started into marriage with good intentions. I expected it would come naturally, that I would fall quickly into contentment, but I never did. Instead I felt stifled and restless, subconsciously suspecting life held other options but ill-equipped to explore them. My friends knew the answer to my uneasiness. "Have a baby," they said; instead I had an affair. Then I packed what seemed essential—some clothing, a toaster, a few dishes—into an Oldsmobile Ninety-Eight and left my hometown.

At that time and ever since, my mother has stood next to me, supporting every decision I've made, even the bad ones. Her love for me cannot be shifted. I have tested it time and time again; it remains solid. And here again, I fully expected her to understand, to put aside her own fears and indulge me without question. She did. But the tears came spontaneously.

At a loss for words, I listened to her sobs until I couldn't stand it anymore, then, desperate to relieve her fear, I asked if she intended to pray for me.

"Yes, of course!" she said.

"Then I'll be fine, right?"

"I'll pray for you every day you're gone. I've already started."

"Then there's no reason to worry."

It worked; she stopped crying. I promised to call often from the road and she promised to keep praying.


"MY MOTHER IS praying for me," I say aloud to no one in particular as I pull back into traffic on my hacking bike—if it were a person, it would be spitting up blood about now. I suggested it only for my mother's sake—the bit about praying—but for some unexplained reason, it calms me also. I'm unsure whether the comfort comes from the idea of a higher power watching over me or simply from the idea of my mother taking care of me. I was an anxious, uneasy child except in her presence. Only one photo of me as a toddler exists without her leg or her skirt lining the edge of the picture. In that one photo, I'm running straight for the lens with a tormented look on my tiny face. My mother apparently held the camera. I assigned her superhuman powers of protection and the first time I realized she couldn't protect me from the inevitable pain of adolescence, I was angry with her. But even as a teenager, when it was not cool to be seen with a parent, I never strayed far from my mother's side.

When I spoke to her on the phone that day I felt the same sense of comfort she provided me as a child. Upon her promise to pray for me, an immediate calm washed over me. My stomach stopped churning, and I slept soundly that night for the first time in the weeks of preparation for this trip. A few days later I saw a television program that spoke of a study with AIDS sufferers who fared significantly better than the control group when people—total strangers—prayed for them. They ruled out the mind-body connection because the people for whom prayers were being said knew nothing of the praying. The study was small, and I'm sure someone can give a rational explanation for the improved health of those who were prayed for, but I didn't want an explanation. I wanted to believe.

I personally have no relationship with God and no expectation that God will watch out for me. I have been known to pray in moments of fear and desperation in an "Oh, God, help me" sort of way, but I'm not one of those who cuts deals with God—just get me off this freeway and I'll go to church for the next twenty Sundays. I have to think anyone, God or not, would find that sort of bargaining unforgivably annoying, enough to smite someone on the spot. For the most part, I ignore the possibility of God in my everyday life. I think about it from time to time, but the issue is never forced. Chances are good that I can live my entire life without having to proclaim and defend my beliefs. Unlike my Mormon ancestors, I've never been given an ultimatum: Keep your faith and give up your home, possibly your life and the lives of your children, or give up your faith and keep everything dear to you. Religious persecution in our country has gone underground now. Still practiced, but much more discreetly than when my great-great-grandmothers were alive. I, and others like me, can live relatively easily from day to day without questioning ourselves too deeply on the difficulties that belief in God or a particular religion would represent. We can satisfy everyone, including ourselves, uttering a timid little cliché—*I believe in some sort of higher power*—while hedging our bets just in case. No one demands more of us.

I'm not averse to the possibility of God. But I don't quite know how to think about God, how to visualize God, how to frame God in my mind. I'm envious of people who seem able to do this without a problem, who seem so sure of God's structure. I've had plenty of instruction in this area, and I've followed it diligently—prayer, faith, fasting, blind acceptance—but nothing took. My gut feeling is that God is nothing like the God of my religious experience, but is instead something I can barely conceive of, something unbelievably simple and overwhelmingly complex at the same time.

Even as a child, when God was presented in probably the simplest way possible, God was utterly confusing to me. I wanted things concrete, understandable, preferably touchable and visible. I wanted clarity. I understood Jesus to be the son of God and there were plenty of pictures of Jesus floating around so that was momentarily clear. A picture of God would have helped. Next thing I knew we were praying to "our Lord, Jesus Christ," and up until then I had understood God to be "our Lord" and we were referring to Mary as the "mother of God" when I thought she was the mother of Jesus and God was the father of Jesus. About that time, the Holy Ghost was introduced and the title alone was more than a little disconcerting and never adequately explained. Every question seemed to get a different answer, and it would all be perfectly clear if I could just see a picture of all the players together. I searched the books in my primary classes, lots of pictures of Jesus, a few of Mary with Joseph—adding to the confusion—but that was it. Soon after that, I had a primary teacher who spoke of God as the trees and the stars and the mountains and the whole damn universe. She did nothing to help me at all. Then we started singing "Jesus Wants Me for a Sunbeam," and that idea scared the hell out of me, so I forced it all from my mind and did what I suspect most kids do in church—go through the motions that keep the adults happy by practicing mindless reverence.

There was a brief period when I was certain about God. It was a Friday night in October of 1969; I was thirteen years old. My older brother and sister were out for the evening, and I dropped into a frenzied state of boredom and frustration that came with much whining and self-pity and eventually tears and a stern warning from my father. I slunk into my bedroom, flopped down on the edge of the bed, and prayed earnestly to God for a babysitting job that would rescue me from a certain slow death of monotony and parental monitoring. About five minutes later the phone rang and the woman across the street, apologizing for the short notice, asked me if I could babysit, and the glory of God dashed through me. I spent the evening with two towheaded children from a born-again Christian family—the five-year-old girl fond of giving me memorized lectures on the true meaning of Christ—glowing in the rapture of the true God, my God, the Mormon God, the God who had arranged my babysitting gig. For an entire week I radiated faith from every pore of my body. I was hesitant to push my luck, to test my standing with God, but the next Friday night found me in the same desperate position. Again I dropped to my knees, pleading to be blessed with a babysitting job one more time, possibly reminding God of the bonus of my influence on the two little lost souls across the street believing in the wrong god. Then I sat on the edge of my bed and waited not-so-patiently for the phone to ring. It didn't. I was devastated, my beliefs shattered. Two days later, I told my Sunday school teacher about it, and I accused God of not answering my prayers.

"God ALWAYS answers your prayers," she told me. "Sometimes the answer is no."

"Why would God answer no?" I asked her.

"Maybe he was trying to teach you something."

"Like what?"

"Like patience."

"Well, he failed."

She gave me the look that let me know I'd gone too far, said too much, and being a fairly obedient child I blushed with embarrassment and stumbled to my seat, where I remained flushed and near tears for the entire class. I worried for a while after that episode that God might show his disapproval of me in some magnificently horrific way, and I watched for signs. Every pimple on my brother's face was an oncoming dreaded disease; every sigh from my mother's mouth I heard as her possible last breath. My idea of God felt like a balloon that had been inflated right to the point of explosion; any wrong move could be lethal. But as happens with balloons if left alone, the feeling started to shrink, first down to normal size and then down to nothing at all. Just a baggy little pouch of nothing.

My sister has tried to show me God. She's been saved—rescued from the Mormon Church and from her sins—born again. She claims to know the exact moment it happened. She prayed and prayed, and she felt it. Whether this took hours, weeks, months, or years I'm uncertain and hesitant to ask, but she eventually felt the spirit of Christ move into her. That's what I want, a very distinct, recognizable moment when clarity floods my brain and soul.

My sister once gave me a Bible with instructions on the inside cover—go to this page and read these scriptures, then that page and read those scriptures, do some praying, and eventually, I guess, one arrives at salvation. I tried it, admittedly half-assed, but nothing that could be recognized as any sort of spirit moved through my body.

The Mormons, who still visit me from time to time, have tried to show me the way also. (Apparently I have endless potential.) They've given me a little card with instructions. A cheat sheet for praying. A four-step process. Step one—address God by name; step two—thank God for blessings; step three—ask for what you want; and step four—close in the name of Jesus Christ. They tell me if I pray *and have faith* I will know God is real and the Mormon Church is true. But the part where the faith has to come first is the stickler.


DEB GAPES AT me in her rearview mirror with frantic eyes and keeps trying the thumbs-up method of reassurance as we cut through Forest Park back to her Central West End condo. I ignore her to let her know that nothing is "thumbs-up" no matter how bad she wants it to be. The bike dies at every red light and lunges down the road in a series of starts and stops. I struggle to keep it on rubber. Sweat pours from under my helmet and trickles down my neck; more flows over my belly into the waistband of my underwear like mountain snow melting into a lake. By the time we exit out of the park and make our way back onto the busy city streets, the bike—clanking loudly—is so badly overheated I'm forced to stick my knees straight out in either direction to keep my legs from roasting, and I'm unable to travel at speeds higher than five miles per hour, making me look like the biggest fool to ever straddle a motorcycle. Cars honk and careen around me. One driver leans out his window and offers this helpful advice: "Get off the road, moron!" At the entrance to the parking lot, the bike quits for good, and I coast into Deb's assigned parking spot teetering from side to side, bouncing one foot then the other off the pavement. With shaky legs I kick at the side stand, lean the bike over, tear at my helmet and jacket, and collapse on the lawn in a heap of sweat, nerves, and tears. So begins my journey.

"WHY WOULD YOU want to do that?" people asked when I told them I planned to travel the Mormon Trail from Nauvoo, Illinois, to Salt Lake City, Utah, by motorcycle. I found the question unanswerable so I would stare at them in contempt as if to say, "Well, if you don't know, I'm not going to tell you." I thought I might be taking the trip simply because I'd set it in motion by talking about it, then found it too late to comfortably back out. Everything about the idea scared the hell out of me—handling the bike, traveling alone, traffic, weather, road construction, strangers along the way, what I might discover about my Mormon ancestors, what I might discover about myself. At every point along the planning process I boasted of my plans to anyone who would listen while I waited for the perfect excuse to stay home—a sick pet that needed my care, a cherished plant that would perish in my absence, an ingrown toenail that would render me bedridden. But relatives stayed healthy, my husband stayed supportive, and all necessary gear arrived in time. No convenient excuses.

Besides the fact that no one and nothing fell into place to let me off easy, something softly but incessantly nudged me toward this trip, toward the trail. I had an internal pattern clicking, seemingly designed by someone else on my behalf, that drove my external preparations. My unconscious mind had tapped in to that pattern. I was like a zombie performing the will of the living—having the bike checked out, acquiring riding gear, poring over maps. Every so often I would awaken into a state of pure panic, then I'd hear my mother's voice—"I'll pray for you"—and I'd calmly continue outlining the shape of my feet on a piece of paper in hopes of acquiring a decent pair of riding boots.

My mother's words did not stand alone. They carried with them the confidence of five generations of Mormon women who came before me, and those women are not easy to ignore. It was they who etched a pattern so deeply into my soul that in spite of leaving the Mormon Church more than twenty-five years ago, the shape remains.


WHEN HANNAH MIDDLETON Hawkey heard the screams of her three- and five-year-old daughters, who were propped on top of their belongings, she dropped the shafts of the handcart she pulled and made her way to the rear where her fourteen-year-old stepson, James, had stopped pushing and dropped facedown in the knee-deep snow. She reached down to help him up. Having stooped for this purpose so many times, she was barely aware of her actions. But this time she knew immediately when she wrapped her hand around his shrunken arm that he had at last yielded to hunger, to cold, to pure exhaustion. Hannah buried James beneath the snow in a grave marked only with the ephemeral prints of her devoted hands, near the icy North Platte River in Wyoming. Forty-three days later, on November 30, 1856, after having walked more than twelve hundred miles, she was brought out of the mountains into the Salt Lake Valley in the back of a rescue wagon sent by Brigham Young, toes burst open from the cold, her two young daughters clinging with frozen fingers to what was left of her tattered skirts. Hannah would remain bedridden for several months; her damaged feet would not carry her another step until the following spring.

Before Maria Thompson turned eight years old, she had twice been bundled into the back of a wagon—likely the very wagon she was born in—and forced to flee with her family under orders such as that of Missouri governor Lillburn Boggs that all Mormons be "exterminated or driven from the state." In 1851, at thirteen years of age and by this time motherless, Maria, along with her father and four brothers, joined other Saints in the Land of Zion.

Following fifteen years behind Maria and ten years behind Hannah, Anna Maria Larsen, pregnant with her first child, placed her young hands on the splintering holds of a handcart piled high with food, cooking utensils, and bedding. Encountering rain, wind, dust, and insects, she and her husband, Hans, averaged about twelve miles a day pulling the cart alongside a Church-organized wagon train more than a thousand miles along the Mormon Trail. One hundred and fifty years later I wrap my much older hands around the grips of a motorcycle to follow the route of Anna Maria, Maria, and Hannah.

None of these women are famous; they are heroic to no one but me. They will not be found in history books, short of being an insignificant piece of the nearly fifty thousand Mormons who traveled all or part of the Mormon Trail from Nauvoo to Salt Lake City—and Hannah's stepson, James, was only one of the six thousand or so bodies left along the way. But they are the reason I find myself traveling on a BMW R 1100 R when fewer than 9 percent of all motorcycle riders in the United States are women. I carry their pioneering spirit. I am their great-great-granddaughter.

Between the years of 1846 and 1866, among a steady flow of Mormons trekking across the country with no intention of stopping before reaching the promised land in the Salt Lake Valley, seven of my eight great-great-grandmothers traveled all or part of the Mormon Trail, mostly by foot. The eighth arrived in Utah in 1873 after the completion of the railroad. These women, their mothers before them, and their daughters after them intrigue and perplex me. Generation after generation of self-assured and steady Mormon women in my family have not only chosen to live within the confines of the Mormon Church, they have, in fact, found liberation and fulfillment there. I am fascinated and puzzled by their ability to reconcile their independent spirits with their dedication to this patriarchal institution.

My great-great-great-grandmother, Welthea Bradford Hatch, packed up her seven children and with her husband, Ira Sterns Hatch, left her prosperous home in Farmersville, New York, to meet up with Mormon Church founder and self-proclaimed prophet Joseph Smith in Nauvoo. There, in a cholera fever, she gathered her family and told them they would find a home in the Rocky Mountains as Joseph had prophesied, but she would not. Her family buried her near Eton's Creek, about twenty miles from Nauvoo. Two and a half years after Welthea's death,

Joseph Smith and his brother would be murdered in the Carthage, Illinois, jail. Four years after her death, the Hatch family would be forced from their home. On a cold wet day in February 1846, they joined Brigham Young's company and started west.

I can trace every line of my family back to the origins of the Church, a continuous and connected whole. Then I count forward again until I get to me. This is where it stops. I've left the Church and I've chosen not to have children, no legacy to pass on and no one to pass it on to. For years these decisions seemed absolutely right for me. Then sometime around my forty-fifth birthday, a creeping sense of unease set in. I'm not longing for children and have no compulsion to return to the Church. But I can't help feeling as if I've broken an essential connection.

Over the years, I've searched for the peace and faith in the Mormon Church that the women before me carried with such confidence. But I never found it. At age eight, two men lowered me into a warm pool of blue water to cleanse me of whatever sins my small soul might have accumulated thus far. The following day, four men rested their heavy hands on top of my small head to confirm my admission into The Church of Jesus Christ of Latter-day Saints. Since then I have stuck close to the women in my family seeking clarification and understanding of my position in this male-dominated society. But thirty-seven years later, I can still feel the weight of those eight hands on top of my head every time I enter a Mormon church. I left the Church simply because the presence of men there was stronger than the presence of God.

# 2

WHEN DEBBIE APPROACHES I PULL MYSELF UP OFF THE lawn more for her sake than mine; she looks terrified. I walk around the bike, looking at it closely to reassure her that I'm on top of things. I jiggle a wire here and there, but the bike is extremely hot so I mostly just look intently at stuff from a squatted position. I think about lifting the seat and unwrapping the little packet of tools that came with the bike, but I don't know what I'd do with them beyond spreading them out on the pavement. This might be a dead giveaway that I'm clueless about the mechanics of my motorcycle. People who care about me get nervous with the idea that I would ride across the country alone on a machine I know very little about. Of course people do it in cars all the time, but I'm told that's different. I do carry a bit of guilt over this. The last thing a woman motorcyclist wants is to fit the stereotype of the woman motorcyclist—the one who can't make tight U-turns, who can't answer the question "How many cylinders?" when she takes the bike for emissions testing, who most definitely cannot fling that tool packet open with one quick movement, pull out a wrench, tweak this and that, and get the bike back in working order.

I once watched a woman get off her bike and have a man drive it up a potholed hill out of a parking lot and onto the side of the roadway where she ran to meet him so she could avoid the possibility of a stop on a gravel grade. I was publicly appalled but privately sympathetic. I know how hard it is to balance a slow-moving bike loaded for touring on a steep slope, and I know from experience how unsettling it is to drop a bike under those circumstances. A stop there requires nothing short of total alignment of all elements of the universe, not to mention all sections of the brain. One piece of the brain tells the eyes to scan the road surface for potholes; another piece of the brain tells the right hand to roll off the throttle and squeeze the front brake lever; another piece tells the left hand to squeeze the clutch; another piece tells the right foot to put pressure on the rear brake pedal; another piece tells the left foot to tap down on the gearshift lever and then drop off the footpeg to the ground, hoping the piece of the brain that was supposed to scan for potholes did its job and your foot meets solid ground before the weight of the loaded bike finds downward momentum. You have about two seconds to accomplish this.

Assuming your brain is operating at full speed and you've managed to pull this off without a hitch, pulling yourself out of this position and onto the road is a breeze as long as you are not prone to tentativeness. Your right foot on the rear brake will keep you from rolling backward, your left foot will keep you from falling over, your right hand will roll on the throttle, your left hand will gently release the clutch, and your bike will deliver you over potholes, through gravel onto a paved highway that welcomes you like a set of clean sheets. Now, you can go ahead and breathe.

I did ride my own bike up that grade and out of that parking lot, but thanked the God I don't believe in that the road was clear and I didn't have to stop. Fact is, I fit the woman-motorcyclist stereotype (as do a significant number of male riders), and I shamefully carry the burden of this. Being one of a relatively small group of women who choose to ride, I feel a sense of duty to do it well—the same pressure felt by all women who have entered a male-dominated arena. I've seen women retrieve a packet of well-used tools and tinker with a temperamental bike, and I'm duly impressed, but I'll never be one of them. Just like I'll never understand the inner workings of my car, my computer, or my refrigerator. I'm capable of learning, but when things are running properly there seems to be no reason, and when they are broken down there's no time.

Will owned a motorcycle when I met him, and occasionally I went for a ride with him. Nothing about those rides on the backseat engaged me. But he was passionate about motorcycles and I was passionate about him, so I kept trying. At a roadside stand on one of those rides, we struck up a conversation with a couple in their seventies. The woman said, "I have a BMW R 65 for sale; do you want to buy it?" At the time I knew nothing about motorcycles but I responded, "Yes, I want to buy it." A month or so after that purchase and after taking a few riding lessons, I started the R 65, backed it out of the driveway with much trepidation, and drove it around the block, never exceeding thirty miles per hour. It's impossible to describe to nonriders—and unnecessary to describe to riders—what happens in those first few moments of riding. From that moment on, I had a personal sense of power that eludes me in so many aspects of life.

In the ten years that I've been riding, I've been asked often why I ride a motorcycle and why I add to the already apparent risk by traveling solo. Although Will has been riding close to twenty-five years, he seldom hears this question. Surprisingly, the admonishments usually come from my own gender. Those who ask point out the obvious dangers as if they were an oversight on my part and once I recognize them I'll come to my senses. "I would never ride a motorcycle," they say with a certain wisdom I obviously lack. All within hearing distance nod knowingly in agreement. I have struggled but failed to come up with a satisfactory one-sentence answer for those who seem genuinely interested. Lately, however, the most logical answer seems to be "I grew up Mormon."

For me, as for anyone else who rides, the motorcycle symbolizes freedom. I've bought into this *Easy Rider* cliché without a moment's hesitation, and I feel it in my gut every time I hear the engine turn over, every time I feel the wind hit my face even if I'm only going to the emissions-testing station. But at the core of riding—especially for women—lies *The Wild One,* the rebel. At least in the beginning. Later comes the joy of riding, the thrill. But no matter how many years I ride, no matter how many reasons I can name for riding, the rebel lingers, travels with me on the backseat. The motorcycle is the crowning answer for every "should" and "should not" a woman has ever heard. A woman should not travel alone. A woman traveling alone should not draw attention to herself. A woman should not attempt to handle large pieces of machinery. A woman should not love speed. A woman should not love power. A woman should worry about the dirt under her nails, about the mess the helmet has made of her hair. The list goes on and on, and for every woman it's a little bit different depending on the family she grew up in, the friends she hung out with, the religion she lived. But the superlative answer for the rebel-woman remains a beautiful hulking amalgamation of metal, rubber, steel, bolts, nuts, and power.

As much as the motorcycle represents independence and individuality, I know few motorcyclists—men or women—who ride alone, truly alone, mile after mile. Motorcycle clubs are common, group rides are customary, rallies are spread across the country, riding with a buddy the norm. I once met a group of five Harley riders on the road, all with tricked-out bikes, all with long hair and long beards, all with chains dangling from their belts, all sporting a denim vest with the logo "The Loners" stenciled on the back.

I TRY TO remember a time when my mother, any one of my aunts, or my grandmothers talked to me about what it means to be a woman—about the things women do and the choices they make. I know this never happened. Although it was expected I would find my place as a Mormon wife and mother like those before me, I still somehow felt their encouragement to explore life, to choose. Unknowingly, I followed a legacy of questioning, of pushing beyond my fears, of finding my own way even when the path looked illogical and dangerous. Crossing oceans and mountain ranges to dwell in the presence of a wet-behind-the-ears, self-proclaimed prophet offering a smooth line of promises must have seemed like the height of foolishness to the families my ancestors left behind. My seemingly unorthodox means of searching is really not all that peculiar encircled by my history—it's almost hereditary.

For many years, my path led directly away from the Mormon Church. The women in my family said nothing as they watched me go. Maybe they always knew that path would eventually loop back to the beginnings, to the place where Hannah loaded her handcart and took her first step to religious freedom on Brigham Young's promise: ". . . let them gird up their loins and walk through, and nothing shall hinder or stay them." (Somehow Brother Brigham's language stayed with our family, and when I was a tired child lagging behind my mother in a store or parking lot, she'd mortify me by calling out, "Gird your loins and get going!" In those tender prepubescent years, the words "gird" and "loins" in the same sentence either reduced a child to hysterical laughter or overpowering embarrassment. For me it was the latter.)

As I stoop by my disabled bike, I ask myself whether Hannah or Anna Maria had moments of doubt as I do. As Hannah loaded her belongings into a handcart the way I load my gear into my saddlebags, forced to make decisions of what to leave behind, did she question her stamina to make the trip like I question mine? Did she question the validity of the trip or did it seem as essential as mine does now?

Hannah had buried her husband in Durham, England, four years prior to leaving, and at the age of thirty-three, her heart and mind were filled with the irresistible promise of life among saints here on earth and reunification with God thereafter. When she saw the notice in the Church-published *Millennial Star* newspaper to join Brigham Young's new handcart movement for $45, she packed her bags and her family for Zion. Hannah and her three children were assigned to the ill-fated Martin Handcart Company.

In his introduction to *The Gathering of Zion*, Wallace Stegner writes, "For every early Saint, crossing the plains to Zion in the Valleys of the Mountains was not merely a journey but a rite of passage . . . the crossing of the plains provided a testing that most proselytes welcomed . . . a labor to be performed, difficulties to be overcome, dangers to be faced, faithfulness to be proved, a great safety to be won." In a later chapter he goes on to write, "The marathon walk of the handcart companies, though it involved only a few thousand of the total number of Mormon emigrants, was the true climax of the Gathering, and the harshest testing of both people and organization."

Maybe I'm looking for the twenty-first-century version of "the harshest testing." When critic Robert Hughes reviewed the Guggenheim motorcycle show, he defined riding as an odd mix of aggression and vulnerability, requiring a degree of both abandonment and intense focus. I could opt to take this journey as others do in an air-conditioned car surrounded by sweet-smelling leather, behind locked doors, protected by air bags and seat belts. I could lower my risk considerably. In a car, I wouldn't have to worry about parking lots and gas stations with their slopes and angles and splashes of oil where I am at the greatest risk of dropping a 517-pound bike loaded with 100 pounds of gear that will require more strength than I possess to put back on two wheels. I wouldn't have to think much about the physics of a curve—how much must the bike lean to make the curve and how much speed does it need to stay upright once it's tipped on the edges of two tires. In a car, my odds of surviving a tire blowout are fairly good; on a motorcycle, considerably lower. I wouldn't need to prepare for every possible element of weather—heat, cold, wind, rain, even snow—if I had the protection of an enclosed vessel. In a car, a sign that reads "CAUTION: UNEVEN PAVEMENT AHEAD" barely hints at any risk at all; on a bike, it warns of severe hazards and demands acute concentration.

Driving the trail—which demanded and took so much from my ancestors—in a car asks nothing of me. I could do it immediately with little preparation. I could daydream halfway across the country singing along with the radio. On a bike, the trail will demand my full attention, my physical stamina, and more. It will demand that I dig deeply for those elusive elements of faith and belief. On a bike, the trail will demand mind, body, and soul. Alone on a motorcycle is appropriate for this trip. For me, too, as for Hannah and Anna Maria, this is not merely a journey but a rite of passage, a test, *a labor to be performed, difficulties to be overcome, dangers to be faced, faithfulness to be proved.*

But faithfulness to what? I ask myself, and it is precisely this question I'm trying to answer on this journey. I have no faith in the Mormon Church, none in the visions of Joseph Smith or Brigham Young (although I'm duly in awe of their achievements), none even to some sort of god. My faith is abstract, hard to define, unattached to an identifiable object or institution, confusing even to me, but it has a lingering presence nonetheless.

I'm not sure what I expect to find in the "restored" streets of Nauvoo, lined with an imposing new temple built to replace the burned original in all its splendor, lined with the still-standing, near-opulent homes of Church leaders such as Brigham Young and Wilford Woodruff—homes abandoned before the bricks settled, now shrines to the plaintive stories of unyielding faith in the face of persecution. I'm not sure what I expect to feel as I wander the graves of dead Mormons buried on the still Iowa hillside at Mount Pisgah or when I stand in front of the plaque at Winter Quarters, Nebraska, that lists names of some of the six hundred or so Mormons who died there waiting for the weather to allow them to continue their journey to Zion. I'm not sure what will be disclosed to me as I walk through the meadow at Martin's Cove, stepping over the bones of those who died miserably from starvation and exposure in the Wyoming mountains. I'm traveling on a gut feeling—call it faith if you will—assuming my ancestors won't let me down.

# 3

I SINK INTO MY SQUATTING POSITION BY THE SIDE OF the bike, feeling solid here next to the ground, feet flat, leg muscles engaged. Heat floats from the bike, the smell of hot rubber wafts from the tires. I breathe deeply and begin to relax, almost feeling as if I could nap in this position. Debbie touches my shoulder pulling me out of my stupor.

"See anything?" she asks, and I remember that's why I'm down here—to look for trouble. I see a blur of gray and black. Focus. I see that the clear coat is peeling off my BMW symbol on the side. I see that splattered bugs can be beautiful—a splash of yellow and gold against a red background. I spot a few more wires to be jiggled, then rise reluctantly.

"Nope. I can't figure it out," I say as if there were some possibility I might.

"Well, kiddo," she says, "you better plan on staying put for a few days."

Debbie grew up in the South, the daughter and granddaughter of Southern Baptist preachers (because she's from the South, she likes to point out that her daddy and granddaddy are not one and the same person) and speaks with a slow, Southern lilt and an unassuming manner that allows her to get away with calling people "kiddo" and "honey." Coming out of my mouth—unless I am in fact speaking to a five-year-old—those words evoke either laughter or scorn. But when they float from her throat people turn into marshmallows, and if she's asking for something she'll get it. I once heard her give the abbot of a Benedictine monastery a lecture on having compassion for all of God's creatures when he threatened to take the monastery dog to the pound after a few monastery ducks disappeared. (In Deb's argument, the dog is a more worthy creature than the duck.) The words were harsh, but they came out sounding like a hymn floating on a mountain breeze. Had that lecture come from me, we might have been invited to leave along with the duck-eating dog.

MY TRIP HAD started out auspiciously. I'd paid the best BMW motorcycle mechanic in Tucson—possibly in North America—to go over my bike in meticulous detail and proclaim it roadworthy. St. Louis is the nearest city to Nauvoo, Illinois, the starting point of the Mormon Trail, and fortunately Debbie would put me up for a day or so while I got organized and packed. I shipped my bike from the Tucson BMW motorcycle dealership to the St. Louis dealership on schedule; flights left on time, luggage dropped effortlessly onto the carousel, UPS packages with riding gear arrived in St. Louis three days before me. Deb picked me up at the airport on Friday night. I planned to pick the bike up Saturday at the local dealership and leave for Nauvoo—two hundred miles from St. Louis—on Sunday morning.

On Saturday morning, in full riding gear, I strode to the door of St. Louis BMW Motorrad, gave it a mighty push just to play up the part of the confident motorcyclist, and almost broke my nose on the glass. I peered in at the darkened show-room, then pulled my head back to read the sign taped to the door that told me they had decided to close Saturday for the Labor Day weekend and would open again Tuesday. That put a bit of a damper on my auspicious beginnings, but I wasn't put off. I had made arrangements with a woman named Betty Honaker to pick up the bike on Saturday, and if I could track her down I figured I could keep my plan intact. There were a bunch of Honakers in the St. Louis phone book, but there was one listing for J & B, and I banked on the B standing for Betty. I put Deb on the phone to do the asking in that way she has, and by the time she finished saying, "Betty, honey, I know you're real busy and all but . . ." Betty had agreed to meet us at the dealership after church on Sunday to release the bike. Only a one-day delay.

With the rest of Saturday open, we jumped in the car and drove out of St. Louis over the Mississippi River on the route that would eventually take me to Nauvoo so I could get my bearings. The day was perfect, unusually cool for early September but sunny and bright with surprisingly low humidity.

At O'Jan's fish stand on the Illinois side of the river, I scanned a menu filled with deep-fried turtle and such things I'd never eaten before, and I didn't particularly feel like my life would be incomplete without them now. Deb suggested crappie sandwiches (pronounced "croppie" although I never could make that pronunciation come out right the first time) and I said sure. The breaded deep-fried crappie, a small sunfish found in U.S. rivers, comes between two slices of white sand-wich bread straight out of the bag. The idea (I gathered from watching Deb) is to pile some raw onions on top of the fish, slather some tartar sauce over that, and smash it all down be-tween the white bread, which works like a sponge to soak up the grease. I gave myself away as being an ignorant out-of-towner by stripping my crappie of its bread, pushing the onions off to the side, and dipping it hesitantly in the tartar sauce. That was likely an embarrassment to my true Southern friend, who has probably known how to eat a crappie sandwich since she was toddling around the swamps of Florida. Regardless, it went down smooth with a bunch of onion rings, a beer, and a few Tums at an outside table on the Mississippi River bank.

We headed north for a while along the river enjoying the views, the air, and the conversation. Here's what I know for sure about folks who live along the Mississippi River in that part of Illinois: They love big front lawns, huge front lawns, several acres of front lawn. And they love riding lawn mowers. To an Illinois Mississippi River dweller, mowing the front lawn is not yard work, it's meditation, it's entertainment, it's religion, it's competition, it might even be art. Old women, adolescent boys, teenage girls, middle-aged men—farmers, housewives, grandmothers, cheerleaders—all out on their riding mowers. If there's not enough lawn to satiate the entire family, they ride on out of their yards and keep on riding, mowing the grass along the highway until they meet their neighbor a few miles down the road who has rolled out of his yard and is mowing toward them.

Once the mowing is done, the Mississippi River dwellers decorate with lawn ornaments. The favorite is a fake deer positioned to appear as if ready to bound across the highway into traffic. It wasn't until we came upon a headless deer ready to jump in front of the car that I realized they were lawn ornaments. Scattered among the fake deer and running a close second in lawn decoration preference are sixteen-inch Dutch people—a little Dutch boy kissing a little Dutch girl or tending to little tulips.

On two-lane roads through Illinois farm country and small towns along the river, we snaked through acres of corn and soybeans that seemed to demand the speed of dawdle. We complied. This comes naturally for Deb, whose endless energy swirls inside a remarkably slow-moving body. Deb drives so cautiously she's a danger to others and has a tendency to do a little tap dance on the gas pedal, which causes the car to go up the road in a small, repetitive lunging motion unnoticeable to anyone but those inside the car. I settled into the passenger seat, content to have the sun bake my right arm as it hung out the window and fantasized about coming back to those easy country roads on the motorcycle.

SLOW CAR RIDES on country roads feel as natural to me as breathing, at times feel as necessary as breathing. When I was a child—from the time I was born until the day I left home—there were only two places in which my father ever exhibited anything that resembled contentment: on the back of a horse and behind the wheel of a car. The rest of the time he was tense and mostly angry, as if he were frustrated by the movement of the world and the only thing that could ease his frustration was his own motion. My instincts for finding my way on country roads are remarkably strong, even in unfamiliar territory, as long as I'm in the West. Once I'm out of the Mountain time zone, my instincts die.

On those days when my father loaded us in the car, when my mother packed a picnic of thinly spread tuna sandwiches wrapped in wax paper, potato salad, and a cooler full of soda pop, we must have looked like one of those family units seen on a Mormon brochure. The father, the priesthood holder, taking his rightful place at the head of the household, the subservient and loving mother, the cheerful yet reverent children. In actuality we didn't come close. Although my father would never consider himself anything other than Mormon, he hadn't set foot in a church since the day he married my mother in the Logan, Utah, temple; priesthood was something he wanted no part of. My mother remained in a state of perpetual sadness, stretched like tied leather in the sun between her love for the Church and her duties as a wife. My brother, sister, and I were stuck between them in an enduring state of angst and confusion, knocked back and forth like a volleyball between my mother's devotion to the Church and my father's disdain for it. (Forty years later, my father will shake his head, apparently perplexed and disappointed in the results of his child rearing, and say, "We should have insisted you kids go to church more.") The only Mormon ideal my father personified was that of head of household. This position he held unequivocally. But on those car trips, meandering through farmland, climbing into canyons, subdued by the flash of white-barked aspen trees in our peripheral vision, we momentarily pretended we were that perfect Mormon family, and to this day, my memories of those car trips are soft and comforting.


DEBBIE AND I floated over the bridge that took us into Louisiana, Missouri, and headed south along the river toward St. Louis. At a roadside fruit stand, we bought tomatoes and okra for dinner and fresh peaches so ripe they weren't going to make it back to St. Louis, so I washed them under a hose, settled back into my seat, and commenced eating them at once. As I was biting into my fourth and last peach, Deb's driving caution suddenly left her. She spotted "Jim's Ribs" painted in bright red on the side of a tiny white building and laid rubber

sliding to a stop before hanging a sharp right into a gravel parking lot, spewing rocks off to our left and making me drop the
last bite of my peach onto the car floor.

"Jim's Ribs is back!" she said.

"Oh," I replied with my head between my knees searching
for my peach pit.

"Jim's dead. I wonder who's cooking?"

I figured they must be damn good ribs for her to drive in
such a reckless way and even though I was full of fried fish,
onion rings, beer, peaches, and ice cream acquired just a bit up
the road before the fruit stand, if they were that good I'd do my
best to suck the meat off a few bones.

"Let's go find out," I said pitching my peach stone out the
window.

We confirmed that Jim was in fact dead and that the new
guy—a guy called Raspberry—was no relationship to Jim at
all, just happened to be occupying the same building and capi-
talizing on his name. Nevertheless, we ordered a slab of ribs
and a half chicken to go and shoved them onto the floor behind the passenger seat. Our good intentions were to taste a little and drop the rest off with Deb's partner, Cindy, who was
pulling a late shift in the emergency room at Barnes-Jewish
Hospital. But after smelling Raspberry's barbecue for the next
hour that it took us to get home, we weren't feeling quite so
generous.

We fixed ourselves a salad, cooked up the tomatoes and
okra, opened a bottle of Merlot, and settled out on the front
terrace to see if Raspberry measured up against Jim. He did. A
strong, warm breeze blew as dog walkers, daters, and pizza delivery boys came and went from tree-shrouded buildings. We
sat for hours licking sauce off our fingers and talking about old
lovers. Harry Truman Capote, Deb's German shepherd, sat

patiently waiting to clean up any piece of food that might slip out of our greasy hands. For that moment life was as good as it could possibly be—safe, simple, and easy. Why question it? Why push it? Why not be satisfied with a good friend, barbecued ribs, and a bottle of wine?

I HAD GOTTEN up early Sunday morning anxious to get the bike and get on my way. But as I pulled on my motorcycle boots, Betty called. She couldn't find her keys, thought she had probably left them on her desk and they were locked inside the showroom. I felt a strange sense of dread, like this trip had suddenly turned bad, but I tend to blow things out of proportion this way so I pushed it aside. Eventually Betty found someone to open the dealership, and when Deb and I got there that someone was already gone, but my bike stood shining in the sun in front of the locked door.

I was momentarily elated, then a shot of adrenaline climbed my spine and jolted me with the realization that I was in St. Louis, Missouri, and expected to ride that bike to Tucson, Arizona, by way of Illinois, Iowa, Nebraska, Wyoming, and Utah—a good three thousand miles before I'd be home again. At that moment it seemed like a harebrained idea, an unnecessary labor to be performed, the dangers insurmountable, the test too harsh. I also remembered something that had been nagging me for the past three weeks. When I delivered my bike to the Tucson dealership, the engine cut out as I was turning in to the drive. I had managed to convince myself this happened simply because I had drained much of the gas out of the tank for shipping, but now I wasn't so easily persuaded.

I pulled my hair into a ponytail at the base of my neck, tugged my helmet on, straddled the bike, and after about three attempts, rolled it off its center stand. I asked Deb about the nearest gas station, and she pointed left up the street. I noted the island in the middle of the street and asked her if there was a gas station in the opposite direction. She shook her head.

I suck at U-turns on a motorcycle. It's not a technical problem; it's a psychological problem. I know all the rules of turning my head, keeping my eyes up, looking through the turn at the place I want to end up, leaning the bike, and rolling on the throttle. Technically, I've got it down. Psychologically, I'm a mess. This stems from dropping my bike in the middle of a U-turn when I first started riding. I'm scarred for life. But my choices were a U-turn to the gas station or risk running out of gas, and it seemed an appropriate way to initiate this trip, like some sort of entrance exam. If I couldn't handle this simple U-turn in city traffic, I couldn't expect to get all the way across the country unharmed. If I couldn't make the turn, I should just load the bike back onto a truck and ship it back to Tucson. I pulled into traffic and moved immediately into the left lane. I executed a perfect U-turn, but as I leaned into it, the engine cut out. Just as the bike was about to hit pavement—along with the entire left side of my body—the engine caught again and pulled me up out of the potential spill. I sputtered to the gas station and pulled up to a pump, already a jumbled mess of nerves and sweat.

A full tank of gas didn't alleviate the problem. When we got back to Deb's house, I started making phone calls in this order: my husband, the mechanic who checked the bike out, and the Tucson dealer who'd said, "I'm sure it's fine," when I told him the problem before the bike was shipped. I'm not sure what I expected any of them to do from Tucson, but it is my style when I'm worried to alarm all friends and family and try to get them to worry along with me. It seldom works, particularly with my husband. He is remarkably sure about my ability to handle things; he simply assumes I'll figure it out. I never know whether to be angry or flattered. Part of me wants him to panic along with me and express his undying love and concern about my safety, and the other part wants exactly what he gives: calm and confidence. After fifteen years, I've started to use his reaction as a reality check on my own emotions. If I hear the smallest amount of concern in his voice, then I know my problem is huge and potentially fatal. Otherwise, I know I've blown things out of proportion to the actual element of danger involved. I also called Will first because he is a levelheaded, rational person who knows what to do in any situation.

"I don't know what to tell you," he said after I got done with my very long explanation of the problem. That's not right. Tell me what's wrong with the bike, tell me how to fix it, tell me it's not really a big problem, tell me you'll catch the next flight to St. Louis, tell me who to call, what to do, how to feel. Tell me I'll be safe and fine. He told me I might want to ride the bike a little and see what happens, and then he hung up with a jaunty "Let me know how it turns out." Next, I called my mechanic and the Tucson dealer for technical advice. My mechanic wasn't home, and the dealer told me to ride the bike a bit and see what happens. At that point I came to my senses and decided to look for help a little closer by.

The *2001 BMW Owners Anonymous* book gives a listing of BMW motorcycle owners across the country who are willing to help out if a fellow rider gets in trouble on the road. There were twenty-three listings for the St. Louis area. I started at the top and went down the list, hanging up on all answering machines until I got a live person—Dean. I asked Dean if he knew anything about R 1100 Rs, explained the problem, and he said I should ride the bike a bit and see what happens.

There seemed to be a consensus on that sage advice, but it must be one of those things that makes sense only to men with some mechanical ability and the confidence to handle a sputtering, coughing, stalling bike in city traffic. I decided to keep trying for an option that better suited my sensibilities, so I continued down the list of phone numbers until I got John. I asked John if he knew anything about R 1100 Rs, and he was noncommittal. I explained my problem, and he asked me if the bike has a fuel filter. I told him with authority that yes, in fact it does have a fuel filter, and it turned out I was right. He said he would be willing to take a look at the bike and gave me directions to his house. Since riding to his house would incorporate all other advice I had received thus far, I took him up on his offer.

WHEN I FIRST began to ride a motorcycle, my father thought my brain had been sucked out of my head, leaving me with the intelligence of a potted plant. For much of my life, my father has questioned many of my decisions and most of my opinions—because they differ from his—but two of my actions stand out in his mind as the undertakings of a lunatic. One was the purchase of a motorcycle, but the first was my decision to leave Salt Lake City for New York City to take a job on Wall Street. To leave the West for the East, in my father's mind, is akin to defecting from one's country and shunning one's family at the same time. He didn't think a Western girl had a chance in hell of surviving in New York City. And he had done everything in his power to make me a Western girl.

When I was five years old, my father became obsessed with the West in a way usually reserved for converts from the East who've read too many Louis L'Amour novels, as if he needed to prove himself worthy of the place he'd lived since birth. But unfortunately, L'Amour novels are read on this side of the Mississippi also, and the myth of the cowboy grows larger every decade and thrives in the minds and hearts of true Westerners who ought to know better. In the midst of this regrettable fallacy, many still hang on to the romantic notion that living in the West requires defining one's own destiny by riding the range like Chuck Connors in *The Rifleman*—doing good deeds while knocking off the bad guys, all the while maintaining the attitude of an outlaw. The rugged-individualist legend manifests itself in various forms seen throughout the attitudes, laws, and politics of the West.

I don't believe my father ever picked up a Louis L'Amour novel, and he often scoffed at the ridiculousness of TV Westerns, but he nevertheless somehow acquired his own idea of the romantic West. It started with the death of his father.

My father's father was a sheepherder, and he spent his days riding through the canyons of the Bear River Range of the Rocky Mountains near Cache Valley, Utah. As a child, my father spent many of his summers doing the same. The sheep my grandfather herded were never his own, and when he died, my father would inherit nothing but a single black horse named Banjo. Until then, he went to college, got married, had children, and became a high school teacher in a small town 175 miles from his hometown of Paradise, Utah.

Our redbrick house sat in a curb-and-gutter neighborhood, and a row of rose bushes bloomed along the cement driveway where I chalked my hopscotch outlines. My mother—slim, dark, and beautiful—doted on me, her youngest and most emotionally fragile child, and until the day my grandfather died, everything seemed just right to me. I couldn't see the smolderings of either of my parents—my mother's for the Mormon Church nor my father's for the Western life. My mother's, in fact, wouldn't ignite for many years, but my father's were about to burst into flame, touching off a fire that burns to this day.

No one on our street had a horse; Banjo was a problem. The easy answer was to sell him, but when my father stood in the doorway between our kitchen and living room he could easily see the boundaries of his land at the end of a little patch of grass in front and in back of the house, he could walk to the end of his land in all directions in less than a minute, and that fact was chipping away at his Western soul.

The arrival of Banjo led to a rented horse corral and barn on the outskirts of town. Then to another horse we named Spider. At five years old, decked out in my new attire of jeans, a snap-button, orange plaid shirt, boots, belt, and hat, I got my first lesson in the ways of the West.

My father saddled both horses, boosted me onto Spider, and mounted Banjo. Before heading up the canyon—our destination for the day—we rode past the house to show my mother how wonderful it all was. As we left the house, my father warned me that we were to pass a road that led back to the barn, and I would have to control Spider to get him to turn in the opposite direction. As we approached the road, my father warned me again, then more insistently: "Turn him! Turn him! Turn him!" My father must have thought turning a horse should come naturally to any daughter of his, but when we reached the place I was supposed to turn him, I had no idea how to accomplish the task. I thought I had been showing Spider the way to go all morning but realized later he had simply been content to follow Banjo until he spotted an obvious path home. Spider turned down the familiar road and headed for the barn on a dead run. I dropped the reins, grabbed the saddle horn, and went for my first real horseback ride. About a half-mile down the road, my father, on a much faster horse, rode alongside me, reached down, grabbed the flopping reins, and jerked us all to a stop with such force that dirt and pebbles flew as horseshoes skidded on the gravel road.

My father dismounted, red and shaking with anger. "God dammit. I told you to turn him." He yanked me off Spider's back with one hand on my upper arm, put me on the side of the road, and stuffed Banjo's reins into my trembling hands. "You have to control him." My father held Spider's reins close to the bit with his left hand and used the loose end of the reins as a whip on Spider's rump. Held close, Spider pulled back, nostrils flared, eyes wild, as he swung his rear end away from the flash of the reins. "Stupid son of a bitch! Stupid son of a bitch!" He was beaten for wanting the comfort of cool shade, fresh water, and green hay. He was beaten because I didn't show him the way to go. Banjo, frenzied with what was happening, tugged at my hands, but I held tight. Equal amounts of fear and resolve pulsed through my small body and from that moment, I refused to accept this new Western life.

4

"YOU CAN STAY AS LONG AS YOU NEED TO, HONEY," DEB
tells me as I trudge up the stairs, stringy and sticky from my
freeway adventure.

"I'm a bad houseguest," I warn her as we enter the condo,
and suddenly my less-than-stellar manners seem hugely significant. Like it's all tied together, every bad or even mediocre
deed I've ever committed, culminating in this one moment.
My manners and my broken-down bike seem inexplicably
yoked. I'm one of those houseguests who leaves junk all over
as if I'm home, and I'd already used someone's razor found on
the edge of the tub that morning. Borrowing a razor—at least
the way I shave, as if I'm late for an appointment even if
I have all the time in the world, leaving my legs notched
and bleeding—has to be akin to sharing a needle with an IV
drug user.

"What happened?" Cindy asks looking concerned.

"I used your razor," I tell her.

"We didn't make it to John's house," Deb says. "The motorcycle broke down on the freeway and we barely made it back

home. Jana's going to need to stay here a few days until she can get someone to look at her bike."

"I used the razor on the edge of the tub this morning. I'm sorry. I forgot mine."

"That's okay," Cindy says, but she's just being nice because I look like a crazy woman with frantic hair surrounding a red, sweaty face, talking about razors instead of motorcycles, and she doesn't know me well enough to gauge what might happen next. (The next morning she'll leave me a new disposable razor next to my toothbrush.)

Bob, the owner of BMW Motorrad in St. Louis, shows up at Debbie's condo fifteen minutes after I call him Tuesday morning with a trailer to haul my disabled bike to the shop. He's all business as he nimbly backs my bike out of its parking space as if it's the weight of a ten-speed, rolls it onto the trailer, and straps it down. I'm moved to tears by his kindness; his swift response signals an unspoken acknowledgment of the uneasiness caused by bike troubles far from home. I follow him around the trailer, expressing my gratitude as he tightens straps. He nods and grunts. My words don't feel strong enough, and I suppress an urge to show my appreciation by throwing my arms around his neck. He doesn't seem like the type who might appreciate lavish outlays of emotion, and there's always the very real possibility that my vision of him as shining knight is blown slightly out of proportion to the situation at hand.

By 3 P.M. Wednesday, I have a brand-new fuel filter and just about enough daylight to make it to Nauvoo. Deb is alarmed by the idea of my abrupt departure and tries to talk me into staying until morning, but I know I need to leave. I'm too comfortable here, sleeping well, feeling as if I might settle in and stay. I race through her house excitedly collecting my gear and hauling it downstairs in several trips. Deb busies herself in the kitchen, worried that speaking to me will cause me to forget some lifesaving step in my preparations. The silence feels good. As I methodically tighten straps and check lights and turn signals, I try to wrap my mind around the journey I've put in motion and think about the women who have drawn me here.

GREAT-GREAT-GRANDMOTHER Anna Maria loved to sew. After she arrived in Utah, she made a living sewing men's suits and women's dresses by hand. Before she started her journey across the plains, those young hands must have loved to brush up against smooth, cool cotton, must have trembled at the textured touch of raw silk. They must have been painfully unprepared to be wrapped around wood that would dry and splinter quickly in the Nebraska prairie sun and ordered to push against two or three hundred pounds. Maybe she considered lightening her load by dropping a blanket along the way, although she'd heard stories about people freezing to death in the mountain passes she would climb in a month or so. By the fourth or fifth week, when she had lost ten pounds in spite of her pregnancy, when she left swipes of red on her cotton dress as she passed her bleeding hands over her small, protruding belly, as she strained to stand up again after a short rest under a scarce shade tree, maybe she considered leaving the bluebird-patterned dishes her mother had tearfully given her when she departed Vollerup, Denmark.

Surely there must have been times when she questioned her faith in the vision of Joseph Smith, when she chided herself for gullibility, when the test was too harsh, the proof of faithfulness too difficult. What kept her going then? What impelled her to pick up the cart one more day, suffering from heat, exhaustion, and possibly morning sickness, and walk the next twelve miles?

Maybe I'm wrong about Anna Maria. Maybe she never had a flicker of doubt about her journey, about her conversion to Mormonism. When the child she carried across the plains was born dead, when she lost four of the next seven children she bore, maybe she never wavered for a second in her devotion to God. The notation—"Needed by God"—scrawled in a firm hand next to the dead children's names in my family history shows no sign of ambivalence. I like to think she questioned and struggled for the answers then as I do now, but there is no record of that struggle for Anna Maria, Maria, Hannah, or any of the women in my family. For that there is no apparent pattern.

In her later life, Hannah told her children that she didn't mourn for her stepson when he died along the trail, that "the Lord took away the sting of death." She was glad for James, that he had been taken from the extreme trial and suffering. When asked if at any time along the trail she regretted her decision to leave her home and come to Zion—maybe in camp at night when she cleared snow with a tin pan to make a place for her children to lie down, when she rewrapped her frozen and bleeding feet, when she could see her tiny daughters growing smaller each day from starvation—she firmly replied, "No, never!" I want to understand a faith that profound.

I BEEP MY horn a few times and wave good-bye to Deb, who has led me out of town to make sure I'm on the right road to Nauvoo. As I swing into the left northbound lane of Illinois Highway 100 around her Mazda pickup truck, I flash a thumbs-up—the sign she has wanted for five days—to let her know the bike is running fine. She pulls off the road to turn around, and tears stream down my cheeks. I pop my face shield to readjust my sunglasses and let the wind dry my face, which it does in seconds. My emotions take me by surprise—a mixture of relief that I'm finally on my way, fear that I'm now alone, and tenderness for Deb's generous friendship and bigheartedness.

I breathe deeply, realizing I'd come near to holding my breath for the last five days, as I shift my weight to the rear of the seat and rest my chest on the tank bag to stretch my back. The ride out of St. Louis had taken me through sixty minutes of city traffic before crossing the Mississippi River at Alton, Illinois, and the stress from that ride now settles into the usual receptacles: my knees, which feel permanently sculpted into a ninety-degree bend, and my hands, which are unnecessarily squeezing the grips as if that's the only thing keeping me from flying off the bike.

I loosen my hold and slap my left hand against my thigh to get the blood flowing through it again. One at a time, I lift each foot from the peg and stretch my leg straight out in front of me. Pain ricochets through my knees, normal for the first day of riding. Things will loosen up after a few days.

By the time I reach Highway 96 at Kampsville, forty minutes or so after crossing the river, the day has turned hot and muggy, the pain in my knees and hands is almost unbearable, and my helmet feels two sizes too small, causing a dull throb just above my eyebrows. I am dressed in full riding gear: jacket and pants made of Cordura nylon with patches of Kevlar—the material used for bulletproof vests—at the elbows and knees. It reminds me of the snowsuits my mother used to pack me in as a child, the kind that make you stand with your arms sticking straight out and your knees a foot apart, which would be fine if it were snowing out or even remotely cool instead of ninety degrees with 90 percent humidity. When I'm on the bike and moving, this outfit makes me feel smart and cautious. When I'm off the bike paying for gas or attempting to go to the bathroom, I feel like an idiot as I lumber through the convenience store, the Kevlar knee pads meeting and screeching with every step amid people in shorts and flip-flops swirling rapidly around me. I feel like John Travolta in *The Boy in the Plastic Bubble.*

The small town of Mozier offers a wide, friendly main street with an inviting shady spot in front of a small inn. I peel my jacket off and drop it onto the lawn, struggle to pull off leather gloves soaked through with sweat, and frantically fumble with the buckle of my helmet. As it comes off, my head feels as if it's expanding like a sponge filling with water. Two young girls— about ten or eleven years old—stroll past. "Nice bike," one of them says knowingly. The other feigns disinterest, letting me know that a motorcycle isn't enough to make me cool with hair plastered to my head and a beet-red face.

The road between Hamilton and Nauvoo runs next to the river. The sun has dropped low in the sky and light skips over the surface of the Mississippi. The river invites a feeling of lazy summer days coming to an end. Shadows fall long across the road; lawns on my right grow big and green. Trees hang over my head, and every so often a leaf floats down to greet me. A large construction site on a hill at the south end of Nauvoo seems a strange sight for the tiny, settled village, and as I ride into town, I'm overcome with melancholy as if I have returned to a place of my youth. I inherently know this place I've never seen before, and its significance in forming my life cannot be pushed aside.

IN *THE VARIETIES of Religious Experience,* William James writes that some people are incapable of religious belief. "They are either incapable of imagining the invisible; or else, in the language of devotion, they are life-long subjects of 'barrenness' and 'dryness' . . . the nature which is spiritually barren may admire and envy faith in others," writes James, "but can never compass the enthusiasm and peace which those who are temperamentally qualified for faith enjoy."

I recognize myself in James's words and it scares the hell out of me. I don't want to be a *lifelong subject of barrenness and dryness,* but here I stand, envious of the faith known to my ancestors but with my "religious faculties checked," as James puts it. Checked, I believe, by the two emotions I most closely associate with religion: anger and sadness, which flowed freely from my father and mother, respectively.

I don't know the origin of my father's anger—his roots in the Mormon Church run as deep as my mother's—but I was inundated with his contempt for the Church from the moment I could conceive speech. He hid none of it from his wife or children. My mother did what she could to infuse balance, but she couldn't do much. My father has a way of making people feel like ignorant fools if they disagree with him in any way. He wore her down quickly and effectively, and I wouldn't realize the depth of my mother's faith and love for the Church until many years later.

When I was small, she gave up trying to attend church herself under his constant ridicule, but she regularly dropped us kids off at the many weekly Mormon services and activities. What for most of my childhood friends must have seemed like a natural extension of their home life, for me was as strange and frightening as if I'd been dropped into a tribal ceremony of cannibals. I forever expected some sort of evil—inspired by my father's rantings—to jump from behind the pews or spew from the mouth of my primary teacher. The rules of "reverence," used simply as a means to keep the screams and laughter of children at a tolerable level, thundered around in my head like a deadly threat. I was possibly the most reverent child there.

I quietly went through the rituals as assigned. I can still recite the names of the books of the New Testament, and I can still remember most of the thirteen Articles of Faith—the basic Mormon beliefs set down by Joseph Smith. I even embroidered a laminated copy of the articles in yellow yarn and hung them on my wall at home. I cross-stitched, knitted, and crocheted in the name of Christ and Joseph. But I didn't believe. I didn't even comprehend.

In my adolescent years, I soon discovered the value of going to church. In a small Utah town like mine, nonreligious things happened in church, and missing church was like missing a week of school—you could quickly drop out of the loop, miss inside jokes, and see your friends drifting away. I had a few Catholic friends who would be carted off to catechism, and they were at a distinct disadvantage in the social strata of the third grade. I continued to attend church well into my teens, but the religious tenets seemed to hover around my body and never enter. By my senior year, the social requirements of churchgoing had diminished, and my attendance became intermittent and soon stopped altogether.

I don't remember feeling anything when I left the Mormon Church. It wasn't a statement of rebellion against the Church or God; it wasn't an intellectual examination and refusal of Christianity; it simply wasn't necessary in my life anymore. It dropped away like an old friend from high school. When I left the Church, it didn't leave a void or an emptiness to be filled. I simply felt freed from unnecessary social obligations, and I was happy to linger in ambiguity through the remainder of my teen years. (I would later find out that in Utah, you are either Mormon or you're not, and I would soon be faced with the choice that still has me flapping about twenty-five years later.)

What lingered in no-man's-land with me, however, was my mother's obvious but unspoken sadness, deepened by my actions. Since the day my father dropped his Mormon facade, shortly after he convinced my mother to marry him in a Mormon temple, my mother's sadness hung around the house like cobwebs. I loved her so obsessively I would have given anything to lift those webs, but it didn't take me long to recognize my impotency when confronted with the depth of her longing for God and the Mormon Church.

ON NAUVOO'S MULHOLLAND Street, the narrow main drag, the sun disappears for the day behind the Hotel Nauvoo, a grand old house painted baby blue with white trim. The Hotel Nauvoo seems to be the center of town, and I find out later it remains so because it features the main attraction—a nightly buffet boasting a hundred or so offerings. I kick the side stand down and carefully lean the bike to my left. It always leans farther than I think it should, especially when carrying a heavy load, and I momentarily panic thinking it is going all the way to the ground. I slowly swing my right leg around behind me and groan audibly as I attempt to get my knee, elbow, and wrist joints unkinked. I peel off my gloves, which combined with my sweat have left my hands stained black from the wrist down.

An elderly man stands on the sidewalk watching this process, while his wife and another couple keep walking, leaving him behind.

"BMW, huh?" he says.

"Yeah," I reply, not sure what else to say.

His three companions stop and look back, obviously annoyed with him. They shuffle a little to let him know they are ready to go, and he takes one step toward them but stops again, looking at the bike and shaking his head. His wife huffs loudly, and I understand that I'm in the middle of something that's been going on for decades. I reach up with black hands in a futile attempt to fluff the sweaty hair that's stuck to my head.

"I only buy American," he tells me. "I'd never buy foreign; too hard to get parts."

So that's what this is about. He has no interest in me or the bike, just wants to scold me for driving into the heartland of America on a vehicle made in Germany. I nod and start rummaging in my tank bag for my wallet.

"I'll bet you have a hell of a time getting parts for that thing," he insists.

"No, not really."

"Well, even if you can get them, I'll bet you have to pay an arm and a leg for them." For some reason I want to give him this, although compared to the American-made Harley-Davidson, not only are the parts, but the cost of the entire bike, more reasonable. I am too tired to explain all of this to him and something—maybe it's the annoyance on the faces of his companions or his obvious need to be right—tugs at me to let him win.

"Oh, yeah," I say. "I just paid four hundred dollars for a fuel filter in St. Louis [not mentioning that the filter is inside the gas tank and takes hours to replace]." He beams satisfaction, and I am happy to make him happy.

"I just bought a Chevrolet Mark III," he says. "Ever heard of a Mark III?" and he points to the vehicle in front of my bike. I assure him that I have not. He starts in on what is likely going to be a lengthy list of the qualities of his big American automobile when his wife decides she's had enough.

"We need to go to the gas station and put air in this tire NOW!" she says, pointing to a low rear tire on the back of the Mark III, and he scuttles away quickly with one last assurance to me that "Yep, American is the way to go."

"Nice talking to you," I say.

I enter the Hotel Nauvoo and sidle up to the front desk, the knees of my riding pants rubbing and screeching, my hair stuck to my head, my hands black from the wrist down. All heads in the dining room turn my way, but no one speaks to me. The desk clerk is beyond cheerful, as if to show me and the gaping onlookers that she's seen it all and that the pitiful sight of me is nothing to throw her off her game. I fill out the paperwork and sign the credit card slip with fingers that barely cooperate. She hands me a key and sends me three blocks down the road to the Motel Nauvoo, a cheerful yellow twelve-room roadside motel squatting behind petunias and a fresh-cut lawn. In the parking lot, I stop momentarily to get my brain thinking again like a motorcyclist instead of like an extremely tired middle-aged woman who just wants to see a bed. The parking lot slopes slightly toward the rooms, which means I need to turn around and back the bike into a parking space. As I maneuver the loaded bike in my usual awkward way, an older couple leaves their room, gets into their SUV, and pulls away. A moment later, they return, showing obvious concern for me.

"Are you OK?" the man asks through a rolled-down window.

"Yeah," I yell through my helmet as the bike slowly rolls back until the rear tire meets the cement abutment.

"Do you need some help?"

I put the side stand down and pull off my helmet. "No, but thanks."

I am at once touched and annoyed that he has come back to help. He says it might have been easier to pull straight in, and I explain to him that indeed it would have been but impossible to push the bike backward up the slope to get back out again. I get off the bike and walk toward the car. I know immediately they are Mormon. For one thing, they are tourists in Nauvoo, and as far as I can tell, Nauvoo sports only one tourist attraction. But more than that, they have that Mormon aura that is recognizable to anyone who grew up in the Mormon Church no matter how long you've been away—an absolute perfect balance of righteousness and humility. The true believers have it, and those of us teetering on the edges can always recognize it.

The other reason I know they are Mormon is because they came back to help. I'm not saying that Mormons have a corner market on being Good Samaritans, but they certainly have perfected it to an art.

"Are you folks Mormon?" I ask them. They tell me they are and from Wyoming and are driving the Mormon Trail. They started in Palmyra, New York, where Joseph Smith started the Church. They ask where I'm from and what I'm doing in Nauvoo, but never ask if I'm Mormon, probably assuming I am not. I don't fit the profile. I tell them I am traveling the trail also.

"Alone?" the woman asks.

"Yes," I say and ask them what kind of weather I can expect in Wyoming in a couple of weeks.

"Are you traveling all alone?" the woman asks again, and before I can answer her husband says, "Yeah, sure, alone," as if wanting to exhibit his understanding of independent women, but his wife's not buying it.

"Completely alone?" she asks again.

"Yes, alone," he says firmly but without anger as I continue to nod my head in her direction.

"Oh, for heaven's sake," she says shaking her head and sounding remarkably like my mother. They promise me good riding weather through Wyoming before they pull away.

I pull a duffel bag, two saddlebags, and a tank bag off my bike, drag it all into the motel room just a few feet away, pull off my riding gear, and collapse on the bed in my underwear. I am among Mormons. This fact brings me a surprising sense of comfort and safety. The solace comes certainly from being close to something familiar when I am alone and far from home, but also from what I know about the Mormon people. They are to be trusted.

# 5

WHEN I LEFT THE MORMON CHURCH AS A YOUNG woman living in Utah, I discovered a world cleanly split into Mormons and anti-Mormons. Although it may have widened some over the years, the middle ground between those two camps in the mid-1970s felt extremely narrow, and the social pressure to form an alliance with one group or the other weighed heavily.

The reasons for such a determined split can be traced back to Joseph Smith and the origins of the Church. Joseph envisioned a fusion of the secular and the religious, a kingdom of God on earth, a state governed by the priesthood and led by the prophet/president. When the Mormons built Salt Lake City and then quickly spread throughout the surrounding territory, there was little to keep Joseph's vision from becoming reality.

Brigham Young, however, being steeped more in practicality than his visionary predecessor, soon recognized the need for a secular government if the Mormons had any hope of repairing the ongoing conflict between them and the federal government. (The conflict was caused in part by polygamy and in part by the Mormons' ongoing resentment of the government's lack of intervention and protection when they were being driven from the United States.) In 1849, the Church set up the supposedly secular State of Deseret and, not surprisingly, elected Brigham Young as its first governor.

Throughout the nineteenth and twentieth centuries, the separation between the Mormon Church and the secular state of Utah certainly widened, but it has never been uncommon to find Mormon men holding many of Utah's significant governmental and political posts. While today's president of the Church repeatedly tries to convince media sources that the Church has no interest or influence in politics, many residents of Utah believe that while the letter of the law separating church and state may have been met, the spirit of the law never has been. This sentiment causes some resentment on the part of non-Mormons and some defensiveness on the part of Mormons. I ran head-on into this simmering contention when I left the Church.

In the mid-1970s, the first thing a person did in any social setting in Utah was determine who "is" and who "isn't." Holding a beer or sipping a glass of wine automatically put you in the "isn't" category and was quite often an open invitation to some Mormon-bashing, most heatedly from those who had once been in the "is" category and who seemed eager to forget everything good about the Church and willing to pass along egregious stereotypes and misconceptions as if they were being tested to get into the anti-Mormon camp. Shortly after leaving the Church, I seized the opportunity to join in, to scoff at the Mormons with some pressing need to distance myself. I didn't necessarily believe the tenets of anti-Mormonism, but it was like reciting the Articles of Faith in church—part of the ritual, a social obligation.

There was then and still is a middle category called "jack Mormon," which basically means nonpracticing Mormon. But in my mind the jack Mormon category was reserved for those who wanted to have a few years of drinking and partying before they became "good" Mormons—which aptly describes 99 percent of my high school friends—or for people like my father who have a beef with the Church but will never consider any religion but Mormonism. I couldn't fit into either of those groups.

Outside of Utah, the categories blur. But still, whenever I identify myself as coming from Utah a further identification is usually requested. I currently refer to myself as non-Mormon, but this is difficult to justify. I've never been excommunicated from the Church and have never asked to have my name removed from the rolls. The institution still claims me as a member, and I'm reminded of this gently but often through visits and letters. I'm obviously not in the same category as a non-Mormon who has never been part of the Church. I'm unable to join this category unconditionally because the technical accuracy of my non-Mormon claim can be called into question—I was baptized and raised in the Church; I'm the daughter of a Mormon mother and a jack Mormon father; and the amount of Mormonism I carry in my genes is staggering.

I have firmly removed myself, however, from the anti-Mormon camp. I am incapable of responding to the disparagement of Mormons because I'm uncomfortable with all possible responses. I'm lost somewhere between the two sides, not willing to concur with the common caricatures of Mormons as oddball zealots and obedient dupes, but unable to defend an institution that I know to be overtly sexist, homophobic, and oppressive. Had I been honest with myself in my

Mormon-bashing days, I would have known I was missing part of the equation. I didn't then and still don't understand the kind of faith and belief Hannah held when she boarded the ship in Liverpool. It cannot possibly be shrugged off as stupidity or ignorance. Religious faith and belief are obviously not reached purely through the brain. They operate at a deeper level; they seep into the flesh and weave the mind together with the heart.

"Even late in life," writes William James, "some thaw, some release may take place, some bolt be shot back in the barrenest breast, and the man's hard heart may soften and break into religious feeling." It is this possibility that forces me back to my Mormon beginnings.

THE SETTING OF the sun, which signifies the end of something to most, feels like a beginning to me. I love the silence of nighttime. I feel alive and vibrant moving through darkness alone, stepping through a quiet world of unconscious bodies. Some of the small, horrible acts cease—the brash fall silent and their victims find peace—and beautiful things replace them: A mother edges up to the side of a crib in a room barely illuminated by a slice of moon; an old woman jots memories in margins of a book in a spot of soft light surrounded by inky blackness; I fixate on the stars and ask unanswerable questions. The hope of finding answers dwells in the darkness but dissipates with the morning light.

Because I'm loath to waste the night in a state of unconsciousness, I sleep later than most in the mornings, and peering out the window of my motel room, I see the sun beam in on the red tank of my motorcycle like a spotlight, then fall flat on the surrounding pavement with nothing else to catch it.

I am not surprised but always disheartened to see a parking lot empty of all vehicles but mine. Anxiety sets in—almost panic—as if I've awakened into the episode of *The Twilight Zone* where all life has disappeared from the earth. There's nothing lonelier than a deserted motel parking lot in the morning. Everyone has moved on without me; they are laughing over a plate dripping with pancakes and syrup and pumping gasoline into their cars.

I shower and dress quickly, stuff my backpack, and rush away from the motel. In one startling moment, the sun disappears and the rain drops directly from sky to ground in globs, then slows to a steady drizzle. I duck into the drugstore across the street and come out with a cheap plastic slicker pulled over my shorts and T-shirt. In less than five minutes, soaked from the inside out with my own sweat, I realize why I'm the only person wearing such a getup. I opt for the freshness of the drizzle and dump the $2 slicker into the nearest garbage can.

By the time I reach the construction site at the end of Mulholland, the rain has stopped and the sun has reappeared. I find a bench across the street and up a small rise on the front porch of the motherhouse of the Benedictine Sisters of Saint Mary Monastery, which has been purchased and will soon be demolished by the Mormons to allow for an unobstructed view of the Mississippi River from the steps of the temple the way Joseph Smith envisioned it more than a century ago. The Mormon temple is only about half-finished and surrounded by cranes and earthmovers sunk into fresh, dark dirt, but none of that can hide its opulence. All Mormon temples are magnificent structures, but this one even more so than usual.

Mormons' unique mix of meekness and arrogance stems from years of persecution and ridicule mixed with the certainty that they are God's chosen people, members of the only *true* church on earth. That fusion has never been more apparent than in the Mormons who have returned to Nauvoo. After 150 or so years away from the small Illinois town, the Mormons are returning in the way only Mormons can—shaking with humility at the same time they construct a fifty-four-thousand-square-foot, six-story, $26 million replica of their original temple, complete with window glass brought from France and Germany, handcrafted doors and window frames, limestone quarried in Alabama, and sun-, moon-, and starstones crafted in four different states and Canada. It will stand on the spot the original once stood—smack in the middle of what was the Mormon city of Nauvoo with a population of at least twelve thousand and possibly as many as twenty thousand (historical records conflict on this point) and is now the tiny town of Nauvoo, population about twelve hundred, made up mostly of non-Mormons whose families arrived during the last century. The Mormons are now returning to Nauvoo the way Mormons have done since their early days—in a large herd.

THE MORMONS FIRST arrived in Nauvoo in 1839 led by their tormented prophet, Joseph Smith, after being driven out of Kirtland, Ohio, and the Missouri counties of Jackson, Clay, Daviess, and Caldwell. They were not politely asked to leave. The Mormons had an uncanny knack for getting on the worst side of their non-Mormon neighbors. The causes are numerous—some factual, some grossly exaggerated by their enemies—but always with the same result: a stern invitation to move on.

Mormons lived in a closed society with a deliberate merging of church and state, and they often voted as a solid bloc in state and national elections. Accumulating members faster than they were covering miles, they had the capability to play havoc with politics in any state they resided and sometimes did. To make things worse, the majority of the Mormon ranks were Yankees whose abolitionist views did not play well in the border state of Missouri at the time, although Joseph did his best to straddle an unstable fence on this issue. In addition, the Mormons' worship of a living prophet insulted the sensibilities of the Christians already in the area, particularly when that prophet seemed so obviously flawed to them. Joseph found himself on the unfortunate side of some financial dealings and was sued and arrested numerous times for inability to pay his debts. Rumors of polygamy started circulating as early as the 1830s (they were denied by the Mormons until the 1850s). But the overwhelming factor in alienating their neighbors wherever they went was something they could neither deny nor hide; it was and still is the very essence of Mormonism: the sanctimonious aura that must accompany the knowledge that they alone are the proprietors of truth, that they firmly grasp the keys to the kingdom of God.

The Mormons fled Missouri amid the tarring and feathering, brutal beatings, and jailings of Joseph and other Church leaders, amid the burning by mobs of their homes and property, amid the slaughter of seventeen Mormon men and boys—including a nine-year-old boy who, while begging for his life, was told "nits will make lice" just before his brains were blown out—at Haun's Mill in Missouri, and amid gubernatorial orders that they be exterminated or driven from the state. The Mormons defended themselves by forming a small, secret militia known among Mormons as the Sons of Dan and among Gentiles as the Destroying Angels. In *The Gathering of Zion,* Stegner aptly describes the Mormon settlement of Nauvoo shortly after their expulsion from Missouri:

*So Mormonism reeled back from Missouri to lick its wounds for one winter on the east bank of the Mississippi, and then, in a dazzling display of recuperative power, gathered again around its escaped Prophet to build the city of Nauvoo . . . In five years they transformed a stretch of high prairie and wooded bluffs, a malarial riverbottom swamp, and a fever-and-ague hamlet called Commerce into the city of Zion, the largest town in all of Illinois and the show-place of the upper Mississippi, with a population of 20,000 and a partly completed temple that was surely the most grandiose building in the Middle West, and would shortly be the most imposing ruin.*

That imposing ruin looms in front of me now, slowly taking back the dignity it lost after being looted and burned by mobs, and finally toppled to the ground by a tornado less than a decade after its first stone was laid. A crane effortlessly lifts a four-by-six-foot, 2,850-pound sunstone to its destination at the top of a column. On its way up, it twists slowly from one side to the other as if to catch the view before being placed into its permanent southern exposure spot, from which it, along with twenty-nine others, each carved from a single piece of limestone, will cast a tranquil gaze upon templegoers and passersby.

Brigham Young led the Saints out of Nauvoo in 1846, seven years after and in much the same manner as they arrived—under the threat of death. But in spite of being gone more than 150 years, in spite of the non-Mormons who have since lived and died in Nauvoo and claim the town as their own, Mormons feel a sense of ownership here. I'm prone to give them that. I've spoken to a few townspeople who are mourning the loss of their small-town life to what is sure to become a steady pilgrimage of many of the proclaimed 10.7 million members of the Mormon Church. No one could understand that sense of loss better than today's Mormons, whose ancestors built Nauvoo from a swamp to a city before they walked away from their homes, their property, and most of their belongings with little or no compensation, as they had done several times before.

I think about my great-great-grandmother Maria during those times. She was one year old when the Mormons were forced out of Missouri into Illinois, seven years old when they were driven from Illinois, and thirteen years old when she arrived in the Salt Lake Valley.

When Maria was five years old, Joseph Smith and his brother Hyrum were murdered. She would have been unable to understand the magnitude of this event, but she surely could not have escaped the raw emotions flowing from the adults around her, who went into a simultaneous spiral of unabated grief and resolve. At seven years old, Maria would stand at the gravesite of her mother, dead after a fall down a flight of stairs, leaving her the only female in a family of six, and at twelve years old, she would bury her new stepmother along the trail to Utah.

Maria's story was a fairly common one among the early Mormons. As there was little time for grieving between the building and the fleeing of homes and cities, I'm sure it was expected she would take it in stride, and left with few options, I'm sure she did just that. During those early years of her life she would come to understand loss—and faith—in a way that gave her a generosity and toughness that will be forever beyond my grasp.

We don't allow ourselves to experience loss in this manner anymore. We have few expectations that a child could naturally understand it, grow from it, and emerge from it full of knowledge and compassion. When a child loses a parent today, we gather her up and rush her off to the child psychologist. When an adult loses a partner through death or divorce, well-meaning friends urge her into "therapy" or "support" as if she will be forever damaged by going through the ordeal in solitude. Ads to make us believe that feeling buoyant and joyful every day of our lives is an inalienable right as easily attainable as swallowing a pill have confused the true condition of depression with the normal course of life and loss.

We've traded faith and fortitude for therapists, support groups, and antidepressant drugs. We treat loss not like the natural process it is, but like a disease to be cured, and we quickly assign the label of victim to the child and expect her to act accordingly. What the child has really sacrificed, what we've all sacrificed, is the opportunity to experience our losses fully and gracefully.

The absence of faith in my life seems most disquieting when I think about Maria during those years and the unwavering faith she carried in her small body, a notion more certain and mature than any sentiment I may have experienced in my forty-five years.

Not much was written about the adult Maria, and I have only two pictures of her, both in later life looking sober, but calm and certain. I imagine her as a seven-year-old child walking along the path where I now sit, clinging tightly to the hand of an older brother, to gaze in awe at the construction of the original temple. Subtract the modern equipment and add a significant number of workers—at its peak the original temple had three hundred workers a day—and the scene must have looked very much as it does now. I imagine her stooping to collect a stone from this site, something small, something she can slip between folds of clothing and carry always, something she will never lose.

Her family lived in Illinois with the certainty—as did all Mormons—that their troubles were not over and their God would once more test their faith with everything they owned and loved. They were up to the test. What was meant to be the dispersion and end of the Mormon Church—the death of Joseph—served to fortify their convictions, to intensify their identity as Saints. After the death of Joseph, the Mormons embraced each trial with a strange sort of gusto, each sacrifice representing one more opportunity to prove their worthiness, nudging them one or two steps closer to the kingdom of God.

After Joseph's death, they worked at a frantic pace to complete the temple in all its grandeur, never scrimping on Joseph's original vision, knowing full well they would leave the magnificent piece of architecture behind before the mortar dried. Ironically, their haste to complete the temple also served to hasten their departure from Nauvoo. Brigham Young, Joseph's successor, had promised Illinois government officials, who were growing uneasy with both the numbers of Mormons flowing into their state and the mob mentality of Mormon enemies, that the Mormons would leave "as soon as the grass grows and the water runs." But the restless Gentiles, eager to be rid of their strange neighbors, grew suspicious as they watched money and labor poured into the building of the temple. To them that looked nothing like preparing to leave. What they did not understand was that the Mormons were not just constructing a building, they were constructing a monument to God and a path to salvation. According to the word of Joseph, only in a temple could God's ordinances and glories be granted to the worthy. The Saints were desperate to flee their enemies' grasp, but they were equally desperate to do so fully endowed with the covenants of the Lord.

• • •

I ROUSE MYSELF from my perch and drop down off the small hill to get closer to the temple. I'm stunned not only with the quiet splendor of the building itself but with the result of Joseph's vision. I say I'm not a believer in Mormonism, although I'm not really sure what I mean by that statement anymore. At one time I defined "Mormonism" as the dogma and the patriarchal institution—neither of which resonate with me. But the culture of Mormonism, the subtle characteristics transmitted from one generation to another—how can I not believe in that? Denying something so pervasive in my life would be impossible, like attempting to erase and write simultaneously when the only tool available for doing so is a single pencil with an eraser tip. So Mormonism remains as elusive in my mind as God. But as I stand in front of this temple that so spectacularly represents the stunning success of Joseph's vision, I have to admit that I'm a believer at least in the dream.

I stoop to pick up a small round stone crusted with dried mud and begin to rub it clean with my thumb. It has no real significance other than being unearthed when the ground was turned for the restoration of the temple, but I slip it into my pocket anyway; it's a small thing that can be easily carried on a long journey.

The Mormons have purchased back much of the property they once owned, including the temple site and the home sites of many former Church leaders. In spite of their past, the Mormons laid brick filled with faith in the future, and many of the city buildings and homes built when Joseph was alive still stand. Others have been restored.

In each of the buildings, one or two senior-citizen missionaries in period garb stand ready and eager to share the story of persecution, a story the Mormons embraced so readily from the beginnings of their maltreatment that it caused an editor of the March 25, 1840, *Chicago Democrat* to stop just short of calling them "martyr mongers," calling them instead "men of sufficient sagacity to profit by anything in the shape of persecution."

Since then the Mormon Church has capitalized on the suffering of its early members in an almost Disney-like manner, building upscale visitor centers staffed with earnest missionaries who have committed the early atrocities to memory and are willing to recite them twenty or thirty times a day with equal emotion at dawn or dusk. Some centers, such as those in Nauvoo and Salt Lake City, are equipped with IMAX-style theaters showing the sad tales of the early Mormons in a series of professionally produced short movies. Unlike other museums and parks, they charge no admission fees; they count their profits in baptisms.

This is not to say the Mormons are insincere in the retelling of their story; they are most certainly genuine. The history of persecution in Mormonism is as much a part of the religion as the theology, maybe more. From the beginning of the Church, the persecution of its members built Mormonism from a religion into a culture, from a sect into a society, in which the members were asked to prove their worthiness and did so time and again. This history is taught alongside the Book of Mormon to every Mormon child, and rightly so.

When I recount the death of my great-great-great grandmother Welthea Bradford Hatch, dead from cholera two days after her thirty-seventh birthday, one year after leaving her comfortable New York home to trail after Joseph Smith, friends are stunned that I bear stories five generations old when they often don't even know the birthplace of their grandparents. Carrying such stories forms the inner landscape of a person;

you don't just set them aside and go about your life. To today's Mormons, the suffering of their ancestors is seen as a gift, much the same way all Christians view the suffering and death of Christ as a gift. To me personally, the gift looms large. I'm continually tugged back to Mormonism because no woman casually chops away at the very foundation that bears her weight.

# 6

MY MOTHER GREW UP WITH THE WHITEWASHED version of early Mormonism, as did her mother and probably her mother before her. Throughout my adolescence, my father would horrify my mother by speaking of Joseph Smith's fondness for women and Brigham Young's fondness for whiskey. Her horrification was what he was after, and when he'd see it on her face, he'd throw his head back and cackle. My brother grew to emulate my father in most every way, and before he was old enough to know what he meant by his words, he'd join in the fun. I'd watch the spectacle with little understanding of the events, but my mother's discomfort meant my discomfort. I don't remember at what age I knew this for certain, but I'm sure I sensed even before I left the crib that my mother was my life preserver in the noisy, blustering sea of my family. Any threat to her was a direct threat to me, and my stomach would swirl every time the sadness of her missed religion pushed through her make-the-best-of-things exterior.

Even now, after the Church's own historians have written candidly about some of the early Church practices, my mother shudders at the mention of Joseph Smith in any tone other than reverent adulation. And when she does, my stomach aches and I want to pull her into my arms and give her a safe place to hold on to her beliefs.

But the fact is, although my father's intentions were wrong, his facts were mostly right. The Mormons have done and continue to do a great deal of whitewashing of their story, preferring to leave out most references to polygamy, whiskey drinking, tobacco chewing, unpaid debts, bitter bickering and jockeying for power among early Church leaders, and their own night-riding militia, the most notorious member being Porter Rockwell. They prefer to concentrate on the martyrdom of Joseph, the unyielding persecution of their members, and their amazing powers of faith and restoration. But there's really no need.

The true story of the Mormons is heartbreaking and incredible enough. That they were unjustly persecuted for their religious beliefs is unchallenged by historians of all faiths. Bernard DeVoto described it as ". . . terrorism, arson, and gang warfare" that "cannot be justified or palliated," and Fawn Brodie called the barbarism of the anti-Mormon persecutors almost unparalleled in American religious history. And that the Mormons held remarkable powers of faith and unquestionable abilities of recovery is obvious when one reaches the other end of the Mormon Trail in the Salt Lake Valley.

The one story of Porter Rockwell the Mormons are fond of telling with a twinkle of mischief in their eyes is Porter's claim that he could prove his innocence when he was accused of the attempted murder of Missouri governor Lillburn Boggs. Boggs had issued an extermination order on the Mormons and was well hated by the lot of them. A blessing given by Joseph to Porter, who was Joseph's and later Brigham's self-appointed bodyguard, allowed Porter, known as a sharpshooter, the freedom to ride and defend with reckless disregard for his own safety. Joseph prophesied that no bullet would ever touch Porter, and the long-haired zealot had been riding wild in the name of God and Joseph ever since. When someone filled Boggs with buckshot, Porter was naturally fingered. Porter's claim to innocence in the Boggs case was the governor himself. According to today's version of the story, Porter claimed that "if it had been me who shot him, he'd be dead."

Chances are it was not the shooter's poor aim but Boggs's own obstinacy that kept him alive—he took three bullets to the head. Still, Porter was held in jail for nine months, then released for lack of evidence.

It might behoove the Mormons to allow a little more of the human aspect into their story. Joseph is portrayed now as a prophet and a martyr, dangerously close to Christ himself. But he was also a man with a disarming sense of humor who loved, in addition to God, three things—women, power, and wealth—and he designed his church to accommodate an accumulation of each of those. Today, historians still argue whether Joseph's doctrine of polygamy resulted from theology or sexuality or a combination of both. But as president of his church, mayor of his city, and lieutenant general of his militia, Joseph was accountable to no one but his own God.

It was from those positions of power that the truly captivating element of Joseph's personality emerged—his infinite compassion toward his followers. Until his death, the control remained his, but Joseph truly loved people and spreading the wealth of the Lord's gifts gave him endless moments of joy, and that mattered to Joseph. "Men are that they might have joy," says the Book of Mormon (2 Nephi 2:25).

A good part of Joseph's appeal as a prophet, and one of the reasons the Mormon Church was attracting members like children to an ice cream truck, was Joseph's guarantee not only of salvation in the next life but his delivered promise of the same here on earth—that all members would contribute and all members would be taken care of. Today's Church still holds fast to Joseph's promise. With a model welfare program second to none, few go hungry in the Mormon Church.

Joseph's God required no vow of poverty. From the time Joseph was a boy, he was drunk on fantasies of finding buried treasure, and even in his early days as leader of the Church, he found himself in trouble and in debt after pursuing some get-rich-quick schemes through questionable land and banking deals. Then, as now, material prosperity among Church members and the Church itself fit right in with the building of the Kingdom of God here on earth, just one of the basic blessings of the Lord.

Many Mormons would prefer not to look too closely at Joseph the man versus Joseph the prophet. Doing so throws some huge and unwieldy wrenches into the faith of the Mormon Church, historically based on the pure thoughts and intentions of Joseph himself. Fear of such scrutiny was evidenced by the swift Mormon condemnation of Fawn Brodie's biography, *No Man Knows My History: The Life of Joseph Smith*, which portrayed Joseph as a ordinary man full of life and laughter, tenderness, sexual desires, and a penchant for power and wealth; and as an extraordinary man of vision, vigor, imagination, tenacity, and charisma. Portraying Joseph in such a state of humanness resulted in Brodie's excommunication from the Church.

In addition to buttressing Joseph's prophet persona for the preservation of the Church's tenets, a history of persecution has taught the Mormons to defend themselves and their beliefs with a fierce will, and they are hesitant to give their critics the smallest opening. I understand this. Not long ago, I was in a meeting in Tucson when a young woman, talking about the 2002 Winter Olympics, said, "Salt Lake City is such a beautiful place; too bad the Mormons have it." I felt a bristle at the base of my skull, reminded once again of the animosity still harbored for Mormons, and I immediately went on the defensive as if I were genetically programmed. "It wasn't a beautiful city *before* the Mormons got there," I snapped back. Unfortunately, the Mormons' insistence on selecting historical facts in such a *saintly* way does them a great disservice; it allows their critics to dismiss them as bleating sheep.

AS I MAKE my way from one historic building to the next, I'm a little numbed by one sad story of flight after another. I'm mostly thinking about food, about the need for a shiny modern hot-dog stand on the corner in front of the historic bakery offering nothing but a tiny sample of an old gingerbread cookie recipe. My stomach is growling, but I've opted to leave the bike at the hotel, giving in to a desire to have my legs straight under me for a day or two before the long journey west begins, and it's a good hike back up the hill to modern Nauvoo and food. Thinking I can handle only one more story before I go in search of nourishment, I stop at the former home of John Taylor, the printer and newspaper publisher of early Nauvoo.

I join a small group of British tourists already assembled and follow them quietly. In the middle of an upstairs bedroom sits a small black carved-wood rocking horse—about eighteen inches high—with a flowing tail and mane made out of horse hair. As the story goes, when the family of John Taylor fled Nauvoo, they took only essentials, leaving the little horse behind. Taylor's small son cried for the first two days of the trip, unable to speak. Finally, the boy told his father he was sad because he would never see his little horse again. To retrieve his son's rocking horse, John Taylor rode two days back to Nauvoo and snuck into town at night, avoiding a riled-up mob of Gentiles celebrating the departure of the Mormons and threatening to kill any stragglers.

I feel an overwhelming and sort of twisted-up sense of grief as I lean against the doorjamb staring at the little horse, tears falling off my face. The man telling the story, a descendant of John Taylor, cries also, and we both stand silently as the British tourists, who had happened upon Nauvoo by accident, turn on their heels and start down the stairs. When the group is gone and the silence between us grows uncomfortable, I smile briefly and force something out of my mouth. "How did the horse get back here?" I ask. He tells me it had remained in his family and had been returned to Nauvoo during the restoration. I nod and leave.

Outside I sit on a piece of damp lawn under a shade tree and try to work through what I'm feeling. My grief seems not to be for John Taylor or his young son or any of the Mormons fleeing for their lives, but for the tiny rocking horse left behind without a young boy to love it. I once passed a park where a rusted toy dump truck had been left behind in a sandbox, and knowing that once-beloved toy would never be retrieved, washed off, and played with again momentarily engulfed me in sadness. Later that night, I asked Will if he felt sadness for discarded inanimate objects like a toy or a book. He looked at me in that way he does sometimes when he thinks I've moved too far from reality and said, "No." But I'm not mourning any New Age phenomenon that might give a spirit to a book or a soul to a rusted-out toy. I'm not sure exactly what I'm feeling, but whatever it is was stamped on my soul at an early age. I emerged from childhood with every doll, every game I'd ever played with, in almost pristine condition, and they remained that way in my parents' home until my two nieces got hold of them and turned them into ratty-haired, clothes-torn dolls and games with missing pieces. When I found them years later in that condition, I cried.

As the moisture from the lawn soaks through my clothing, I begin to rise. But a story I recall reading, stuffed among the many scraps of paper my grandmother scrawled upon, forces me back to the ground. When she was a child, her mother and father once took her to a Christmas party in their small Idaho town. She described the room as one filled with happy but poor farming families and a beautifully decorated tree on which hung gifts for the children:

> *The first thing my eyes spotted was a beautiful doll on the tree. It had a red and white striped dress, a red crocheted bonnet and boots. That was all I could talk about, and Mother and Father just grinned. When Santa Claus took it down I lost my breath and sat down weakly. Then I remember seeing Mother and Father smile to themselves again. When Santa read my name, I was wild with joy for that meant the beautiful doll was to be mine. It was certainly a nice Christmas, and I was never more happy in my life. I loved that doll through life and finally gave it to my sister Annie's girls.*

The doll has long since disappeared, but the story has not. Maybe this is the source of my empathy for inanimate objects—the longing of a little girl who wants a chance to love a doll in a crocheted bonnet. I have a hunch that my not having children plays a part also in my love of this story of my grandmother's and the sentiments I'm feeling after hearing the story of the rocking horse left behind in Nauvoo—loss, unease, fear—but if I were to be asked in what way, I wouldn't be able to articulate an answer. The decision not to have children and the decision to leave the Church seem equally dangerous to me right now. Yet even as I write this, I know the opposite choices are not right for me, either.

I've been surrounded by people for whom the decision to have children seemed as simple as deciding what kind of bread to buy at the grocery store. They get married and have children as if one were an inevitable consequence of the other—like garden blooms after a rainfall. But the decision seemed monumental to me, the most important choice of my life. What single decision has more impact, more permanence?

In my first marriage, which lasted seven years in the late seventies and early eighties, people routinely accused me of selfishness for my decision not to have children. Outwardly I shrugged their comments off, but inwardly I was confused and hurt. They assumed that I didn't want to devote my time to a child, that I would prefer to be free to travel or even just to go to movies. They assumed I'd rather spend my money on clothes and cars than on diapers and college savings accounts. None of those things entered into my thinking about children. In fact, the reasons for having children seemed overwhelmingly selfish: wanting the unconditional love of a child, the total dependence of a child; wanting to understand my own capabilities for love and devotion. The Mormon Church provides an unselfish reason for motherhood—there are lots of souls up there waiting for a human body—but that didn't ring true with me.

The decision to bring a human life into a society filled with violence and fear, consumption and waste, was daunting to say the least—it felt a little like throwing a newborn baby into the middle of a *Terminator* movie sequel. The choice to introduce another into a species whose membership is lavishly abundant, a species quickly devouring its own habitat, seemed overwhelmingly selfish and almost ludicrous.

The decision, then, whether to bear a child rested either in ignorance or faith. As with my search for faith in God and religion, so went my search for faith in motherhood. I expected the compelling reason to believe, and the compelling reason to bring a child into the world, to present itself, to clearly emerge from the collision of destruction and sadness in the world around me. It never did.

So, at forty-five, I stand godless and childless, and that's frightening. I am now starkly aware that a piece of myself lies buried, a piece that can be accessed only through motherhood. It is a piece of myself that I will never know. As with many things, ideas that seemed lucid and obvious twenty years ago become muddled with age and wisdom. And it occurs to me at times when I can't push away feelings like those I'm now experiencing in this town built by my ancestors on the Mississippi River that maybe faith doesn't work the way I've been expecting it to work. Maybe a person has to do more than just wait patiently for it to show up.

I go home to Utah three or four times a year, and my mother and I spend days digging through paper stored at her house— stacks of genealogy and family histories, poems and stories scribbled in my grandmother's and great-grandmother's handwriting, letters describing sickness and hardships, brief glimpses of despair that always end with faith in God, in the "true prophet of the Lord, Joseph Smith," and in the Church itself.

While we sort through the papers, my mother and I cling to each other as if we know we are coming to the end of something. This has nothing to do with carrying forward the legacy of my family. With thirty-two first cousins who have more than 240 offspring of their own, there is little danger of losing the family history. What I'm feeling is much closer to the bone. It resides within and between my mother and me. I stand before her, a childless apostate. She and I have shared a connection that engulfs the conviction and sacrifice of five generations of Mormon women. This tether that has gently held me, guided me, and given me plenty of slack has been cleanly snipped by me. I'm holding the two frayed ends in my hands. Part of me wants to let them drop, and part of me wishes I knew how to tie a good knot.

# 7

MORMON GARDENS ARE MAGNIFICENT—LUSH AND colorful—and the Monument to Women Garden near the Nauvoo visitors center is no exception. When I lived in Salt Lake City during my most radical Mormon-hating phase, I would be drawn once or twice a day from my downtown office building to the gardens of the temple or the Church headquarters, feeling a mix of smugness and guilt that I could sit in a spot of beauty provided by the Mormons while cultivating my hostility toward them. I wanted badly to detest them as they walked past with their proud smiles and "beautiful day" remarks, but I loved them for giving me fifty different kinds of flowers to walk among, to stroke, to feast my eyes on, to stick my nose in. And I loved them for allowing me to sit day after day, hour after hour, without ever once disturbing my peace with anything more assertive than a friendly nod. I'm baffled to this day by the myth of the aggressive, foot-in-the-door Mormon missionary; that has never been my experience with Mormons.

In the abundant and kaleidoscopic Monument to Women Garden, sculptures of women lurk around me, many of course devoted to the Mormon female ideals of childbearing and child rearing, but a surprising number reflect women in artistic and business pursuits unadorned by man or child. A nice attempt, but at least ten out of thirteen pieces in the garden were sculpted by men.

Theology aside, my rift with the Mormons resides here, in this garden, among the perky daisies and dainty columbine, here at this beautiful yet feeble gesture toward Mormon women. In practice, the leaders of the modern Mormon Church show no respect for a woman unless she has a baby attached to her breast and a toddler wrapped around her knee. Casting women in bronze and planting them among the peonies won't fool anyone who doesn't want to be fooled into thinking Mormons revere their women.

From the time of Joseph Smith's death in 1844 until today, the power of Mormon women within the Church has been evaporating faster than a splash of rainwater in the Great Salt Lake Desert. Scholars have found evidence that Joseph intended women to play a strong role in the leadership of the Church, not only through the Relief Society, which he set up to be governed entirely by women in a structure parallel to the priesthood, but also through certain ordinances of the priesthood. Brigham Young also acknowledged the collective and individual intellectual and spiritual power of women, and encouraged them out of their kitchens and into schools and positions of authority within the community. In a 1869 sermon, Brigham Young stated, "We have sisters here who, if they had the privilege of studying, would make just as good mathematicians or accountants as any man," and he made sure they did have that privilege.

But in the early 1900s, after both Joseph and Brigham were dead, Church leaders began calling the Relief Society an "auxiliary" organization. Priesthood ordinances such as blessing the sick, performed by women since the beginning of Mormonism, were at first discouraged and eventually banned. Right around the time of the 1960s feminist movement, the leaders of the Church passed directives to discontinue the Relief Society magazine and place all Relief Society funds, publications, operations, and curricula under the auspices of the all-male priesthood, thereby removing all women from any decision-making position, including those for even the "auxiliary" female organizations. The Relief Society Declaration, a manifesto for Mormon women announced in 1999, was conceived, drafted, and approved by men.

The Mormon Proclamation on the Family identifies the role of men as that of "presiding over their families." Women have a responsibility to follow their husband's counsel and instruction as long as those instructions fall within the doctrines of the Church (established by men). The primary role of women is to bear children, and "mothers are primarily responsible for the nurture of those children." The proclamation doesn't address the role of childless women in the Mormon Church.

In the Mormon publication *A Parent's Guide*, Church leaders preach that "girls ought to be taught the arts and sciences of housekeeping, domestic finances, sewing, and cooking. Boys need to learn home repair, career preparation, and the protection of women." The rule of Mormon men permeates the Church from the elegant Salt Lake City offices of the president and his twelve apostles right down to the bishop in charge of the smallest congregation in the smallest town.

The women of my family have lived with this increasingly stifling doctrine for generations. When I was younger and more certain about almost everything, I assumed the Mormon Church was dictating the facts of their lives, that they were simply too weak to extricate themselves from the Mormon legacy they were swaddled in from birth. It was a lofty position I held in my twenties and thirties—certain of my own superior judgment and intellect. But in the face of my rational arguments, the women in my family never wavered in their commitment to the Church. They also never wavered in their devotion to me, never chided me, never dismissed me, and never turned away from me. Humility is a difficult thing to teach, but the women in my family never give up.

As the years passed, my exalted certainty on this issue and so many others began to dissipate and was replaced by curiosity, by wonder, by possibility. I found myself contemplating the idea that the women in my family were, in fact, making choices—fully aware and conscious of their decisions.

After my father came clean about his feelings for the Church shortly after marrying my mother, he forbade her to wear temple garments—the undergarments worn by all Mormons who have been through a temple ceremony—because he didn't find them sexy. He threw his own aside like a dirty old T-shirt. This stunned my mother right down to her soul. Temple ceremonies are considered the most sacred of all Church rituals, and no Mormon goes through a temple marriage lightly. Mormons have to prove themselves worthy and get a "temple recommend" from Church leadership before they can enter a temple, so my father had fooled more than just his wife. A temple marriage, unlike a Mormon marriage that might take place in a meetinghouse, seals the two people together beyond death "for time and all eternity." It is believed the temple garments act as a physical and spiritual shield, a protection against the power of the destroyer while on earth, and as a reminder of the covenants taken in the temple ceremony. My mother took the wearing of them and her temple vows as seriously as anything in her life.

My father threw a fit when she tried to pay tithing. He left the house during the visiting teachers' monthly call—a common Mormon practice to check in with members—and went into a sarcastic tirade each month when the deacons knocked on the door to collect fast offerings, an additional tithe associated with a day of fasting each month.

My mother was torn in half, loving the Church more than she loved her husband, at the same time trying to follow Church doctrine that taught her to worship him and respect his wishes. She sought guidance from her sisters, who, operating under the same principles, encouraged her to stand by him, believing always that God would guide my father back to the Church. She eventually stopped going to church, worn down by my father's scorn. But she quietly simmered with her love for Joseph Smith and the God he had shown her ancestors and they in turn had shown her. Eventually, the simmer came to full boil again—I don't know the source of the heat—but thirty-six years after her marriage, when God still hadn't intervened with my father, my mother donned her temple garments, walked past my father on her way to church, and threatened to leave him if he stood in her way. He stepped aside.

Most of her life now revolves around church activity and commitments. She feels liberated and fulfilled. I asked her once if she didn't see the irony in finding liberation in an organization that grants men master-status among women, in finding fulfillment in an institution that bestows its highest honor—the priesthood—upon twelve-year-old boys but never upon women. I asked if she didn't see the irony in finding freedom in an organization that kept her in a difficult marriage for fifty years. Yes, she said, there was a bit of irony there, and she laughed quietly.

My mother shines in her work with the Relief Society. I have seen her organize twenty women into a legion of caretakers, chefs, chauffeurs, financiers, and diplomats when tragedy strikes a local family. I have seen her drive forty miles through a blizzard to get to the Salt Lake temple to do church work. I have seen her share a meal with a reclusive woman who wouldn't let anyone else walk through her front door. Since her return to the Church, I have seen her face change; I have seen lines fall away and return in exquisite softness. I have seen her at peace. I don't know the source of her peace—her return to the Church or the reclamation of a life. But watching my mother and the other women in my family, I am beginning to understand that the paths to liberation and fulfillment are many, and they are never clear, never simple.

American women are used to making decisions for themselves while operating within the confines of a patriarchal structure; we do it every day of our lives on a grand scale. And while some of us take on the daily burden of change—working to fix the political system, lobbying for women's rights, struggling against violence, putting ourselves in a position to challenge the patriarchy every day—most of us do not. We believe the equality ideology, we might send a little money to the National Organization for Women or Planned Parenthood, we might insist on keeping our own names after marriage, we do what we can when an opportunity arises and go on with our lives in a making-the-best-of-things sort of way. And we are quick to condemn women like my mother. Her willingness to comply with her subservient role in the Mormon Church is baffling at best, infuriating at worst. Or we simply assume she is no more than a pathetic gudgeon with a brain shrunk to the size of a pea from years, generations, of indoctrination.

However, those generations of indoctrination are not what one might expect; they are not without contradiction and complexity. In spite of my departure from the Church, Mormon women have a hold on me in ways that might surprise some people. They are my feminist role models. My mother and her sisters, typical Mormon wives and mothers all of them, planted in me and continue to nurture ideas of boundless imagination and passion; Maria, Anna Maria, and Hannah teach me about loss and perseverance. And the lessons of Mormon women don't start or stop with my own family.

Louisa Barnes Pratt, a Mormon woman who left Nauvoo with her four children, teaches me that equality is not a luxury; it can and should happen anyplace, anytime. On June 7, 1846, camped near Bonaparte, Iowa, during the exodus to Utah, Pratt wrote in her journal, "Last evening the ladies met to organize . . . Several resolutions were adopted . . . If the men wish to hold control over women, let them be on the alert. We believe in equal rights."

Susa Young Gates, daughter of Brigham Young and his twenty-second wife, Lucy Bigelow, teaches me balance, conviction, and sacrifice simply by being who she was: a wife; a mother of thirteen children; a prolific writer, editor, and publisher; a musician; a historian; a teacher; and a public speaker at such places as the 1899 International Women's Conference in London, where she spoke about women's rights and equality. Susan B. Anthony once asked Gates to give up Mormonism, which Anthony found too controversial for politics, and become the secretary of the National Council of Women. The decision was obvious to Gates; she remained a Mormon.

The editorials of Emmeline B. Wells in the *Women's Exponent*, an independent newspaper owned, written, edited, and operated by Mormon women of which Wells was editor for thirty-seven years, teach me the power of free speech and the written word. In July 1872, Wells had this to say about a woman's position on the pedestal: "See the manner in which ladies—a term for which I have little reverence or respect—are treated in public places! . . . She must be preserved from the slightest blast of trouble, petted, caressed, dressed to attract attention, taught accomplishments that minister to man's gratification; in other words, she must be treated as a glittering and fragile toy, a thing without brains or soul, placed on a tinseled and unsubstantial pedestal by man, as her worshipper."

Stories about Sarah M. Kimball turning Relief Society meetings into suffrage rallies and lessons in political procedure and law in the 1870s, 1880s, and 1890s teach me about activism. Wells, Kimball, and others formed associations with national women's rights leaders Anthony and Elizabeth Cady Stanton to campaign not only for the rights of women in Utah but for the rights of women everywhere. Wells was invited to speak at the National Women's Suffrage Association convention in 1879.

Indeed, Wells and Kimball might have seen themselves and other Utah women years ahead of the rest of the nation in terms of women's rights. From the time they arrived in Utah, Mormon women built and managed cooperatives; grew, harvested, and stored wheat; organized and ran the Deseret Silk Association to promote their own silk industry; invested in real estate; filled teaching positions; served on community boards and as directors and officers of business corporations; and pursued degrees in higher education.

Utah women started voting in 1870, fifty years prior to the passage of the Nineteenth Amendment, and held the vote until the U.S. Congress passed the Edmunds-Tucker Act in 1887, which, in an attempt to weaken the Mormon Church on many levels, banned polygamy and abolished the Utah women's vote. They became political activists in Utah's fight for statehood, making sure the proposed state constitution included women's suffrage, and they regained the vote when Utah became the forty-fifth state admitted to the Union in 1896, the third state in the Union with female suffrage. In the first state election, when Utah voters elected Dr. Martha Hughes Cannon, a physician and a Mormon plural wife, to the state senate, she was the first woman in the nation to hold such a position—and she defeated her husband, who was running for the same seat. The Utah voters also elected two women to the statehouse the same year.

But outside women's rights circles, among the general population of women in the East, Mormon women were rarely acknowledged as the feminists and political activists they were. In fact, the practice of polygamy often characterized them as the most severely oppressed women in the nation.

Among the Mormon women themselves, polygamy drew mixed responses. Some experienced it as an opportunity for independence by sharing housework and childcare responsibilities with sister-wives, allowing them to further their education or take jobs outside the home, and they embraced the intimate friendships they forged with the women they shared their lives with. In 1869, almost 50 percent of the students at Utah's University of Deseret were women. Polygamy allowed many Mormon women to attend medical school, and they were among the first women in the nation to receive medical degrees. These Mormon women saw polygamy as a true statement of feminism—women living their lives without need of a man's continual attention and daily approval, as evidenced by this excerpt of a September 1874 article in the *Women's Exponent:* "Is there nothing worth living for, but to be petted, humored and caressed, by a man? That is all very well as far as it goes, but that man is the only thing in existence worth living for I fail to see. All honor and reverence to good men; but they and their attentions are not the only sources of happiness on the earth, and need not fill up every thought of woman."

Other polygamous marriages, however, were fraught with jealousy and unequal distribution of material goods, leaving some women impoverished and miserable. Such were the arrangements that received national attention. Outside the Church, the response to polygamy was almost universally condemned as a practice that degraded and enslaved women. However, Elizabeth Cady Stanton had this to say about polygamous arrangements after a visit to Utah: "As I stood among these simple people, so earnest in making their experiment in religion and social life, and remembered all the persecutions they had suffered and all they had accomplished in that desolate, far-off region, where they had, indeed, made 'the wilderness blossom like the rose,' I appreciated, as never before, the danger of intermeddling with the religious ideas of any people."

In spite of the fact that only a small minority of Mormons actually practiced polygamy—exact figures are unknown, but estimates range anywhere from 3 percent to 20 percent—during the fifty or so years it was endorsed by the Church, and in spite of the fact that the doctrine was banned by Church officials in 1890, it remains one of the most controversial and notable "Mormonisms" today. I'm continually surprised by the number of people I meet who believe it is still commonly practiced in the Mormon Church. I've been asked if I come from a polygamous family, and when I tell people that Mormon Church members haven't practiced polygamy in more than one hundred years, they look at me as if I'm in on the secret and the cover-up. The polygamous colonies in Utah and Arizona that hit the news on a fairly regular basis and make for sensational stories are often reported as "Mormon sects," adding to the confusion, but although some of their members may be descendants of Mormons, they have either been excommunicated from or never were members of the official

Mormon Church. Regardless, polygamy has gone a long way in characterizing Mormon women as oppressed, pathetic creatures, a characterization that persists today in the minds of many non-Mormon feminists.

Today's leaders of the Mormon Church have done their best to make that characterization a reality, using the enormous wealth and power of the institution to immediately squash any dialogue, idea, or person suggesting that Mormon women are anything less than delighted with their role in the Church. As President Gordon B. Hinckley said in his September 8, 1998, interview with Larry King when a caller asked about the possibility that women might hold the priesthood in the Mormon Church, "I don't anticipate it. The women in the Church are not complaining about it . . . they're happy."

Many women to date have left the Church because they see no possible way to reconcile the devaluation of women there with their personal lives. I can identify with these women. But many strong women remain in the Church today taking on, with indomitable perseverance, the nearly hopeless struggle for change. They are feminists and scholars and writers who speak and publish fearlessly, and they are mothers and grandmothers with high hopes and expectations for their daughters. And in the face of a nasty little habit Church leaders have for excommunicating feminists who get too uppity and scholars who dig too deeply, they offer comfort to women like my mother who believe in the basic tenets of the religion, who simply love the Church and find a way to worship God there in spite of the inexorable shortcomings of its leaders.

What Joan Chittister, a Benedictine sister, writes about the Catholic Church in her book *In Search of Belief,* holds true for Mormonism also: "People currently considered 'excommunicated' or 'suspect' or 'heretical' . . . believers are, in many ways, among the most intense Christians of our time. They do more than sing in the choir or raise money for the parish center or fix flowers for the church. They care about it and call it to be its truest self. They question it, not to undermine it, but to strengthen it. To question is not to deny," says Chittister. "It may, in fact, be the truest type of faith a person can muster."

# 8

I SPENT MOST OF MY CHILDHOOD SHRINKING INTO MY mother's narrow protective shadow and lying low in corners to avoid the Richman men: my father and my brother who, I believe, modeled my father from the moment he exited my mother's womb. My father is not a physically imposing man. He stands about five feet eight inches with a slight build. But during my childhood he was prone to regular temper outbursts upon little provocation—a spill at dinnertime or a question not answered swiftly enough—and he made up for his small size with a booming voice that frequently spewed forth a line of obscenities or invoked his favorite disciplinary tool: humiliation. Noise swirled around my father like flies swirl around the barnyard. Even when he wasn't speaking or yelling, we could hear him coming long before he arrived—the twisting groan of the outside water hose being turned on to wash the dirt from his boots, the clomping footsteps meant for a much larger man, the slap of work gloves thrown into the corner, the clanging and banging of doors—all became warning signs in my world. My father was never physically abusive, but he struck terror in me right down to my core.

But in 1963, when I was in the second grade, prompted no doubt by something hugely significant but long since forgotten, I made my first stab at gender equality by deliberately adopting some of my father's language. I have no idea what I expected this to do for me. I just know that my brother, who was three years older than I, and ten times louder, had been using my father's language on a regular basis, and if he could do it, then by damn, so could I. My favorites, which were also my father's and brother's favorites, were "goddamn," "sonofabitch," and "asshole." I would string them together like I'd heard my father do and use them whenever the opportunity presented itself. If my friends complained that our teacher had given us too much homework, I would respond with "That goddamn sonofabitching asshole!" and my face would burn with shame and delight. I made no discretion in my use of it—children and adults alike were fair game—and it made quite an impression in our little Mormon neighborhood, not only on my friends but on their parents as well.

My mother's father was a quiet, gentle, religious man who was killed in an accident when my mother was thirteen years old. She longed for the peace she had known with her father and always seemed somewhat startled and perplexed by her surroundings in our family. This short attempt at liberation on my part set her to hand-wringing. She was mortified, but my father was initially amused and strangely proud until, as kids will do, I carried the practice to an extreme. When one old gentleman overheard my conversation with friends as we walked past his house on our way to school, he suggested that was no way for a little girl to speak, and I told him he was a stupid asshole. When my father found out about the incident, he told me to shut my goddamn mouth and stop my goddamn swearing. My attempt at equality and self-determination a dismal failure after less than a month, I shrank back into myself and pasted myself once again against my mother's side, where I remained for the next ten years and where a piece of me is lodged still.

OVER DINNER A few months ago in a Salt Lake City restaurant at the foot of the Wasatch Mountains, one of my aunts spoke indignantly at the idea that a Mormon woman could be picked out of a crowd, that she could be identified on looks and mannerisms alone. When I moved from Salt Lake City to New York City, my mother drove across the country with me. At the home of a couple in Westchester County who had offered me temporary residence, my mother left the room to wash her hands for dinner and one of them exclaimed, "Your mother is quite a modern woman!" I had told them my mother was Mormon, and they apparently expected a pioneer woman in a bonnet. None of the women in my family fit the dowdy, ultra-conservative Mormon-housewife stereotype. Even now—at seventy-five my mother is the youngest of the four sisters—the women in my family are sharp, well-dressed women with stylish gray hair framing their beautifully made-up faces, earrings dangling from their ears and rings decorating their aging hands. They are no exception among Mormon women. But those of us who grew up in Utah, those of us who are not expecting Mormon women to carry the appearance of a blank-eyed, opinionless dupe, can, in fact, pick a Mormon woman out of a crowd. She's the one with a strong air of confidence and certainty, mixed with a tiny bit of defensivenss but ready to be affable as soon as she determines it's safe.

At the information desk in the visitors center, I seek directions to the Wilford Woodruff house from such a woman. She begins to give me driving directions, so I interrupt to tell her I'm on foot.

"Oh, shoot!" she says. "My husband just took the car to run uptown for a minute. I'd be happy to give you a ride."

"Thanks, but I enjoy walking."

"Are you sure? He'll be back in just a few minutes and we'll jump right in the car and I'll take you right down there," she says as if she's known me thirty years instead of thirty seconds.

I'm touched by her offer, and I'm again flushed with a sense of safety and comfort among these Mormon women, in one sense complete strangers, in another, as familiar as family. I eventually convince her I'll be fine walking, and she sends me out the door loaded with brochures and a map.

I wander down the hill checking my brochure as I go, blindly dropping into small holes and stumbling over bumps in the grass. The theme-park feel of historic Nauvoo has become almost unbearable. I'm hesitant to hear one more missionary in 1800s attire wringing out one more persecution story, but I want to see the home of Wilford Woodruff, one of the early Mormon hierarchy. The Woodruff house is set apart from the others and, therefore, lacks the steady stream of tourists. Maybe that's why it seems to draw me, although I'm often happy shuffling through the rooms in a group where I won't garner much attention or be expected to twist my face into an emotion appropriate for the story being told.

The skies have turned dark and the wind pushes against me one minute, then shoves me forward the next, requiring a couple of quick steps. This suits me fine. After fourteen years in the Arizona desert with a consistently "hot and sunny" forecast, I've acquired an appreciation for intense weather of any other kind.

Sister Johnson of Canada, costumed in a floor-length dress with ruffles at the sleeve, takes me out of the wind at the door of the Woodruff house as if I were an old friend who has traveled many miles to have a cup of tea with her. No one else is here, and I suddenly wish a passing car would stop and take the pressure off me to be the perfect tourist. She walks me through the eight-bedroom home adorned by eight fireplaces with stories of Mrs. Woodruff and the kids. Mr. Woodruff spent most of his Nauvoo days away on a mission in England and spent fewer than a hundred nights in his home before he was forced to leave it. He sold his home for $600—far less than it was worth but more than most received—and legend has it that after he and his family had crossed the river to the temporary Mormon camp on Sugar Creek, he remembered a leaky spot in the roof and felt compelled to return and repair it for the new owner.

Nothing particularly different about this story, but Sister Johnson tells it with such earnestness and intensity, I have to turn away. I thank her for the tour and start to leave, but she hears the catch in my voice and stops me. I lift my eyes to look at her and her eyes, also filled with tears, meet mine.

"Are you a member?" she asks.

"No," I say. And the silence hangs under the once-leaky Woodruff rafters. I rush to fill it, not wanting to disappoint Sister Johnson. "Though I was once."

She seems surprised. I'm sure they don't get many former members coming through Nauvoo; most former members I know don't get within a hundred yards of anything Mormon.

"Are you traveling alone?" she asks, and I tell her I am. She looks at me with pure tenderness on her face. Then she tells me she was nineteen—forty or so years ago—when she discovered the Church, that she prayed to God and asked him if the Mormon Church were true and she soon knew the answer. I'm unmoved by this because it is the same story every Mormon tells—convert or not. But then she tells me she used to collect coins as a young woman, and when she got a lot of money she'd hide the coins for safekeeping. But she would forget where she hid them, so she'd ask God where they were, wait a few minutes, then walk directly to the coins. And she would hide them again and forget again. And she'd say, "God, I'm sorry to bother you, but I seem to have misplaced my coins again and if you wouldn't mind . . . ," then she would walk straight to them. Then she would misplace her keys, and it got so that she pretty much depended on God up to a half-dozen times a day just to find stuff.

This is the God I need, the God of Sister Johnson. It's not the big life-changing, catastrophic events I need help with. Those are the kinds of things I'm good at; I'm totally competent in a crisis. I want a God to help me find my lost eyeglasses, to fix a bad haircut, to repair a malfunctioning alarm clock, to set a digital thermostat that needs to be programmed. Like having twenty-four-hour access to the toll-free turkey line on Thanksgiving. I want the kind of faith that lets me know that it is perfectly all right to ask God to produce my misplaced favorite pen; I want the kind of God who cares that I have a perfectly golden piece of toast to start my morning.

I stop laughing long enough to swipe my face dry with the palm of my hand. I want to stay longer, maybe forever, there in Wilford Woodruff's house with Sister Johnson, perfectly safe while the wind thumps a branch against the brick. But I suddenly become uneasy with my own feelings, worried about how Sister Johnson might perceive them. I thank her for the tour and turn to leave. She reaches for my hand, holds it between both of hers, and says, "Have a *good* trip," then pauses and adds, "Be extra careful." I turn away quickly and rush out the front door.

I walk briskly across the grass under the trees, and when I realize I have no destination in mind, I drop onto my back on the lawn. From here I can clearly observe the skirmish the wind has picked with the giant black walnut tree swinging over my head. Like the Mormon who possibly put it in the ground, the tree, taking a ruthless battering, seems to welcome God's test of its strength and stamina with fierce determination, even though it stands within sight of dangling limbs half-torn from its relatives. I wonder about the wisdom of lying under a tree in this kind of windstorm, but I'm betting on the tree to hold its own. After all, I've not seen so much as one leaf ripped from its grasp, although each one is being twisted and tortured in ways that mystify me.

I wonder if this is the kind of thing Sister Johnson would pray about—to keep her safe under a tree in a windstorm—and maybe this is something I could pray about if I felt so inclined, and for a brief moment I think I might try. But the practical part of my mind kicks in and asks, why would God keep you safe under this tree when it would be just as easy for you to move? After all, God helps those who help themselves, a phrase that according to *Bartlett's Familiar Quotations* has been articulated in some variation by Aesop, Aeschylus, Sophocles, Euripides, George Herbert, Algernon Sidney, and Benjamin Franklin. Can't really argue with those sources. And although at many a Mormon funeral I've heard utterances of "It was just his time to go," I've been told by a Mormon bishop that Mormons don't believe in predestination. They believe in free will, in unfortunate accidents, and in getting killed or maimed out of sheer stupidity.

I can't hear or see the Mississippi River from this spot, but I am aware of its closeness. It is probably dark and brooding now—no longer gleaming with the stone-skimming surface of yesterday. I close my eyes to see it, and instead find myself alone on the shore of Stansbury Island in the Great Salt Lake. The wind blows hard—cold and insistent. The black-blue clouds hang near my head, threatening to compress me into the slippery rocks under my feet. From here it's an easy glide into the morbid gray waters of the lake, angrily lapping the shore near my soggy shoes, reaching for me. Two boys in my high school went onto the lake in a rowboat on such a day. Their bodies were later found on that shore, bloated beyond recognition and crusted white with salt. I didn't know them well; to me they were simply the incarnation of the darkness that possessed the lake on stormy days. In my twenties, I loved to stand there on that shore on those days, full of fear, close to death. Not in a suicidal way; I never had any intent of going in. I just wanted to be near it, to be close enough to brush up against it—a futile attempt at understanding my small life.

I open my eyes to let some light in, expecting the darkness to dissipate. Instead, I'm struck with an almost desperate sense of bereavement, which will emerge time and time again on this trip whenever I stand on a spot that puts me dead on the actual Mormon Trail.

# 9

EACH DAY OF RIDING STARTS OUT WITH SOME TREPIDA-
tion, some doubt. I check myself. I remind myself of the rules:
head up, eyes level with the horizon, anticipate potential hazards, make decisions and execute them without hesitation. I
remind myself to ride defensively but not tentatively. Motorcycling requires an aggressive attitude, and once I finally understood that, I became a much better rider. Driving allows for a
good deal of coasting—both literally and figuratively. Motorcycling does not. A car and driver are like an old married couple:
relaxed, comfortable with habits, one able to compensate effortlessly for the other. The relationship between motorcycle and
rider is more like an affair: intense, charged with energy, demanding a great deal of attention and an acute sense of awareness. A relatively small mistake can have large consequences.

A few miles into every ride, though, the energy stays and the
apprehension gives way. Like my father, I find peace in movement. The early morning sun flashes on broad green lawns and
the mottled shady road. The sun drops down through the trees
like splatters of spilled paint on a gray canvas. The silent passage

of the waveless river merges with the buzz of the bike and lulls me into the moment. My bones settle into the seat, muscle and flesh relax around them. I'm only going a short distance today, so I've left most of my gear in my Nauvoo motel room. Without the load, my bike feels nimble and light, like a scooter with power, and without the armored suit, riding in only jeans and a jacket feels like swimming in the nude.

This is why I ride—because I don't want to watch the moment through a safety-plated windshield; I want to be part of it. The morning's air collides with my chest, then swoops around me and through my clothing. It slips through the slivers of space at my temples and touches my ears with a low growl. It rushes at my nostrils, begging me to inhale. I do, and it offers a combination of dank leaves, freshly mowed grass, last night's rain mixed with oil spills, and muddy river water. I pop up my face shield and stick out my tongue. The morning tastes cool but slightly musty—like spearmint ice cream left in the back of the freezer a little too long. The sun plays with wet leaves stuck to the road, teasing them with promises of drying heat and fluttering possibilities before darting behind a slow-moving cloud. The road glides beneath me as smooth as polished granite, and the roadside grasses nod as I pass. Soon, the elements begin to coalesce—wind with flesh, body with bike, tires with asphalt, road with river. Smells are sucked into the engine, grasses and leaves blur, and I'm just along for the ride.

The Carthage jail is a short thirty-minute ride from Nauvoo. In lieu of another missionary-guided tour with a group of eager pilgrims, I'm foolishly hoping for a dilapidated shack accessed through a field of overgrown weeds where I can sit among the grasshoppers. But it is not to be. The Mormons would never miss such an opportunity. The Carthage jail is where Joseph Smith the man and Mormon leader became

Joseph Smith the martyr, the charismatic prophet whom his de-tractors, by their violent behavior on June 27, 1844, would turn into an legend.

I park my bike next to a Kawasaki loaded for touring and the owner appears out of nowhere to greet me—George from Grapevine, Texas. We exchange the usual motorcycle small talk about bikes, gear, how long we've been on the road, weather we've encountered, what direction we're headed.

"You're kind of a strange sight," he says.

"Why's that?" I ask although I already know what he means.

"Are you traveling alone?"

"Yeah, are you?"

"Yeah, but you're the first woman I've ever met traveling alone across the country by motorcycle."

I usually get one of two reactions from people I meet when I'm traveling alone by motorcycle—awe for my courageous-ness or sympathy for my stupidity. Neither reaction is entirely appropriate nor inappropriate. The advantage of meeting an-other motorcyclist on the road is that no explanation is needed. The why question is never asked. Trying to explain the small gifts of moving through landscape on a motorcycle to someone who has never experienced this movement is like trying to explain the color green to someone who has been blind since birth. The cliché of wind in the hair barely scuttles around the edges of the experience. And it's not as easy as putting someone on the back of your bike and showing them. That misses entirely the heightened consciousness induced by one solo ride through the scarred insides of a dynamite-blasted mountain cut open by a two-lane road for your con-venience.

In addition to the merging of body and nature, the bike it-self plays a significant part—the power of the throttle thrust deeply into your right hand, the tank tucked securely between your knees, a gentle hum sent along your spine. The elements of human, machine, and universe clash, then weave themselves around and through one another, creating a moment for you alone.

You can assume almost every motorcyclist—especially those with bikes loaded for touring—gets this. It creates an unspoken bond between strangers who would otherwise pass each other in a parking lot unnoticed. It's the reason motorcyclists wave to passing motorcyclists as if they are old friends—a confession of shared consciousness.

"There's no other way to travel," George says and I nod; nothing else needs saying.

AS WE WALK toward the new visitors center now attached to the old jail, George asks me what exactly happened at this place. He was looking for an obscure museum he'd read about in a travel book when he happened upon the sign for the Carthage jail. I tell him he'll soon hear more than he probably wants to hear, so he opts out of the visitors center and attaches himself to the tail end of a group just entering the jail. I would be wise to do the same, but I'm a little neurotic about starting at the beginning of things—tours, books, newspapers, and so on—and following through to the end.

Consequently, I find myself to be the sole touree of Sister Taylor, who sits me down in the middle of a sort of art gallery meant to tell the story of the origins of the Church. Many of the pictures include Joseph, and at the entrance stands a pair of three-foot, full-length paintings of Joseph and his brother Hyrum side by side. I've seen many paintings of Joseph throughout my life, and he was a handsome man—over six feet tall with light features and a rather large nose—but in this particular painting he's drop-dead gorgeous.

"He was strikingly handsome, wasn't he?" I say to Sister Taylor.

"Oh, yes," she answers like a love-struck teen in a momentary state of rapture, never quite returning to her composed seventy-something state as she tells me the tale of Joseph's life.

In spite of the sad and lovely story told by Sister Taylor, in which Joseph is nothing short of flawless, the charges that landed Joseph in jail on this occasion—there had been others—could not be summarily dismissed. His death, however, was cold-blooded murder.

Sister Taylor begins her story of Joseph at the beginning of Mormonism in 1823 in Palmyra, New York, where Joseph, seventeen years old at the time, is visited first by God himself and his son, Jesus Christ, and next by the angel Moroni, all of whom sort of hover over Joseph as he kneels praying in a grove of trees. After a few such visits over the next four years, the angel Moroni reveals the burial place of the golden plates that will eventually become the Book of Mormon. Such was the beginning of The Church of Jesus Christ of Latter-day Saints, aka the Mormon Church. Sister Taylor recites this story matter-of-factly, as if it is no more sensational than a story about driving to the next town to visit relatives.

This is where non-Mormons begin to scoff and roll their eyes at the gullibility of Mormons. During my time as a young Mormon, it was a difficult story for me to tell with conviction, and during my time as an anti-Mormon, it was a handy story to trot out in proof of my superior judgment. But it no longer bothers me; in fact, it's a good story filled with fascinating characters and riveting suspense. The angel Moroni teased Joseph with the existence of the plates before actually allowing him to extract them in 1827 from the mountain where they were buried. Joseph, twenty-one at the time, had not yet learned to write, but he translated the golden plates through the use of the Urim and Thummim, two magic "seer stones," attached to a breastplate, with the help of his wife and two others who wrote down what Joseph dictated. From this translation, the Book of Mormon was published in 1830.

This is not a particularly sensational story for its time and place. That area of New York State in the early 1800s was swarming with evangelists conducting limb-jerking, mouth-frothing revivals, and new prophets were sprouting faster than wheat. Many who might mock the story's extravagance are the same people who have told me the stories of Adam and Eve, the Immaculate Conception, the burning bush, the parting of the sea, or the Resurrection with the same matter-of-fact tone Sister Taylor now uses.

Whether the story is truth or fiction, whether the Book of Mormon is divinely inspired history or a dully written novel borne out of a lush imagination remains fodder for generation after generation of scholars determined to make a reputation for themselves by crumbling the foundations of the monolithic institution the way the mobs crumbled the walls of the Nauvoo temple. In spite of evidence soundly on the side of the scholars, the foundation shows few cracks.

I find the question to be of little significance at this point. As Fawn Brodie wrote of Joseph, "The source of his power lay not in his doctrine but in his person, and the rare quality of his genius was due not to his reason but to his imagination." Millions have chosen to follow Joseph over the last 175 years filled with a love for him and a faith in God that is quite real regardless of its origins. The institution itself has and will continue to survive as a social organization, full of judgments and imperfections, but also full of compassion, good deeds, and good intentions, far from the strange and evil distinctions the Mormons have acquired in circulating myths.

The story left untold there in the shadow of Joseph's comely portrait would include the reasons Joseph and the others—his brother Hyrum was killed the same day—found themselves out of the protection of the Nauvoo Legion, a Mormon army of four thousand and the wing of the Illinois militia of which Joseph was lieutenant general, and in the city of the Carthage Greys, another wing of the Illinois militia primed for Joseph's blood. In the months leading up to that fateful day in June, Joseph followed one bad decision with another. By the spring of 1844, Joseph had alienated his first and second counselors, one of whom was a bit of a scoundrel and easily dismissed, but the other was a man by the name of William Law.

Law, a prosperous and well-respected man in Nauvoo, was a devout Mormon in spite of being critical of Joseph's autocratic rule, which included all business dealings for the city of Nauvoo in which there was no pretense of a separation between church and state. In an attempt to guide the Church and its true but misguided prophet back to the righteous path, Law, a man known for his integrity, made his concerns public, resulting in his swift excommunication from the Church. But instead of packing his bags and slipping quietly out of Nauvoo, Law bought a printing press and in his rational, respectful way issued the first edition of the *Nauvoo Expositor*, accusing Joseph mainly of abusing his power and using tithes for his own speculative land deals. For good measure, Law threw in accusations of polygamy, at the time still being denied and kept secret. (Law carried the sting of having his own wife, Jane, proposed to by the prophet.) Since Law could not be easily dismissed as a fool or a vengeful miscreant, Joseph responded by sending the

Nauvoo Legion to destroy the printing press, which they did with zest. Law and his fellow apostates fled to Carthage.

With news of the destruction of the printing press, anti-Mormon sentiment flared again and spread rapidly through Illinois and into Missouri, where it had never really been extinguished. Blood-hungry mobs started to form under the auspices of the Illinois militia, including the riled-up Warsaw militia and Carthage Greys.

In an effort to avert a bloody civil war, Governor Ford of Illinois asked Joseph to appear and answer the numerous charges against him, which included among others the fusion of church and state, polygamy, suppression of freedom of the press, and inciting a riot. Joseph's request to bring an escort from the Nauvoo Legion was denied for fear their appearance in Carthage would further antagonize the Carthage and Warsaw boys. Joseph's first instinct was to flee across the Mississippi into Iowa and he did just that for a couple of days, but loyalty to his city and his followers took him back to Nauvoo to prevent the mobs from annihilating it. On June 24, 1844, Joseph Smith, knowing full well he would not likely see Nauvoo again, rode to Carthage and turned himself in.

Three days after Joseph's incarceration in the Carthage jail, Governor Ford foolishly or deliberately left the Mormon leaders (in addition to Joseph, Hyrum Smith, John Taylor, and Willard Richards were also being held) under the guard of the Carthage Greys while he rode to Nauvoo to calm the fanatically loyal and increasingly antsy Nauvoo Legion. When Joseph heard of the governor's departure, he sent Willard Richards, who was free to come and go from the jail, with an order to Jonathon Dunham to rally the legion and bring them to Carthage. Richards did as he was told, then returned to his prophet. For whatever reason, Joseph's order was never acted upon. The Warsaw militia, which Governor Ford had disbanded and sent home, waited until the governor rode out of sight, then turned back to join the Carthage Greys at the jail.

I SIT ON a bench in the wood-paneled room on the top floor of the Carthage jail. A quilt-covered bed fills the corner. The room was that of the jailer and his wife, which on the second night he offered to Joseph and the others so they wouldn't have to sleep in the "dungeon cell," a windowless room furnished with bars, chains, and shackles. The window in the middle of the wall looks onto the courtyard below. A shaft of light shines through the bullet hole in the heavy wood door. My tour guide, an elderly gentleman missionary, hits a button and a recorded voice tells the story of Joseph's last hours. The voice starts strong in my ears then fades to the background.

Boots thud up the stairs—dozens of them. Joseph, Hyrum, and the other two brace themselves against the door. The first bullet comes through the closed door and catches Hyrum at the side of his nose, travels through his brain, and out the back of his skull. He'll take three more when the door is flung open and one from the mob below as he staggers back toward the window before dropping dead. Willard Richards stands beside the door knocking down gun barrels with his cane and will miraculously avoid all shots. John Taylor will be hit five times. The shot meant to kill him instead hits the pocket watch in his breast pocket. He'll recover to preach the legend of his martyred prophet. Joseph sees a trickle of blood drip down the face of his brother. He falls over Hyrum's body and empties a smuggled six-shooter into the open doorway, hitting but not killing one or two men. Once his gun is empty, he'll rush to the window to stare down for a split second at the bizarre scene of a hundred painted faces behind bayonets pointed directly at him before a bullet will tear through his body from behind. His grip on the windowsill will give way, and he'll drop out the window to the ground, rolling onto his face. He'll be dragged into the center of the courtyard and propped against a brick well before four men will empty their weapons into his slumped body.

Legend has it that one of the militiamen then moves forward with bowie knife drawn to collect a souvenir of Joseph's hair. As he reaches for Joseph's head, the sun will break through the clouds and beam directly upon the shredded body of the prophet, causing the militiamen to drop their weapons and scatter. The body of Joseph will lie slumped against the well for some time before a shocked Willard Richards will find the wherewithal to drag it up the stairs and rest it beside the body of Hyrum. The charismatic visionary, the man who formed my destiny, lay dead at the age of thirty-eight on the spot where my feet now rest. His presence inhabits the room and brushes against the recorded words now coming back into focus.

I wander back into the visitors center and stand alone facing his painting. I would have been a sucker for Joseph Smith— every bit of him. His power, his compassion, his ambition, his vision, his playfulness, his audacity, his charm, his imagination, his arrogance. His easy laugh, his love of women, his insatiable sexual appetite. The thick sandy-dark hair brushed back from the strong face, the probing eyes, the too-large nose, the mesmerizing voice, the strapping body muscled from his love for hard work and play. His seducement of the women in my family—even those who never met him—is no mystery to me.

I MAKE MY way down one side of the thirty-foot-long table at the "world-famous" Hotel Nauvoo buffet, passing the fried chicken, fried catfish, raspberry pork loin, ham, turkey, and roast beef, anxious to get to the mashed potatoes and chicken gravy for my third helping. Once I've reached my goal, I join three young Mormon women at a corner table. They are in their twenties—Christy, Christina, and Sarah—two recently back from missions, one on her way out. Over the last two days, I ran into them from time to time on one tour or another. They befriended me. I marvel at the closeness of strangers when I travel alone, the connection I feel to strangers who offer nothing more than a smile or a nod as they pass. I know a lot of people like to describe themselves as loners and I've never described myself that way, but I do keep my circle of friends close and small. I shirk most social invitations, so I was surprised to find myself delighted when the three young Mormon women approached me in the parking lot of the Carthage jail and invited me to dinner.

We talk about faith and the Mormon Church. Not a flicker of doubt passes before their eyes when they tell me Joseph Smith was a true prophet of God, when they tell me the Mormon Church is the only true church on earth. They tell me this without a hint of arrogance in their certainty, instead humbled by the privilege of being part of the Kingdom of God. I find myself faced with my own stereotypes of Mormon women, especially the young ones, and challenge them to do more than bear the testimony they were taught as soon as they could speak. They are up to the challenge. They speak without hesitation about politics, about world affairs, about history, about other religions. They think. They form opinions. They choose to be Mormon.

# 10

WITHOUT THEIR PROPHET TO GUIDE THEM, IT WAS
expected the Saints would either scatter or seek revenge. They
did neither. Even when Joseph's murderers were tried and ac-
quitted, the Mormons did not react. In an obituary of Joseph
Smith, the *New York Herald* predicted Joseph's death as the beginning of the end of Mormonism, only to retract that view
two days later fearing that the murder of Joseph might
strengthen instead of subdue Mormon fanaticism. The latter
view, of course, proved accurate. The Mormons mourned their
fallen leader—more than twenty thousand filed past his and
Hyrum's velvet-wrapped bodies the following day—and pro-
ceeded to wash away his multitude of sins as they turned him
into a martyr, a legend, and a prophet to rival Moses.

Many of Joseph's apostles made claims to his throne, but
soon after his death, Brigham Young emerged as the clear
leader. Joseph's vision and imagination, assisted by the renewed
antagonism of the Gentiles who were dismayed to see Mormonism hanging together after Joseph's death, would send the
Saints west; he had prophesied several years before his death

that they would build Zion in the shadow of the Rocky Mountains. But it was Brigham's pragmatism and organization that would deliver them to the barren valley of the Great Salt Lake.

When the Saints left Nauvoo, Joseph's first—and publicly only—wife, Emma, and their sons stayed behind. A strong and outspoken woman, Emma played a large part in the formation of the Mormon Church while married to Joseph. I remember her name prominently from my days of churchgoing, spoken of as "Joseph's wife," as if he had no other, in a saintly and revered way. (The fact that she separated herself from the Mormon Church upon Joseph's death would require a messy explanation and, therefore, was never part of the lesson plan.) She was the first president of the Relief Society, and legend has it she had something to do with the passage of the Mormon tenet that disallows the use of tobacco and liquor. Soon after she grew weary of Joseph and his fellow Church leaders drinking liquor and spitting tobacco on her floors, Joseph got a message from God outlining the "Word of Wisdom." But although Joseph's wanderings with other women remained discreet, Emma was not influential enough to stop him entirely on that front. Still chafing with and denying the unbridled rumors of Joseph's polygamy (records show he had taken more than forty wives before his death), Emma found in Brigham—a loyal apostle who embraced the principle of polygamy from the beginning and promptly set about creating his own impressive list of wives—the perfect recipient upon which to unleash her pent-up resentment over Joseph's indiscretions.

Emma never cared much for the stocky, direct Brigham, who was fond of profane language and delivering fiery tongue-lashings to the unfaithful, and she promptly assigned the rise of polygamy to Brigham, cleansing Joseph's name and denying Joseph's involvement until her last breath of life. Joseph's sons lined up behind their mother, and young Joseph III eventually took over the leadership of a small sect of former Mormons known as the Reorganized Church of Jesus Christ of Latter-day Saints.

To an outsider, I imagine the differences between the two churches are barely ascertainable, but to someone comfortable with the strangeness of Mormonism, entering the Reorganized Church makes a person feel a little like she has inadvertently entered into the middle of a family squabble. One side walked away with the family fortune and now finds it easy to be gracious; the other struggles to get by and remains a little embittered by its inferior position. This offshoot of Mormonism holds close to the tenets set out by Joseph, sans polygamy, but doesn't hold the power, wealth, or appeal that the Mormon Church wields. Today called the Community of Christ and with about 250,000 members, this sect still owns Joseph's homestead and mansion house in Nauvoo and holds to them tightly, referring at every opportunity to Emma as Joseph's *only* wife.

The intent of Brigham was that the Mormons would leave in an organized and orderly way. He and the Quorum of the Twelve Apostles (a unit of Church leaders set up by Joseph), would attempt to plan the exodus right down to the two pounds of tea allowed each family (the Mormons were still enjoying a cup of tea or coffee at that time). The actual departure was something between the structure Brigham imagined and panicked exodus. Heightened occasions of burnings, tarrings, whippings, and verbal threats from mobs of restless Gentiles convinced many that they must leave before wagons and teams were ready or sacrifice their lives.

In addition to threats from the restless mobs, the leaders themselves felt the probability near of their own incarceration on one charge or another if they didn't soon leave Illinois, so Brigham made the decision to depart before the intended spring departure. On February 4, 1846, while the Mississippi River chugged with ice cakes, the first of thousands of Mormons rolled their hastily built wagon onto a makeshift ferry that would carry only one family and one wagon per crossing, loaded down with as many personal belongings and livestock as they could take across the icy Mississippi, and deposit them on the frozen Iowa bank, their only source of warmth the memory of their martyred prophet and their burning faith in God.

The ferry will operate along with some flatboats and skiffs from dawn to dusk as weather permits. Some wagons, oxen, and worldly possessions will be dumped into the icy waters and lost on this first wet, cold crossing, and a few human lives will be lost as well. At least nine women in a dangerously precarious condition will cross the ice-choked waters and give birth to nine crying babies in blowing wet tents pitched on the frozen banks of Sugar Creek, Iowa, where the Mormons set up the first of many camps on the road to Zion. Before the end of February, the temperatures will drop so low that the Mississippi River will freeze from shore to shore, and the Mormons still patiently waiting a turn at the ferry will coax their oxen, their children, and themselves one step at a time onto the miraculously frozen waters—no doubt in their minds they are witness to a divine intervention—and they'll stream across the Mississippi as if carried on the shoulders of angels. Once on the other side, however, they will realize this wonder of God is dangerously close to freezing hundreds of misplaced Saints just as solid as the river itself.

My father might have made a good Mormon under Brigham Young's rein. He likely would have hated the golden-haired Joseph, who moved people through inspiration and charm, but

Brigham had just the sort of irascible temperament my father could respect. A swearing, drinking Mormon—that's my father's kind of Mormon. Although Church members were devastated by the death of their prophet, in hindsight the change of leadership at that particular moment was a stroke of luck— or as the Mormons would prefer to see it, the hand of God. Charm alone could not have moved fifty thousand believers— regardless of the depth of their beliefs—across a couple thousand miles of unknown territory dotted with unimaginable threats to settle in the crusty wasteland of the Great Salt Lake. For that, they would need the severe toughness and unquestioned discipline they found in Brigham Young.

THE RAIN SLIPS down the back of my neck while I load the bike. By 8 A.M. my bike stands alone, as do I, in the motel parking lot. Water mixed with oil trickles down the slope of the empty lot toward me in shimmering purples and golds. After three days in Nauvoo, it seems doubtful that the considerable amount of junk spread around the motel room ever fit comfortably on the bike in two saddlebags, one small duffel bag, and a tank bag. Things fit only one way—the laptop and books in the right saddlebag; easily accessible cold-weather gear in the left; clothing in the duffel; maps, eyeglasses, face shield cleaner, camera and film in the tank bag. I pull out today's map, study it for a moment, and fold it to fit in the clear plastic top pocket before placing the magnetic bag on the tank. I center the duffel bag on the backseat and tighten down the straps. The darkened sky to the west puts me in a somber mood.

Parley's Street slopes gently toward the river, toward the place where thousands of Mormons solemnly streamed out of Nauvoo in the shadow of the temple on the hill. As she left

Nauvoo in 1846, a woman by the name of Bathsheba Smith wrote, "My last act in that precious spot was to tidy the rooms, sweep up the floor, and set the broom in its accustomed place behind the door. Then with emotions in my heart . . . I gently closed the door and faced an unknown future, faced it with faith in God . . ."

The road allows me to ride fairly close to the river's edge, but I stop well short of it, chilled to the bone by the sight of the dark, choppy water. I linger only momentarily before swinging around and heading east to the other end of Parley's Street. In a gravel parking lot, I get off the bike, perch my helmet on top of my tank bag, and, in a consistent rain, climb the hill on a well-worn dirt path through the trees. In a gazebo at the top, names of Saints who never left Nauvoo fill every wall.

On the other side of the gazebo I step out among headstones, slicing through tall, wet grass until I find a broad, flat tree stump to sit on. According to the names on the wall, I sit among the remains of two of my great-great-great-grandmothers, but according to our family records, one of them is actually buried about twenty miles from here in a since-forgotten spot along a creek. The cemetery rambles around and down the hill for several acres. Most of the stones are weathered to streaky smoothness and many are crumbled, unseen until one stumbles upon them in the overgrown grass or piled together on top of other stones. Somewhere behind me an industrious woodpecker breaks the silence, obviously unaware of the sanctity of his surroundings.

I find peace among the dead and comfort in the idea of resting forever on this grassy hillside. I crumble into the tree stump like the headstones have crumbled into the grass, too weak to stand against the weather, too tired to give what is expected of me. The rain continues to drizzle but I'm protected by the trees and by my waterproof riding gear, and for a short time I convince myself that my ancestors have taken me into their tranquillity. But they have not; instead they push me forward. Soon the stump feels hard and knotty against my hip and a cold breeze gently taps my face urging me off the hillside to begin my journey.

The journey again feels impossibly large and impossibly dangerous. I imagine it felt the same to Maria, who might have lingered near this spot, gathering strength into her small bones from the nearby remains of her dead mother.

My mother has never been to Nauvoo, although she has wanted to see the city built by her beloved prophet of God since she was old enough to know of this place. She has been nearby—cattle business of my father's—but he didn't bring her here, and she didn't insist. She would never insist.

In my late twenties and early thirties—my brief period of transcendent certainty about all things—I wanted my mother to insist. Upon anything. That the waitress take back the cold potatoes, that the car repair shop reimburse her for repairs they didn't make, that my father stop treating her like his servant and show her some respect, that the Church she devoted her life to do the same. She is too pliable, I thought. I was embarrassed by her foolish weakness.

But I turned out to be the foolish one, saturated by my own narrow-minded "knowledge" of the way a woman should behave in the second half of the twentieth century. I was blinded to her strength. My mother's strength was not to be found in assertiveness and activism, but in unrestrained love, compassion, and understanding. Forty-five years' worth of this has been given to me, flowing unfettered through me, making up for my own deficiencies. In his essay "Letter Much Too Late," Wallace Stegner wrote that his mother had a "softness that proved in the long run stronger than what it seemed to yield to." I think the same of mine.

She now suffers from aggressive rheumatoid arthritis and congestive heart failure. Quite often she passes out while she's giving or receiving the Relief Society lesson in Church. This has happened so often now, they simply make her comfortable on the floor, prop her feet up on a stack of Books of Mormon, and go on with the lesson. She is my source of strength, and every day she gets physically weaker. Maybe I'm draining too much from her.

I look straight ahead as I ride toward Hamilton to avoid looking into the shadowy waters of the Mississippi. Wet, slippery leaves plaster the road amid fallen branches; dark clouds hang on my shoulders. On the bridge that will take me to Keokuk, Iowa, I'm unable to resist looking down into the dark water. Leaving Nauvoo unsettles me. The bleakness descends upon me as if I'd been cast out of my own home, as if the Gentile mobs were on my rear tire. What I'm feeling is not just empathy for my ancestors but rather a loss of my own security. It confounds me to recognize so clearly that I find refuge in the company of Mormons. As the dirty spray from passing cars covers my face shield, a sense of isolation covers my soul. I badly want to turn back to the safety of those capable Mormon women brimming with stories of the faithful.

THE CEASELESS MISTY rain soaks the Iowa bank directly across the Mississippi River from Nauvoo. From this point, the Saints paused momentarily to look back on their cherished city and temple standing high and proud, a monument to their resolve, a prophecy of their endurance. That temple must have seemed an absurd sight in 1846 to non-Mormons—an extravagant show of arrogance. The mobs would soon destroy the temple and smugly congratulate themselves for clearing their country of a fanatic scourge, but the short history of Mormonism should have told them the all-American religion would gather fortitude with every turn of the wagon wheel.

Two fishermen downriver carefully watch me. I suppose I look a little strange loitering in the rain in my padded pants and bright-red jacket, staring longingly across the river. But it took considerable effort to find this spot and I aim to linger for a while.

The Iowa Mormon Trails Association has marked its portion of the trail with interpretive panels. To help me find them, I have a book, notes, and maps all stuffed into the clear plastic pocket of my tank bag, but because I need both hands and both eyes for riding, I rely mostly on memorized directions and instinct. I have an OK sense of direction, but I'm from the West—we find our way by bouncing off mountains. In Iowa I question my direction at every turn, but after an hour or so of twisting along pretty country river roads, I find the first panel. The panel itself is unexciting, but its mere appearance feels like finding treasure at the end of a scavenger hunt, and I'm momentarily elated.

From the riverbank, however, as I look across the dark water at Nauvoo, the joy of finding the site quickly fizzles, the morning's shadows return, and I feel as alone as I ever remember feeling. Desolation creeps in and almost paralyzes me. I plop down on a soggy log, unsure of my next move. I'm to go from this point on the Mississippi River to the Salt Lake Valley alone on a motorcycle. The odds of joining the six thousand dead Mormons buried along the way feel overwhelmingly high. I stumble around in my head for options.

Maybe if I sit on this log long enough, Will will come for me. But I know better. Besides the pure absurdity of the thought, besides the fact that Will has no more than a vague idea of where I am and is not expecting me home for weeks yet, I know from experience that succumbing to helplessness and waiting to be rescued never works with Will. He knows me, and he intuitively knows that a woman who spent many years of her life—well into adulthood—as a frightened little girl needs moments such as this. Our relationship works as a mix of accommodation and recklessness. I know him as an open-minded, thoughtful, politically liberal man with an undercurrent of Latino machismo and Marine Corps–induced virility. He knows me as a tough-minded feminist woman, a veneer barely coating the inner shell of a quivering, insecure girl. There are moments when I want to be pulled in by him and given reassurances that he'll take care of things. Out of respect for me, he does not accommodate these moments.

I reach in my pocket and pull out the stone I picked up from the temple site, swoosh it in a nearby puddle, and dry it on my pants. It is wholly unremarkable in the palm of my hand—an ordinary rock—but it is enough to touch me with the strength of those who broke this trail. I roll it in my fingers for a few seconds and place it flat against my cheek before sticking it back in my pocket. I wave to the staring fishermen and without waiting to see if they wave back, I walk toward the waiting bike.


LINGER LONGER PARK, now a roadside bathroom stop, was known by Mormons as Poor Camp, the first campsite of the third and last wave of Saints to leave Nauvoo. The earlier parties had established a camp about seven miles farther up the trail on Sugar Creek, but this straggling bunch of Saints were in no condition to travel that far. They were the last to leave Nauvoo for a reason: They were simply too sick, too weak, too old, too young, or too poor to go. They had stayed in Nauvoo

not because they held out any hope of fending off their persecutors but simply because they had no other option.

In early September of 1846, the Gentiles launched a full-
scale war against this pitiful group of about a thousand remaining Mormons. They marched into Nauvoo with about two
thousand men armed with cannons, rifles fixed with bayonets,
pistols, and swords, roused the sick and old out of their beds,
marched them down to the river and onto skiffs and flatboats
with literally nothing but the clothes on their backs. They were
the lucky ones. Those too wasted away to walk were taken to
the river and simply tossed in. They gathered on the opposite
bank, huddled together alternately in mud and rain, daytime
heat and nighttime cold, without much food or shelter for
about three weeks.

I've found no record of how many died in Poor Camp, but
considering the sorry state they started in and the extreme conditions of the camp, death must have been both frequent and
welcome. However, God had not entirely forsaken this
wretched bunch. Unbeknownst to them, Brigham, even before
hearing about the final expulsion from Nauvoo, had sent ten
wagons back along the trail to rescue his faithful followers, an
act he would find necessary to repeat many times before this
magnificent gathering would be complete. And God himself
would pitch in to help. On October 9, 1846, just as the rescue
teams were loading the last of the Poor Camp into the wagons
to head west, a flock of quail—possibly exhausted from a flight
across the river—literally dropped into camp and every man,
woman, and child sat down to their first real meal since leaving
Nauvoo, an event that would go down in Mormon history as
one more nod from God toward his chosen people.

The Mormons' first camp on the trail, Sugar Creek, was
from all accounts filled with an even mix of misery caused by

days of sleet and snow alternating with crystal clear nights of subzero temperatures, and something close to gaiety induced by the absurd Mormon embrace of ordeal. The first group to arrive, led by Brigham Young, was well equipped with good wagons and supplies they had been gathering for months. However well prepared, they could not have found much comfort in tents and wagons when the temperatures dropped to right around twelve degrees below zero. Maria Thompson's future husband, my great-great-grandfather Orin Hatch, was in this first group of about three thousand Saints who streamed out of Nauvoo in February and March. Seven-year-old Maria likely left Nauvoo with her father and brothers in the late spring or summer of that year with the second and largest group, an estimated ten thousand or so.

Brigham had organized the groups to travel with precision, broken into companies of tens, fifties, and hundreds, with an able man assigned to captain each cluster. It was an admirable idea and an idea that likely kept the death toll in the thousands instead of the tens of thousands, but broken yokes, unruly oxen mired in mud, sick and dying family members, and buffalo stampedes often challenged Brigham's plan and strung the Saints across Iowa like a ragged clothesline from the Mississippi River to the Missouri. The Nauvoo group must have been a sight to see, but Iowa settlers would continue to see Mormons trail across Iowa—mostly converts from England and Scandinavian missions—for another thirteen years until the railroad was built to the Missouri River.


AS I TURN off Highway 218 onto Highway 2, traffic disappears, the rain stops, and the sky clears. I pop up my face shield and breathe deeply, wanting the cold wind to gush through me like a drain cleaner through a clogged drain, clearing out debris and allowing things to flow again. It works. The scenery softens to rolling green pastures and grazing horses, signs advertise hay for sale, and around each smooth turn in the road sits a model white farmhouse. I ride into a stand of pine trees in the Shimek State Forest and the road runs yellow with wildflowers. I reach out as if I might touch them and each one, in turn, gestures with a dip of its head. The bike sways through gentle curves, leaning slightly to the right, then slightly to the left, asking little of me. Here, I rediscover what I've always known: The movement stills the mind, makes the impossible possible.

A bike requires the body to wax and wane against the force of air it collides with. A bike asks the body to partner with it as it tilts and sways. It asks for an understanding of its ways—momentum is everything, halfheartedness cannot be tolerated. With momentum, a pavement-rubber contact width of two inches will give you the flow you long for. If you can't offer understanding, it asks for trust and faith.

A bike insists that you know your edges, that you respect the edge but that you go out on it from time to time and take a look around. A bike won't let you pretend the edge is not there, won't let you do your laundry and cash your paycheck and utter your perfunctory little prayers without recognizing the existence of the edge, without acknowledging life—and death.

# 11

SHORTLY AFTER MY FATHER INHERITED BANJO, MY
sister and I were yanked out of the 4-H club devoted to baking
chocolate chip cookies and placed, along with my brother, in a
4-H club devoted to fattening steers. We three were the club's
only members, and my father was our club leader. His rented
corrals expanded to hold three small, frightened steers that
would soon be haltered, tied, and left for hours on a short
rope to learn submission. They would then be grained, fat-
tened, named by my sister and me, tied some more, led around
the corral on the end of a rope, awarded a blue ribbon at the
Tooele County Stock Show, then slaughtered. Each year the
cycle was the same.

I have seen my father beat animals. I have seen him tie a
steer to a post and beat it with the dull side of a pitchfork because it pulled back too often against the lead rope. I have seen
him beat a horse with a shoeing rasp because it got tired and
lost its balance after standing too long on three legs during the
shoeing process. With its head tied close to the post, all it could
do was swing its powerful rear end from one side to the other,

uselessly trying to avoid the crack of the rasp on its ribs and back. I have seen him kick a dog for seeking warmth against the outside of a sliding-glass door on a cold winter's night and for still being there and in the way when my father happened to step outside. I have seen a dog hang itself by jumping over a fence on a short rope after being tied up for days. I have felt relieved when a cat's instincts and quick movement have saved it from a hard, swift boot simply for being a cat—one of the most hated animals in my father's world. I have seen my brother repeat these acts. I am not innocent of them myself. I can close my eyes and see deep red blood seep through the white curly hair on the fleshy underside of a steer's chin where I have snapped the halter chain tight around the pinched, bloody jowl again and again. I have smeared its blood on my hands and my clothes and felt my stomach lining tear with its useless, short life. I have hated the fat, awkward nine-hundred-pound animal that yielded to the seventy-pound girl and her Western life.

I CROSS THE Des Moines River and enter the town of Bonaparte, Iowa, from all accounts a flourishing town in 1846 when the first Mormons came through. I pull off the shoulder of what appears to be the shortest main street in America across from an old flour mill turned restaurant. An adjacent park, small and forlorn, runs along the river in the town, which initially appears deserted. I squat next to a dead lawn ornament—a plaster deer lying on its side—to rest my knees, and before I leave, I snap its picture for no particular reason.

A nearby marker tells me the Mormons chose to cross the Des Moines River here because the bottom is lined with rocks. Before reaching Utah, the Mormons would become experts at crossing rivers, often stopping to build ferries or bridges for the many that would follow. Here, however, they just slogged across the river in snow, rain, and mud. One journal entry claims it took twenty-five yoke of oxen to get one wagon up out of the river.

Back at the bike, I tighten the straps on the duffel bag as cars pull up on either side of me. I solicit a lot of stares—none of them friendly. I assume this is either because I'm a stranger in town, even worse a biker, or because there is an unspoken rule—now apparent—to park diagonally, which I have ignorantly broken. As I swing a leg over the duffel bag and begin to pull my helmet on, I search for road markings to tell me in which direction I should go. There are none. I tug the helmet back off and pull my map out of my tank bag to take a closer look. A car pulls in next to me and a pretty woman about my age toting two kids offers the first smile of the day.

"Which way to Bloomfield?" I ask. She points down the road.

"Stop in Bentonsport, then don't stop again till you get to Bloomfield, 'cause that's all that's worth seeing."

In Bentonsport, a pretty street—anchored by the Mason House Inn, believed to be built by Mormon craftsmen—follows the river. Many 1840s buildings along the Iowa portion of the Mormon Trail have remarkable similarity in craftsmanship to buildings in the city of Nauvoo. It was a common occurrence for the Mormons to stop and work for pay or supplies as they traveled.

I buy walnut fudge in the general store from a nice woman who encourages me to stay for a while and enjoy the beauty of her small town. They are a proud bunch in Bentonsport and have gone to great lengths to chronicle the town's history and to make strangers feel welcome. I feel calm and safe here as I wander out onto a footbridge that arches over the Des Moines

River. The day has turned clear and sunny, and a cool breeze blows off the river. From the bridge I spot a flower garden in the public park filled with roses and what I think to be gladiolas, but I could be making that up. I really don't know a thing about flowers except that I love them, and it brings me almost to tears that the folks of Bentonsport find enough value in the beauty of flowers to plant and maintain a public garden for folks like me who might need a moment of celestial bliss on their journey.

My grandmother Hatch likened gardening to churchgoing. Getting up at the crack of dawn and digging in the dirt for a couple of hours served God about as well as any pursuit could. For a month or so each summer, my mother would ship my sister and me to Cache Valley to spend a few weeks with her mother in Logan, Utah, and a few weeks with her oldest sister, Agatha, on her dairy farm in Cove, Utah. My grandmother would arise at 5 A.M. to start gardening and attempt to get us to do the same. We were unforgivably resentful about the idea and thought her nothing more than a loony old bird. We faked death in our beds to avoid such an undeserved encroachment on our summer vacation. She eventually gave up on us, gardened alone, and woke us for breakfast around 7 A.M.—an hour that still summoned our indignance as she laid a full breakfast of pancakes, bacon, and eggs in front of our sour little faces.

She never said so, but I have a hunch she blamed our ungodliness on my father, and, of course, she would have been accurate. My sister and I both should have been dragged from our beds into the morning light by our elbows. I think now, as I wander among the flowers I cannot identify, of that missed opportunity to acquire her gift for growing things, to acquire her knowledge of Utah land and dirt. I threw away my opportunity to know her, to set aside my adolescent arrogance and listen to the woman I thought of as too devoutly religious to teach the likes of me anything useful. By the time I had matured enough to realize my loss, my grandmother was dying in a rest home. Slumped in her wheelchair on the patio of the home, she would breathe honeysuckle into her nostrils and smile in a way that yanked my heart to the surface of my skin. Her face, which had been half-paralyzed since the accident that injured her and took her husband when she was forty-four, seemed to hold buckets full of grief and sadness. What she could have taught me about faith during those years I chose to slumber as a spoiled child instead of digging dirt by her side is forever lost to me.

Back on the road, I ignore the well-intentioned instructions to avoid all stops until Bloomfield and find my way in spite of myself to the next Mormon spot on my map, the courthouse in Keosauqua. I make what I think is a wrong turn and suddenly seem to be heading straight north on a road that looks like it won't offer much chance for diversion. When I pull over to figure it out, I find myself stopped directly in front of a Mormon Trail marker behind the oldest standing courthouse in Iowa, the sight of several concerts by Captain William Pitt's Brass Band, made up of British Mormon converts.

Before I left for my journey, I attended a Los Lobos concert at the University of Arizona. Dry summers that hover around 110 degrees have taught Tucsonans the fine art of moving slowly and then only when absolutely necessary. We are the embodiment of "laid back." So when Los Lobos was unsuccessful at getting more than about ten folks out of their seats to dance in the aisles, they made a joke that the audience must be full of Mormons, which got a big laugh.

Again, I found myself in the strange position of wanting to set the Mormon record straight in almost an obsessive way, as if

I had been personally misunderstood, accused of something unjustly. Who cares if the world thinks Mormons don't dance? Apparently, I do. I found myself leaning over to total strangers in front and in back of me to tell them that this is a fallacy, that Mormons dance, that they love to dance, that there are lots of things Mormons don't do, but dancing is not one of them. For a brief moment I think maybe I should send a letter to the manager of Los Lobos so he can set them straight and they can make their apologies. Mormons are peculiar enough without taking on every counterculture designation ignorant people want to assign to them, and it matters to me in a way that continually takes me by surprise.

The Mormons' love for music and dance, and their capability for using both to rise above the suffering of this journey, cannot be overstated. For the first wave of Saints, the journey from Nauvoo to Keosauqua had been, and would continue to be all the way to the Missouri River, an arduous one. The same snow, rain, and mud that kept the wagons bogged down and the oxen mired up to their bellies would cling to the hems of women's long skirts and climb like a rose bush up a trellis until the women felt as if their legs were wrapped in blankets that had been plunged into the icy waters of the Mississippi River, and they dragged them over the trail as if they were carrying the weight of the Lord's cross. They traveled no more than four or five miles a day, and it took them more than two weeks to go the fifty or so miles to Keosauqua.

Many an evening, the music of Captain Pitt's Brass Band would woo the cold and disheartened out from wagons and tents where they huddled in misery. They'd tap their feet to the rhythm and soon be dancing a full-scale jig that in addition to carrying precious blood to frozen fingers and toes, released the spirit of resolve once again into their souls.

Behind the Keosauqua Courthouse, where I loiter on a bench, things are quiet—possibly things are always quiet in Keosauqua, Iowa—with the exception of steady foot traffic in and out of what appears to be a small law office across the street. I lean back against the courthouse and close my eyes. Pitt's Brass Band was commissioned to play two concerts here at the courthouse to standing-room-only, non-Mormon crowds, and the Saints were able to purchase much needed supplies with the money. I attempt to conjure up the sound of the band in my head, but musically speaking I am pathetically hopeless, and this is a useless effort. The breeze is cool and I think I might sit for a while, when I notice several people staring at me from windows across the street. My peacefulness is pushed away by that creeping feeling of loneliness that comes from being alone in a crowd, that feeling a person gets among people who are not willing to either ignore her or engage her. I feel like a Mormon about to be "invited" to move on.

I make a stop in Bloomfield to snap a picture of a log cabin built by the Mormons. They made dozens of these along the way, got so they could cut the trees and put one up in less than a day. As I stand in the town square—something many Iowa towns have in lieu of a simple Main Street—ogling the ornate Davis County Courthouse in the center, a man bursts out the front door of the local tavern across the street, strides straight for me, shoves a brochure in my hand, says, "Welcome to Bloomfield," and strides right back into the tavern.

The brochure tells me the courthouse architecture is French Renaissance, and another brochure I have tells me it is "hailed as one of the finest examples of Second Empire style architecture in the United States," but its real claim to fame is being the only building that ever defeated the "human fly," Henry Poland. In 1924, he fell twenty-five feet while trying to scale the north side of the courthouse. After getting his hips back in working order—one broken and the other dislocated—he returned in 1932 and took exactly eleven minutes to perch himself on the blind goddess who adorns the top of the courthouse.

I make idle conversation with a couple reading the same brochure and alternately gazing upward. They tell me they are from Tucson, and in my current state of aloneness I come close to pulling them both into a group hug. We discover we live less than a mile from one another and shop at the same grocery store. I ask them what brings them to Bloomfield, Iowa, and they say they are headed to the Ozarks to square-dance. I picture the proximity of Tucson, Bloomfield, Iowa, and the Ozarks in my mind, picture the two of them dressed in a matching plaid dress/shirt combo doing a do-si-do, allemande left, then promenade, and suddenly I'm in the middle of one of those bizarre dreams where nothing connects. I bid them a confused farewell and ride on to Centerville, remembering the boy I was partnered with in my elementary school square-dancing exhibition. He was a good six inches shorter than me and his hand had a tendency to slide up from my waist until his thumb was lodged in my armpit. I pop my face shield to blow myself out of this strange square-dancing extravaganza.


I'VE MADE RESERVATIONS for the night at a bed-and-breakfast in Centerville with a charming website, so I ride with visions of the picturesque Bentonsport in my head. But the instructions for getting to the B and B—through town past KFC, Taco Bell, Hardee's, Texaco, and right at the Dairy Queen—should have told me Centerville was not going to have the quaintness of Bentonsport.

The One of a Kind Bed and Breakfast lives up to its name if not its website. It turns out to be charming in a rough-around-the-edges-stuff-more-junk-into-a-house-than-one's-senses-can-tolerate-thrift-shop-meets-antique-store-meets-county-boutique sort of way. I settle in to my little room—the smallest, cheapest, and least comfortable in the house—sit on the ruffle-skirted bed, take a look at the peeling paint and rattling window-mounted air conditioner, and allow the desolation I've been fighting all day to engulf me.

I pull the Nauvoo temple rock out of my pocket, place it on the bed, extract myself from my riding gear, lie down next to the small stone, and begin to cry. This sort of loneliness and despair is new to me. I have no plan for it, no instincts for it, no idea what is expected of me.

After a good cry, I take the stone in my hand and remind myself that my mother is praying for me. And it occurs to me that I could do the same. I sit with that thought for a while—it has been many, many years since I've uttered a prayer with any real sincerity—and the idea seems at once absurd and logical. I think about calling my mother instead but have a hunch the sound of her anxious voice would take me further into this unfamiliar abyss. I'm alone in a ten-by-six room, at least a thousand miles from anyone who cares the smallest bit about me. Praying feels unnatural and awkward. But it's beginning to feel like an only option. So I try.

"Our Heavenly Father," I say aloud, and I'm transformed into a skinny six-year-old girl standing in front of a congregation, arms folded tightly into digging fingernails, head bowed to the point of neck strain, eyes shut into a face-squinching slit, heart beating rapidly, repeating the words whispered by Sister Johnson, the Sunday school teacher. "Dear Lord," I try again, but am transferred to the third grade and Mrs. Deacon's exclamation of "Dear Lord" each time a nose was wiped on a sleeve or an answer was blurted out of turn. "Our Father who art in heaven" brings me back to adulthood but takes me to a beloved Benedictine monastery and the rituals of Catholicism, which seem inappropriate here.

How could something that must have come so easily for five generations of my ancestors be so awkward for me? I wonder if they would be ashamed of me now, so lost after they had struggled to clear a path. Somehow I don't think so. I think they would stroke my hair with their callused hands and tell me to try again. So I do. I slide down off the bed onto my knees, close my eyes less out of reverence and more out of a need to block out the depressing-overlaid-with-cheerful room, squeeze that temple stone in my hand, and start again with "Dear God." I pause there for a moment, unsure of what should come next and in what sort of language, then, like the day's clothing shed at bedtime, the self-consciousness falls away and I speak as if God and I were sharing a cup of tea. I tell God, "As desperate as I feel, I won't be cutting any deals or making any promises I can't keep. But the truth is, I could use some help. I'm alone and I'm scared. I want to feel the strength of Will's arms across my back and the softness of my mother's face next to mine. But more than anything I want to make this journey with some semblance of the courage and grace of the women who traveled before me. Amen."

I stay on my knees for a moment. The prayer feels unfinished. I start again. I explain to God that I'm not entirely convinced about *his* existence (as much as I want some other image of God than a man, it's simply the only one available to me at the moment), that I'm not one of the faithful, but I'm not averse to the possibility and if he'd like to send some sort of sign, I'll be watching.

I climb back up on the bed and pull out my papers to map tomorrow's ride. I'm unwilling to look too closely or think too deeply about what I feel. I feel nothing specific, no great feeling of comfort or safety, no burning in my soul, no sudden knowledge. I just feel a little lighter is all.

After looking at my maps, I opt to stay put for two nights instead of one. Many of the sites I want to visit are within fifty miles of here. They are also on dirt roads, the condition of which is unknown, but unloading the bike and traveling light appeals to me.

I'm the only guest at the One of a Kind Bed and Breakfast, so I snoop through the other, much larger vacant bedrooms to find a hodgepodge decor of Martha Stewart's country living interspersed with a few couches and love seats in 1970s gold, orange, and lime-green velveteen. Then I spread out in the common area of the second floor among the stuffed country ducks and miscellaneous knickknacks. Religious symbols dominate the knickknacks, faith fills the books scattered deliberately on small antique tables. I grab one of the nearby books and open it at random to this quote by Ralph Waldo Emerson: "Our faith comes in moments . . . yet there is a depth in those brief moments which constrains us to ascribe more reality to them than to all other experiences."

Before I go downstairs to make arrangements to stay an extra night, I duck into the small bathroom by my bedroom, sit down to empty my bladder, and begin to read: "Lord lift me up and let me stand, by faith on heaven's tableland, a higher plane than I have found, Lord plant my feet on higher ground." The bathroom walls are papered with sheet music from old church hymns. For a brief moment, I entertain the idea that the bathroom walls are a sign from God, and I wonder if this is one of those moments Emerson was speaking of. If God were really all-knowing, he would know this would be appropriate for me, just the right touch. A visit from an angel would freak me out, and a leaf dropping into my hair at just the right time would be too subtle. But wallpaper that reads *Let me hide myself in thee* seems about right. The bathroom walls are not saying, "Look, you idiot, here's proof of God"; the bathroom walls are simply saying, "Just pay attention and let the possibility exist."

# 12

THE PROPRIETRESS OF THE ONE OF A KIND B AND B HAS
prepared scrambled eggs with cheese, toast, sausage, fruit, orange juice, and tea, which I eat at a tiny round ruffle-covered
table under the careful watch of antique dolls and teddy bears.
While I eat, the husband of the proprietress sits at the next
table and tells me about his days as a traveling salesman, their
son, the shady side of antiques dealing, and the weather. She
sits with him and adds a helpful detail from time to time. I appreciate their company.

Trying to hold up my end of the conversation, I tell them
about Arizona's "stupid motorist law" that says if you drive
around a barricade to cross a flooded wash and your car floats
away and you have to be rescued, you can be fined under
the law.

"They're probably all Mexicans, right?" he says. I swallow
quietly, not sure I've heard him correctly and not really wanting him to repeat it because I want to like them, but he repeats
himself. I assure him that Arizona has plenty of stupid white
motorists and let it drop there. I don't tell him that my husband

is Hispanic or point out the ignorance of his thinking; I'm not feeling strong enough to alienate the only human contact available to me at the moment.

A light rain falls as I attach the tank bag to the bike and pull on my helmet. A few miles south of Centerville on Highway 5, the sky turns ominously dark and the rain becomes heavy and steady. My directions take me into farmland, past country churches and graveyards, and soon put me off on a muddy road that runs through Iowa pastures. I downshift and mentally adjust to the way the bike moves around as if I have no control, no traction. It is initially disconcerting and I take note of each farmhouse, far and few between, calculating how far I might have to go in case I need help. The road feels precarious, as if I will likely end up in a ditch, shiny side down with my tires spinning. The consolation is that if I do crash, I likely won't be going fast enough to kill myself, and the ditches are cushioned with long, green grass. I find out soon, though, that dirt roads in Iowa are common enough to be treated as secondary highways by residents who drive them at highway speeds—plenty fast enough to kill a person on a bike—and treat them as one-lane roads going conveniently in the direction they happen to be moving. At one point, I am pushed rather close to the ditch and barbwire fence to avoid the grille of a 1980s Oldsmobile.

The pastures I ride between are greener and more richly abundant than anything I could possibly dig out of my arid-West memory, but the sight of grazing cattle moving slowly with their noses to the ground, a sight that at one time instilled anxiety and fear, today instills familiarity and calm. In spite of spending more than a decade of my adolescence fighting against the Western life my father had immersed me in, I emerged from it with an unrequited love for the West. Only three years of my life have been lived elsewhere. During those years I spent in New York, I knew I was not a resident of that place, only a long-term visitor. My love for the West fills me with a dull ache whenever I'm not there, and it's that ache that today keeps me moving along this journey toward that place.

My father's quest for a Western life grew from a single horse into a small, dilapidated cattle ranch with frenzied speed, and my life of hopscotch in the driveway and a game of statues on the grass was blown to bits. My summers went from bicycling between manicured yards, something I was rather competent at, to herding cattle, castrating bawling calves, and riding horses—a life for which I had already proven my ineptitude. But my father aimed to cure me. This daughter of a cattle rancher and granddaughter of a sheepherder would not grow up behind a cement curb and gutter.

My mother was dragged along into this life. She didn't kick and scream about it—she never would—but she never embraced it, either. She had been raised dirt-poor, the daughter of a farmer, and she held no romantic notions of that particular Western life. That little patch of grass between the house and the curb was as large a piece of the West as she ever would have needed. In her new role as rancher's wife, she usually did just enough to keep my father's temper from reeling out of control—although at times that was hard to predict. I kept her close to me, and she did what she could to protect me.

As this life of ours took on the largeness of the West itself, I developed what appeared to my father to be a strange paranoia of large animals—particularly cattle and horses. Moving the cattle from the upper pasture to the lower pasture at our ranch required herding them a good ten miles out on the dirt farm roads. My father would gather the cattle and ride behind them while my mother drove the farm truck, dropping each of her children at a fork in the road to head the cattle off in the right direction.

When my brother and sister were out of the truck standing in the dirt as we drove away, and I knew the next fork in the road would be mine, my mother would look over to find tears streaming down my dust-stained face and my hands clutching the seat. At the next fork in the road, she would park the truck in the middle of the undesired lane and we'd sit and wait together. As the cattle approached, she'd nudge me out, telling me she'd be right there if I needed help. I'd stand in front of the grille trembling, knowing that if I lifted my arms too soon, the cattle would turn back on themselves, and that if I lifted them too late, they would rush past me in the wrong direction. Mostly I just stood in a state of paralyzed panic while the cattle turned down the other fork as if I were a barbwire fence. I loved my mother for never leaving me, but it only partially alleviated my fear. What I seemed incapable of verbalizing, even to her, was that I had no fear of cattle or horses. My fear was of my father. Since my first experience on horseback, my incompetence as a rider or a cowpuncher had opened up a bunch of new opportunities to incite his temper. Seeing my mother there with me would only serve to divert some of his anger away from me toward her. I realized years later there was no need to verbalize the true source of my fear to her. She always knew.

AFTER A GOOD forty minutes on this dirt road, I suspect I may have missed the sign marking the place where the Mormons camped on the Chariton River. When I'm about to turn back, the marker jumps from behind some trees on my left. I slide to a stop and make a teetering U-turn, dragging both feet in the mud to avoid dropping the bike. It is pathetic by all motorcycling standards—I'm glad no one is around to see it—but it gets me where I want to be, in a grassy pullout, bike turned toward the direction I just came.

The rain continues and the skies remain dark. Such a day is appropriate for visiting this spot. The first wave of Mormons camped here ten days in relentless wind, rain, and mud. It took them days to get the wagons across the river, using ropes as brakes to lower the wagons down one steep bank and using ropes again to pull them up the opposite side. The night a woman named Zina Hunnington gave birth to a son was described this way by Lorenzo Snow: "A moment there came a gust of wind and blue the tent flat to the ground . . . The rain came down in torants so fast that it put out the fire. In a few minutes all was darkness, and it was so cold that it seemed as though I must perish . . . The rain wet me through and through, and I never felt in my life as though I must perish with the cold more than I did then."

Zina named her baby boy Chariton in celebration of being born in good health on the tormenting banks of that river. The notes from my research on this section of the trail tell me others were not so lucky; there are three Mormon graves nearby.

I climb through the barbwire fence into the pasture ignoring the no-trespassing sign and wander toward the river in search of the graves and still-visible wagon ruts. A trail guide says I'll find them a quarter of a mile from the road. Although I'm an avid hiker, I have no sense of distance—the term "quarter mile" is almost meaningless to me—I just head toward the grove of trees that presumably line the banks of the river. A cow trail leads me down off the hill through the tall, wet grass, and I'm soon enclosed in trees and a silence that is almost eerie. I've gone more than a quarter mile, but I'm time and again pulled just around the next bend. I reach the river after walking about forty-five minutes. I expect it to cut an angry gash through steep banks; I expect it to show to me the same kind of austerity it showed the Mormons. But deep in the briar (I am fortunately protected by Cordura riding pants and knee-high riding boots) I reach what might be the most quiet, peaceful spot I've ever stood upon. The river flows noiselessly, curving gently around giant trees, sweeping slowly from side to side like a ballroom dancer. As I reach its banks, the river invites me into the dark shelter of the trees reaching tenderly across its waters. I drop to my knees in the wet grass and feel, with no doubt in my mind, the faint presence of something that is far beyond my understanding. I don't feel the suffering the Mormons experienced here, nor do I feel the sorrow that has gripped me at other points along the trail. What I feel on the now-placid banks of the Chariton River is reverence.

In her book *In Search of Belief,* Benedictine sister Joan Chittister writes, "We are bound to one another, each generation a link in the chain, each generation a standard for the one to come . . . we weep for those whose faith has formed our own . . . Our souls stretch always forward, yes, but our hearts stretch always back. The chain of life never breaks, the shape of soul never strains beyond what formed us, what filled us with life in the first place."

I was eight years old the first time I was forced to think of myself as something other than an attachment to my mother. It was 1964, a clear summer Saturday, when my mother committed the simple act of driving to the grocery store without me, an act she had never taken in the prior eight years of my life. Up to that point, in my mind, I had physically and emotionally affixed myself to her and her to me. When I emerged from my bedroom on that sunny day to find her missing, when my father so casually said, "She's gone to the store," I felt as if a pump slowly sucked the air from my body. I returned to my bedroom, stuffed myself in the narrow space between the bed and the wall, and wept as if she were gone from my life forever. My despair over this simple break in tradition was melodramatic to be sure but real nonetheless. I felt as if whatever bound us had stretched and snapped. I knew from that moment it would be easy, almost normal, for her to drive away without me.

What I felt then and what I feel now is precisely what Chittister claims can never happen—the shape of my soul straining beyond what formed me, what filled me with life in the first place. But as she says, my heart stretches always back.

I fumble in my pocket, pull the temple stone out, and dip it and my hands momentarily into the cold water, unzip my jacket, and dry them on my shirt. "My mother is praying for me," I whisper to the river, "and it's possible others are also."

I return to the bike without ever finding the graves or the ruts, but it matters not. A car passes while I'm studying my maps and slows to look. I couldn't possibly appear more lost or more pitiful—wet hair plastered to my head, tiny rivulets running down my face, mud caked so heavily on the bike the color is barely visible—so I'm thankful when they continue on their way without stopping. Actually, I'm not feeling lost at all. I feel as if I'm exactly where I should be.

# 13

THE SKIES DARKEN AS I HEAD WEST. I'VE NOW thoroughly tested the waterproofing capacity of my riding gear and am pleased to note that other than what soaked my hair and trickled down my neck when my helmet was off, I'm bone-dry. The temperature is cool but not cold, the rain stays steady, traffic is light. Riding in the rain suits me; everything feels perpetual and rhythmic. I slice through the water with the grace of a diver. The wind splits the tiny droplets down the middle of my face shield, like parting hair, and pushes them to either side before they rejoin the atmosphere. The water sprays out from under my tires symmetrically, sounding like Alka-Seltzer dissolving in a glass, then quickly and quietly settles back into the grooves on the road. I feel as if I'm scarcely disturbing the air, as if the space I'm creating closes so quickly behind me, it's barely noticeable. This seems right to me—to move along the trail of my grandmothers as quietly and unobtrusively as possible, to make little noise of my own so I can hear what there is to hear.

A turn south takes me on another gravel road and I shoot down it like an old pro. About five miles down the road sits a small country burial ground called Tharp Cemetery. The cemetery itself has nothing to do with the Mormons—all of the dates on the headstones mark passings that occurred after the Mormons were already settled in the West—but the cemetery sits on one of the more famous Mormon sites in Iowa. Here on April 14, 1846, William Clayton penned what would become the Saints' marching song to Zion and would generations later swell any congregation of Mormons full with pride. Clayton wrote the song when news of the birth of his son back in Nauvoo gave him a much-needed emotional lift out of the Iowa mud.

As I walk through the little wire gate into the cemetery, the rain stops and the sun breaks through the clouds and hits me like I'm a character in a Hollywood movie. I wander through the headstones softly singing Clayton's hymn—the only hymn to which I know the words:

> *Come, come ye saints*
> *No toil nor labor fear*
> *But with joy wend your way*
> *Though hard to you*
> *This journey may appear*
> *Grace shall be as your day.*

> *'Tis better far for us to strive*
> *Our useless cares from us to drive*
> *Do this and joy your hearts will swell*
> *All is well! All is well!*

Or as we used to sing it as kids right before cracking up:
*Come, come ye saints, no toilet paper here, butt with joy, wend your way.*

I sit on the wet grass among the dead non-Mormons, back against one of their headstones, face toward the sun, and sing with feeling at the top of my lungs. It's one of those songs that demands a deep voice and the swing of a fist to go along with it, so I give it my all. I imagine those among whose remains I sit appreciate it in spite of the fact that I've been asked to never sing in public.

I love cemeteries, always have. I've always felt peaceful in them. I imagine that has something to do with my Mormon indoctrination of an afterlife in the celestial kingdom, although according to the Mormon rules, I'll certainly never reach that high. My image of the celestial kingdom is draped in goodness and light, like gauzy white linen that never yellows, and filled with a bunch of surprised Mormons (not the ones who expected to be there) and their friends all dressed in white. Every once in a while, the door swings open and a few more float in, but the place never fills up and never feels crowded.

When I was thirteen years old, I did my part to get a few more folks through that door. My Mutual class (Mutual is short for the Mutual Improvement Association, organized by Brigham Young in 1875 to keep young Mormon women and men from following the evil ways of the outside world) was assigned the task of being baptized for the dead, which at the time held no more meaning for me than a field trip into Salt Lake City from our rural town forty-five miles away. Had I known then it would be my only opportunity to be inside the Salt Lake City temple, I would have paid closer attention. Those of us who needed them—me included—were issued baptism clothing, then ushered to the girls' dressing room to change. Being the age we were, some were eager to show off the fact that they were wearing bras and the rest of us were eager to hide the fact that we were not, so we were shuffling to find corners accordingly. All this posturing came to a halt when it was discovered that one girl had forgotten her change of underwear, and just as we were acting out our mortification that she would have to return home pantyless after getting her only pair wet, we discovered the panties she wore were blue. We were equally scandalized by that because the rules of baptism didn't allow anything but white.

Our teacher ended our tittering with the executive decision to ignore the all-white rule, told the young girl to put her baptismal clothing over it, and marched us out to the baptismal font, a big bowl that rests upon twelve golden oxen, a daunting structure to a thirteen-year-old. One at a time, we walked up the stairs to the top of the font and down another set into the warm water, got prayed over and lowered into the water by a couple of men, then sent to the back of the line—I think there were about eight of us—shivering until our turn came to do it again. In the midst of the shivering came much snickering every time the girl emerged from the water with her blue panties clearly visible under her white clothing. We were each dunked about sixteen times.

The Mormon ritual of baptizing the dead, intended to offer those who may not have had the chance to embrace Mormonism on earth a go at it in the afterlife, became controversial when it was discovered the Mormons were routinely baptizing Holocaust victims and other Jews—mostly famous ones such as Albert Einstein and Irving Berlin—along with other well-known historical figures regardless of their religious backgrounds. After some Jewish groups and others expressed outrage at the arrogance of this practice, the Mormons agreed to baptize only those spirits whose Mormon descendants have made such a request. I have no idea whose names were read over my head before being lowered into the water, but I can't imagine that the likes of me standing in for the deceased could give them or their descendants much comfort, even if I was dressed appropriately in white panties.

• • •

A DETOUR SIGN keeps me on gravel roads as I find my way to Corydon. I top the first hill and about halfway down the other side glance in my rearview mirror, expecting to see nothing but my own tracks behind me. I'm stunned and more than a little disconcerted to see the words "WIDE LOAD" across the grille of a semitruck so close I can see nothing else, not his windows nor his tires. I speed up considerably to make it to the next uphill grade, thinking maybe his brakes have failed, maybe he will not be able to avoid me, and what the hell is he doing out here anyway? One of the reasons I avoid freeways and major highways is that I've had my fair share of truckers who like to mess with motorcyclists just because they can. I've been squeezed off to the shoulder, tailgated, and shouted at. There's a good possibility that this particular trucker is getting a kick out of scaring the hell out of me, but if a cow were to wander across the road—certainly not an impossibility in this part of the country—I would hit my brakes and the truck would hit me and that's the end of the story. The fact is, I can stop my bike in less than a tenth of the distance it will take him to stop that truck. He knows that but apparently doesn't care.

I put some distance between us as I glide up the next hill, but as I slow down for the intersection with Highway 2 he again bears down on me. I downshift and slow enough to see that the road is clear and, ignoring the stop sign, begin a left turn onto the highway. Patches of wet gravel scattered on the pavement at the intersection would normally slow me down, but the problem behind me seems more threatening. Well into my lean, I can't avoid a patch of gravel and my back tire slips. The bike takes a dip toward the pavement—my stomach dips with it—before finding traction and righting itself. At about the same time, I hear the truck screeching and sliding to a halt. I glance in my mirror and see the nose of the truck well into the intersecting lane of Highway 2. I pull immediately into an empty parking lot on my right to take a few deep breaths and find myself at the Prairie Trails Museum in Corydon, Iowa.

In front of the Prairie Trails Museum, I find a Mormon Trail interpretive panel. Finding every last one of them with less-than-adequate directions has become something of a challenging sport, testing not only my sense of direction and my ability to spot hidden treasure in the oddest places but also my riding skills. So far I'm ten for ten.

I have the Prairie Trails Museum to myself with the exception of the two nice ladies running the joint, who point me in the direction of the Mormon Trail exhibit and then leave me alone to browse. The Mormon Trail exhibit plays a steady rendition of "Come Come Ye Saints" in a voice much better than my own. It is a perfectly fine and informative exhibit but seems small and meager after the extravagant Mormon Church exhibits of Nauvoo.

But the remainder of the museum can in no way be accused of being small. The Prairie Trails Museum of Corydon, Iowa, the county seat of Wayne County, occupies several acres of space in two huge buildings and is stuffed full of good junk. The collection runs the gamut from over ninety thousand artifacts of trail memorabilia to a substantial collection of paperweights, a less substantial but still good collection of salt and pepper shakers, county fair trophies, high school sports uniforms, and a miscellaneous collection of stuff that looks as if the folks of Wayne County cleaned out their attics and barns and delivered the contents to the museum. A big attached barnlike building holds a bunch of old farm equipment, an old hearse, some embalming tools, and an electric car called the Mars II from the 1960s with a trunk stuffed full of batteries. But the best is this: an impressively large collection of dogs. Ceramic, plaster, plastic, stuffed dogs of all breeds, shapes, sizes, several thousand dogs lining the walls and floor of a glassed-out room built to hold them. The dogs alone are worth the stop.

On my way back to the One of a Kind B and B, Swan's Family Restaurant on the east edge of Promise City, Iowa, catches my attention. I pull in between two pickup trucks and realize too late that the gravel lot has a slight downward slope toward the restaurant. What this means to a woman my size— about 115 pounds after riding in the rain all day—is that I've just made a pretty big mistake. I won't be able to push my bike back out of here, especially with gravel under my feet. As I'm contemplating my situation, two guys looking fresh from the cornfield in jeans and ball caps walk out of the restaurant and smile. I sit still and smile back. They jump into a pickup truck next to me and back out. They are the answer to my prayers. Their departure has left me with enough room to turn around without having to push the bike backward. This incident causes more anxiety than it actually should; I'm in no danger of being mortally wounded in the parking lot of Swan's Family Restaurant, but I can feel the sweat roll down the middle of my back on this chilly late afternoon.

Inside the restaurant sits one Iowa family of four in a place the size of a bowling alley. The entire family—mom, dad, brother, sister—turns to look at me, which I figure is a normal thing to do when someone walks in the door. But they keep looking, and after I sit down and remove my jacket they are still looking. I think about asking them why they find me so curious, but they don't look all that friendly or good-humored. Each of them puffs on a cigarette except the son, who looks to be about thirteen. A lot of people smoke in the heartland.

The waitress asks if I want a menu, and my gut feeling says no but I say yes. She's pleasant in that mind-your-own-business-and-I'll-mind-mine sort of way. I try to strike up a conversation with her, mostly just to let the staring family know I'm human and nothing out of the ordinary, but she has no interest. I say something inane like "It's cold here in Iowa," and she says, "Sure is today," writes down my order, gives it to the kitchen, and joins the other four waitresses who are smoking at a table next to the family.

I know the key to eating well in any small roadside café is to order something fried, and since I like fried food I usually do just that. But it's been weeks since I've eaten anything green, and all the grease I've eaten brings to mind my mother's old Crisco can that collects grease to be used over and over again and remains today in its spot in the back of the fridge, where it's been for at least thirty-five years. I'm feeling as if I'd taken a spoon and eaten out of that can like it was ice cream.

My salad arrives on a small dinner plate—iceberg lettuce that had been shredded for sandwiches, most of it still green, some of it a little rusty, and a cup of ranch dressing on the side. I chase this with a rubbery piece of grilled chicken on a white bun. The family eats their burgers and fries with gusto, craning their necks between bites to keep an eye on me.

When I get back to Centerville, tired and hungry, I kick at some of the larger chunks of mud hanging off my bike, but it has dried to clay capable of breaking a toe. Some motorcyclists hold suspicions about a clean bike running better than a dirty one, but I'm not one of them. The first wave of Mormons were bogged down in this Iowa mud for weeks, "clinging in five-pound masses to each foot," wrote historian Bernard De-Voto, so I decide it's not such a bad thing to carry with me for a while.

I LOAD THE bike in an increasingly hot morning sun and head west out of Centerville. A few miles down the road, at the top of a hill, I pass another motorcyclist—the only one I've seen since leaving the Mississippi River—stopped by the side of the road. He's not bent over his bike; he's just leaning against it, arms folded, as if he's waiting for a bus. I don't see him until I top the hill, so I'm well past him before I have the chance to stop. An unspoken rule among riders says that you don't pass up a fellow motorcyclist who may need assistance no matter what the circumstances. And because I often ride alone, this rule means a great deal to me. He appears to be waiting for someone, he doesn't appear to need help, his bike is not loaded for touring so I assume he's not far from home; still, I know I should turn around and check. But I don't. My bike *is* loaded for touring and going back requires two U-turns on a two-lane road with no shoulder and not much visibility in either direction. The minute I make the decision to go on, the minute I roll on the throttle, my gut tells me it's the wrong decision. But I keep going, muttering along the way to myself, to the man at the side of the road, to the universe in general, "I'm sorry, please forgive me."

Chittister writes that "the way we live ripples across time, touching people we never see, changing places we never went, singing a sound that never ends." I know she's right about this; no single life escapes this opportunity or burden, however one chooses to view it. She goes on to say that "it is what we believe that sculpts and guides us," and I know she's right about this also, which is why a woman needs to be clear about what it is she believes. I know that the beliefs held by the women who now guide me matter—it mattered 150 years ago and it matters now.

# 14

RELIGION SCARES ME. SO MUCH OF IT SEEMS STIFLING, restrictive, oppressive, judgmental. Some of that, of course, depends on the person practicing it, but some just comes with the territory. If I believe, as Mormons do, that the Mormon Church is the only true church on earth, that the only road to eternal salvation is through the rituals and practices dictated by the Mormon hierarchy, how then, am I to look upon my non-Mormon neighbor? Seems it leaves me only two options: I either look upon him with pity because he's not bright enough to see the truth, or I look upon him with disapproval because he knowingly chooses to deny God's path.

I've seen my born-again Christian sister go through the same thing. If she's absolutely certain she's found the path to eternal salvation, which she is, and if she truly loves me with all her heart, which she does, how can the two stand separate? Out of pure love, she must do everything in her power to guide me along her path, never giving up no matter the risk to our relationship. Anything short of that is either a failing of love or a failing of faith.

There's a part of me searching for faith—an easier concept for me than a search for God—and there's a part of me foiling that search at every turn for fear of finding it. My experience with the faithful has been that lives get torn apart, that family relations become strained, that friendships necessarily end. I have friends who have returned to the Mormon Church after years away, and in addition to my sister, I have friends who are now born-again Christians. Our relationships have changed. As much as we didn't want them to, as much as we worked to keep them together, they changed. And not in one instance did they change for the better. We are suddenly strangers meeting for the first time, struggling to find common ground but never succeeding. In most instances, we have simply given up and parted ways. I don't know if it's the religion or my reaction to it that changes the relationship; it doesn't much matter. The loss to me has been great; less so for them, I believe, because they are in the position of faith. Less concerned, I imagine, with earthly needs such as human fellowship. Even if I could count myself among the faithful, religion still prevents me from maintaining certain relationships. My born-again Christian friends look upon Mormonism as a non-Christian cult, the devil's work, and my Mormon friends are understandably a little defensive about that.

What happens to my life if I find faith, if I find God? Can I continue to live with an agnostic husband whom I dearly love? Can I keep my nonbelieving friends? Will they want to keep me? What are the day-to-day requirements of faith?

The question of Christ is a whole different matter and one I'm not ready for. The word "Christian" has been appropriated by the religious right—the born-agains—and the people who used to be considered "Christian"—the Catholics and the Protestants, for example—are looked at in kind of a lackadaisical way, as if they haven't put forth enough effort to hold the title because they haven't been through a transformation. Being born into a religion is not the same as being born again into a religion.

I find a considerable number of people who feel the need to proclaim their religious beliefs to one another these days. I'm not sure why. I met a man for the first time a few weeks ago, a business acquaintance of my husband's, and within an hour or so of meeting, I knew his religious beliefs. He was one of the I-don't-believe-in-organized-religion types but not quite the I-have-my-own-spirituality type. He strongly believed in the traditional, biblical God, and that is something the spiritual-but-not-religious types won't readily admit. They believe in "some sort of higher power" or "some force in the universe." I know this because I'm guilty of such utterances. I don't have a clue what that huge abstraction, "a force in the universe," really means, and I see no reason not to name it "God."

I'm also guilty of the I-don't-believe-in-organized-religion cliché, which is very popular these days. Religion is responsible for so much violence and war, I've said on occasion—also a very popular notion. But my gut feeling is that human beings, not organized religion, are responsible for violence and war. Few religions teach violence, although by their very nature they teach superiority and intolerance, which may escalate to violence. But I believe that human beings are capable of stopping war, violence, poverty, and injustice, and that human beings choose not to.

But what do I mean when I say I don't believe in organized religion? Do I mean I'm against the people of my Utah hometown coming together in the church on the corner to sing, to pray, to eat, to laugh? Or do I mean the hierarchy of the Mormon Church, the institution itself, the one that so neatly excludes women from its top ranks? Possibly. But that same institution feeds hundreds of thousands of hungry people each year. The Mormon Church does not publish financial data, but a Church spokesman estimates it spends about $12.7 million in cash and about $65.2 million in material assistance on humanitarian aid each year. Am I so selfish that my exclusion as a woman from the ranks of power would set me against the "organized religion" that accomplishes this? The Relief Society of the Mormon Church visits thousands of shut-ins every month, offers hope and comfort, tends to the sick and grieving. Is this what I'm opposed to when I proudly proclaim, "I don't believe in organized religion"? How would such things be accomplished if no such organizations existed?

I just try to be the best person I can be, I tell people. That should be enough. Enough for what? Enough to get me into heaven in case there is such a place? Certainly not enough to stem violence or injustice. Certainly not enough to end wars. Certainly not enough to repair or even stop the damage we've done to the environment. That statement is too easy, it holds no conviction, and it's false. I'm not the best person I could be; I don't even try. I'm nice to my friends, I extend common courtesies to strangers, I'm pleasant to coworkers, I try not to hurt anyone, and I try to do minimal damage to my habitat—but so what? Does that really say anything about me at all? On a day-to-day basis I barely even think about my actions unless someone confronts me with them. Until the person asking for money on the street or the person with the broken-down car in the middle of the intersection forces me to make the "good" choice or the "bad" choice, what is it that defines my character? That paltry little sum I give to charity every year? The canvas bags I smugly carry to the grocery store?

Eventually, the conversation with my husband's business acquaintance turned back to business, which is where it started.

Turns out, he attributes his good business sense, his financial gains, all of it, to God, and he drops to his knees every single day to thank God for his big house and new SUV. I thought that was awfully kind and maybe even humble of him to give God all the credit, but I just can't figure God actually works this way.

WHEN MARIA THOMPSON reached Garden Grove, Iowa, in 1846 with her brothers and father she would have been close to celebrating her eighth birthday. They stopped for a rest and remained in this spot for five years before continuing to Salt Lake City. My family records give no reason for the delay, but William Thompson, Maria's father, was never a wealthy man, and after losing his home and property first in Missouri and again in Illinois he likely lacked the resources to get his family through the Rocky Mountains. William and two of his sons—David, fourteen, and William Jr., ten—went to work to earn money. Daniel, eleven, had taken on cooking, cleaning, and care of Maria and her younger brother, Orvil, since the death of their mother when Daniel was nine years old. He apparently had quite a knack for domesticity. In a letter written to his family in Scotland shortly before fleeing Nauvoo, William reports that Daniel "cooks and washes and keeps the house and takes care of the two youngest and does better than some women would."

The first group of Mormons led by Brigham Young founded Garden Grove. As the Mormons would do all along the trail, they stopped to build shelter and put crops in the ground before reloading their wagons and moving west again. This system of western migration—with one eye scanning the western horizon for the promised land and one eye looking back to the east to the promised people still to follow—was unique to the

Mormons. At each way station, they left a handful of able men and women to tend the crops, along with a much larger cluster of the sick, poor, feeble, exhausted, and starving.

Bogged down by mud, rain, cholera, whooping cough, fever, childbirth, malnutrition, rattlesnake bites, starving ox teams, and a steady procession to bury the dead, the second cluster of Saints to come from Nauvoo seemed capable of bringing the whole operation to its knees. That it didn't is a testament to the sheer will of Brother Brigham to deliver Joseph's and now his followers—in whatever sorry state they might arrive—to the Land of Zion, the exact location of which was no more than "somewhere in the West" at this time. On more than one occasion, Brigham sent wagons full of furniture, dishes, and clothing out to non-Mormon settlements to trade for food to keep his people going a bit longer.

He exhorted those who were well-off to share their provisions, he instilled faith in those who had lost all sense of purpose by reminding them of their chosen status, and time and time again he sent a rescue party of his strongest men east on the trail to yank the faithful out of the miserable slumps they'd surrendered to. In the end, he delivered on his promise of Zion. That he not only got the majority of Saints from Nauvoo to Salt Lake City alive, but kept the trail operation going for twenty more years to bring more than fifty thousand Saints west to build the Lord's kingdom on earth, seems nothing short of a miracle.

Garden Grove's pretty little Main Street runs between the Mormon Trails High School—home of the Garden Grove Saints football team—and the Mormon Trails Café to the west end of town, where the original settlement was built. On this spot, the first wave of Mormons left sixty or so "duplex" cabins; many acres of plowed, planted, and fenced fields; and wells, roads, and a bridge over the creek. They stopped only two weeks to build the town of Garden Grove before starting west again. The settlement is now a big meadow, and near the entrance the grass has been cut to show the outlines of the cabins that would each house two or more families.

As I have been at most stops along the trail, I'm alone here. The wind has picked up, but it is still warm, so I sit on the grass for a while and watch the movement of the cows across the road before walking down off the hill toward the line of trees surrounding the pasture. A trail leads me into woods, and the air becomes suddenly still and quiet. I have a heightened awareness of my isolation and my heart rate momentarily quickens, but immediately calms again. Maria no doubt walked in these woods 155 years ago. I have a feeling, in spite of her losses, that she found happiness in those five years she spent in Garden Grove.

Shortly before the Thompson family left Garden Grove and started west again in 1851, William married the widow Mary Ann Hale, whom he had known in Illinois. On the cusp of her teen years, Maria must have been overjoyed at the prospect of having a mother again. Although Maria was adored by her father and brothers, the notion of making the long journey west in the company of another female must have been a great comfort to her. But her comfort would be fleeting. She would help bury her new stepmother less than a year later on the trail near the Platte River at Ancient Bluffs, Nebraska.

As I walk through the grove that once heard the dreams and disappointments of my great-great-grandmother Maria, I think mostly of her great-granddaughter, my mother. Her life has always seemed burdened with the sadness of never-realized dreams. And her dreams were so small: a modest house shared with a husband and children who were filled with love and joy for The Church of Jesus Christ of Latter-day Saints. The dream was granted to almost every young Mormon girl in Utah, but it was not to be granted to my mother. Even I, in spite of harboring an obsessive love for her that gushes from every cell of my body, couldn't grant her even a tiny portion of that dream.

In the summer of 1987, I sat across from my mother in the brand-new Golden Corral Restaurant in Tooele, Utah, as we both ate from our second piled-high plates filled at the all-you-can-eat salad bar.

"I was pregnant when we drove from Salt Lake City to New York," I told her. "I had an abortion in Stamford, Connecticut, a week after you left."

I blurted this out with no lead-in, no warning. Our first plate of salad had gone down easily, accompanied by conversation about nieces and nephews, the weather, and crops. Three years had passed since I'd moved to New York and we had traveled together across the country. I had driven while munching on saltines and sipping Pepsi, trying to quell a bad case of morning sickness, and she had worried about me. It was worrisome enough that I was moving away from home, but watching me pull over to throw up every couple of hours did nothing to make her feel OK about leaving me two thousand miles away from Utah—the only state I'd ever lived in.

When I decided to come clean at the Golden Corral Restaurant, I was firmly entrenched in a Wall Street career and engaged to be married to Will in three months. I had no apparent reason for this outburst. I would like to attribute it to my inability to lie to my mother, to hide anything from her, but I lied to my mother throughout a good part of my adolescence. *(Have you been drinking? No. Were you in school all day today? Yes. Have you ever been to one of those keg parties? No.)* In later years, after my first marriage ended, my reasons for lying changed, but I still lied to her. *(Are you doing all right? Yes. Are you happy? Yes, very.)*

Of course my mother knew I was lying, and I knew she knew. That's what made it all right. But this thing seemed to hang over us in a threatening way, like something we would continually bump our heads against if we moved too quickly. So I put it on the table next to the tired iceberg lettuce and the pickled beets, then we sat in silence for a moment.

"Why didn't you tell me?" she asked.

"I didn't want you to worry more than you already were."

"I would have stayed with you." Her eyes began to tear up. "I would have gone with you; it breaks my heart to think of you going through that by yourself."

Her words had the power to stop blood flow to my brain. I realized something I should have always known—her love, once given, would never be retracted. The words "I had an abortion" did not faze her. She did not spout doctrine from the church she has devoted her life to, she did not talk about right and wrong, she did not even for a moment weigh her own moral values against mine.

"I would have gone with you," she said. I didn't tell her that I wasn't alone, that he was there, because I realized she was right. I should have let her help me. I should not have deprived us of that.

# 15

BACK TOWARD THE MEADOW, A LOUD CAR RADIO PLAYS rock and roll, and I worry about the gear I've left on the bike and, in fact, the keys I've left in the ignition, so I pick up my pace. The source of the noise is not in sight when I top the hill. It comes from around the bend, from the small Mormon cemetery, which is where I planned to walk next. I feel animosity for the people who own the radio although I've never met them, never even seen them, but I loathe them for not respecting what feels like sacred space to me.

I hesitantly start around the hill to the cemetery and soon spot a Ford Explorer jacked up on the left rear side like a male dog at its favorite tree and a beat-up white pickup truck parked behind it. A blonde woman smokes behind the wheel of the Explorer and tunes the radio to another station before she notches up the volume, seemingly in an effort to avoid conversation with the long-haired man tugging at the lug nuts between draws on a cigarette and swearing loudly at regular intervals while he walks back to his pickup truck, throws his tool in the back with a clank, and rummages for another. They spot me as I try to slip by unnoticed to get to the cemetery marker in the middle of the grass.

"Here visiting the park?" the guy asks. I nod and think no, you idiot, I'm lost and looking for you. "Nice little place," he says. I nod and keep quiet again. Yes, it would be if you weren't here and she wasn't here and the air didn't stink like cigarettes and the radio wasn't gutting the silence. I snap a few pictures and walk back up the hill, hoping they will be stuck there together for many hours to come.

THE NEXT INTERPRETIVE panel sits twenty or so miles up the road in the empty parking lot of the Clarke County Historical Museum in Osceola, Iowa. The museum looks closed, but I haven't seen a restroom all day so I try the door. Three feet inside, a man sits on a folding chair reading. He wears jeans and sneakers and fluorescent pink socks. I ask if I can use the restroom and he says, "Sure," and points the way. I glance around the museum on my way. It's a huge open space jammed full of showcases displaying little pieces of small-town life and personal memories—wedding photos, swimming trophies, jackets worn by Future Farmers of America who have long since sown their last Iowa cornfield.

"Get a lot of Mormons through here following the Mormon Trail?" I ask when I return.

"We don't get a lot of anything through here," he tells me, and I wonder how long he's been sitting here without a visitor. Days? Weeks? Months?

The Clarke County Historical Museum in Osceola, Iowa, just like the Prairie Trails Museum in Corydon, Iowa, opens its door day after day without any expectation of a visitor. I'm moved by the character of those who insist upon this regardless of the number of patrons, regardless of the historical value the rest of the world places on it. I'm touched by the man who gets up each morning, puts on the fluorescent pink socks that must give him a certain kind of joy, and spends his day sitting on a folding chair alone in the Clarke County Historical Museum. There's a piece of me that wants to spend hours looking through the museum to validate their efforts, to let them know that having a museum in Osceola, Iowa, matters in life. But they don't need me to tell them that; they understood it long before I did.

FORTY-FIVE MILES northwest of Garden Grove the lead Mormon companies stopped again to build another town. A sign at the start of the gravel road leading to Mount Pisgah tells me the road is "graded," which I'm initially happy about until I realize that "graded" in this case means huge clods of dirt, grass, and rocks have been graded not off the road but into the middle of the road, where they are then scattered by passing cars. I spend the next several miles delicately picking my way through dirt clods the size of gallon milk jugs. At the next turn, a sign tells me I am embarking on a dirt road that is "not maintained." The smooth dirt road takes me through a farmer's yard and welcomes me to the site of the Mormon settlement of Mount Pisgah.

Mount Pisgah was built on a hillside overlooking the Grand River valley. Today in spite of its history of disease and death, the place is remarkably peaceful and beautiful. With the same organization and industry shown in Garden Grove, in less than a week the lead party of Mormons had cleared, plowed, planted, and fenced more than a thousand acres of land and started building cabins that would eventually house thousands of Mormons at the time spread across the state of Iowa from

Mount Pisgah back to the Mississippi River, not to mention those to come later from across the ocean.

According to Iowa historian L. Matthew Chatterley, at various times Mount Pisgah was home to as many as five thousand Mormons. Chatterley also puts the Mount Pisgah death toll at about eight hundred. During the first few months of the settlement, people were dying so fast—most from scurvy and malaria—that the Mormons simply gave up trying to keep adequate death records. It was all they could do to keep up with the burials. The makeshift headstones the Mormons sometimes left are gone now, and a monument that the Mormons erected in 1888 tells the story of the frequent deaths with notations no more detailed than "two more children" and "a stranger, not a church member."

I sit on the grass surrounding the monument and look down off the hill into the valley, trying to feel the enormous amount of loss and suffering endured at this site. But a warm wind blows and the trees bend gently around me. The sun shines through the trees, making delicate patterns on the grass, and the meadow in front of me travels farther than my eyesight. Mount Pisgah was also a place of rest and hope for many, and that sentiment now pervades this site with no hint of the misery endured here.

I linger until the sun becomes intense—I am, after all, dressed in something resembling a snowsuit—then gingerly pick my way through dirt clods back to the main road. At the McDonald's in Creston, Iowa, I stop to make a phone call, and Dave Nichols gives me directions to Nichols Farms in Bridgewater, Iowa.

HAD I NOT spent so much time being first frightened of and then angry at my father, I would have realized early on that he was born to be a rancher. His career choice of schoolteacher made no sense at all—hell, he didn't even like his own children. His knowledge of cattle and horses seemed to grow organically from within—he was good at it—and over the years he turned his run-down ranch of 51 Hereford cattle into a decent, well-respected cattle operation. He turned his attention to newer, more productive breeds, and soon had a small herd of 120 Simmental cattle.

He was one of the earliest ranchers in that area of central Utah breeding cattle through artificial insemination, purchasing bull semen through mail-order catalogs as if he were buying socks from Montgomery Ward. In our basement stood a small steel tank filled with liquid nitrogen and contributions from those listed on the tank's cover: Red Zinger, Big Sky, and Monarch.

In the planning stages of my trip, I shamelessly pursued friends and relatives of friends and relatives who might be willing to put a stranger up for the night. During this time, my father remained mum on the issue. It wasn't until several days before I left that my mother told me my father had served on the board of directors of the American Simmental Association with a rancher in Bridgewater, Iowa, which sat dead on the Mormon Trail, and he had recently purchased a bull from this rancher. That was enough for me, and I asked my mother for his phone number.

My father, however, disapproved of the idea on several levels. One, he's quite certain that people who ride motorcycles are too stupid to live and altogether an undesirable bunch. My father has little capacity to appreciate any act in which he would not participate, assuming he alone possesses common sense and everyone else is a fool. When he finds someone to agree with him about the asininity of, say, motorcycling or golfing, the diatribe can continue for hours. To have a daughter who doesn't have enough sense to stay off a motorcycle and through the very act of riding has joined the riffraff of society leaves my father bewildered. And I now insist on further embarrassing him by calling upon his friends and acquaintances—total strangers to me—in hopes they will extend their hospitality and put me up for the night.

This is another of my father's peculiarities. He believes all humans dislike overnight guests and only invite them to stay out of a strange sense of unwarranted obligation and an inability to say no. He might not be entirely wrong about this, but I'm traveling alone on a tight budget, and I'm tired and lonely enough to take unabashed advantage of anyone unwilling to tell me no.

"I hope you look like your mother, not your father," Dave tells me on the phone with a hardy laugh, and I assure him I do. "I'm so glad you're coming," he says, and I know immediately that he wouldn't say it if he didn't mean it. He gives me directions to Nichols Farms and says to "come on ahead."

Dave's directions shoot me off on another gravel road, and I warily try to pick a path to keep me out of the thick of it, but the bike pretty much wanders the road at will. I don't worry too much about this until I top a hill and see a large farm truck barreling toward me at around fifty miles per hour. I move to the side and struggle to stay upright in deep gravel as the truck speeds past and the driver waves and smiles. Another follows on the bumper of the first and waves also. I nod my head but dare not take a hand from the grip. I'll find out soon that all of these trucks belong to Dave.

The Nichols Farms office sits on what probably looks like a little hill to most people but an insurmountable hill to me. Three or four pickup trucks are parked on a steep grade, and I scan the area quickly, looking for a level place to stop while bouncing over rocks and deep ruts left by recent rains. Pure luck keeps me upright long enough to work my way to a small road that goes directly in front of the office—still on a grade, but level enough so that the side stand will hold the bike.

The first thing to register as I close the farm office door behind me is not the people whom I must immediately acknowledge, but the smell. The Nichols Farms office smells like a farm. The most identifiable scent, of course, is cow manure, but there's more to it than that. I guess some people might find it objectionable, but the rich smell of cattle and manure mixed with mud, wet boot leather, and hardworking men tugs at my emotions. My childhood memories—some nostalgically wonderful, some traumatically horrible—are steeped in the smells of that farm office, and it takes me a moment of inhaling and exhaling before gathering my wits enough to address the small group of people standing in front of me.

I introduce myself and Dave's wife, Phyllis, a thin woman wearing jeans, T-shirt, and sneakers, offers her hand and follows quickly with a generous offer of a bed, food, and even the use of her car, understanding without a word from me that I might want to get off the bike for a couple of days.

Phyllis is a hard woman to describe other than to say that she seems to be at terms with the world around her more so than most and moves through it with a certain accord. She's tough, but that toughness seems to emanate from sheer will rather than nature.

Phyllis hollers at Dave in the back office then introduces me to Lillian, Dave's sister-in-law and partner in Nichols Farms, and a few guys standing around the office, who each stick out a callused hand, shuffle their feet a little, ask a couple of questions about my trip, then launch back into a more comfortable conversation about water, mud, and cattle.

Dave rounds the corner wearing sneakers, beltless jeans fastened under a round belly, a beige button-front shirt sporting a few spots and stains, sleeves rolled away from the wrist, and a ball cap advertising something for someone. He peers at me over the top of wire-rim reading glasses and says, "Oh, good, you do look like your mother," before taking my hand. I like Dave, Phyllis, and Lillian immediately, although Dave was about to severely test my riding skills.

Several folks in Bridgewater, Iowa, have done exhaustive research on the town's history and the sections of Mormon Trail that went through it, and since the town has only two hundred people in it, Dave knows all of them. I change out of my riding gear, and we set off to see a few things and talk to a few people, but before we leave, Dave suggests putting the bike in the shed so it won't get hit. He has disappeared into the shed, so I get up a good amount of speed to get me up the grade and over the ruts without a spill and head toward the spot where I saw him disappear. As I get to the door of the shed, he runs out waving his hands, forcing me to totter to a stop.

"That's not going to work. Pull it up there on the lawn in the shade," he says pointing to a nearby house. "That's Lillian's house; it will be fine there." I know where he means; I also know I'm not capable of getting it there and back out again without help. Instead, I park in an easier-to-get-to spot on the front lawn—the only level spot in sight—with the front tire pointed in the direction I intend to travel when I leave. From here I can drop down off the lawn and go straight off the grade to the gravel road. The only problem will be stopping on the grade if one of Dave's farm trucks happens to be barreling down the road, but I'll worry about that in a day or so.

We drive two or three miles to the farmhouse and Dave helps me carry my bags upstairs to the spare bedroom. "I like to hang dead animals on the wall," Dave tells me, pointing to a deer head hanging next to an antelope head, "so people won't think I'm vegetarian—or Democrat."

Dave, a history buff, a non-Mormon, and a self-described semiagnostic, figures he's done more missionary work for the Mormon Church than most Mormons. He's probably right. Whenever anyone comes to town showing the slightest interest in history, he takes them out to see Jake Pote's cow pasture. Starting at the top of the pasture near Jake and Beverly Pote's farmhouse and running to the river along the bottom of the pasture is a clear demarcation, a place where the land has been ground down. To an untrained eye like mine, it could simply be the lay of the land, but those who farm the land know there are reasons behind such land formations. The reason behind this particular indentation is thousands of Mormon wagons leaving ruts in the soft Iowa dirt.

At one time many such fields in Iowa bore the historically significant scars, but Jake Pote's cow pasture now remains one of the few pieces of land in Iowa unplowed, unplanted, and undeveloped since the Mormons passed through on their way to Zion. At the time the Mormons came through this part of Iowa, undisturbed tall-grass Iowa prairie covered nearly 80 percent of the state. Today it comprises less than 2 percent of Iowa. The first Mormon wagons reached Adair County in the late spring and early summer, leaving much of the muddy travel and swollen-river crossings behind them. Journals describe endless prairies through this part of Iowa, days of travel without seeing a tree, but the wide-open prairies welcomed them with pink clusters of wild roses and blue tufts of phlox bobbing in the spring breezes. They were able to travel two or three times faster than they had in eastern Iowa. Women's skirts caked in mud were washed in rivers and dried under the prairie sun. Misshapen leather boots—what was left of them—

were set out to dry for the first time in months before going back on over blistered and peeling feet.

Historians from the national Mormon Trails Association and from Southern Illinois University surveyed the field and confirmed that the marks are in fact wagon ruts on the Mormon Trail. They posted a small wooden sign along the barbwire fence in front of the pasture—large enough to make note, small enough that it doesn't draw hordes of Mormon pilgrims trampling over the fence and through the field. Dave has petitioned the Mormon Church to purchase the property before Jake Pote dies and someone plows the ruts and plants corn on top of them but hasn't been able to attract anyone's attention.

"Sure as can be," Dave says, "as soon as Jake Pote dies someone will see fit to plant a little bunch of corn or soybeans right over the top of those ruts." He feels like he just hasn't gotten to the right person, but my gut feeling is that while the Mormons are all for preserving history they seldom do it in a small way. If they can't build a visitors center and combine history with a little missionary work, then it's unlikely they'll find it worth the effort. Dave is still sore over a plot of virgin Iowa wildlands near his farm that had been deeded to the Reorganized Mormon Church with the agreement it would stay wild for as long as the owner lived. Upon her death, it was planted in corn faster than she was planted in the local cemetery. "Like we need another damn cornfield," he says. Getting a flavor for Dave's politics as we drive the Bridgewater back roads (as Phyllis points out, Bridgewater only has back roads) in an attempt to visualize the old Mormon Trail, I tell him if he's not careful someone might mistake him for an environmentalist.

Over the course of the day Dave good-naturedly tries several times to goad me into political discussions, but I refrain for several reasons. Although Dave loves people to underestimate him as a good ole' Iowa farm boy, a bit of a country bumpkin, it doesn't take long to figure out he hardly fits the stereotype. Dave reads three or four newspapers a day, devours several books a week, and runs an international farming and cattle operation, which sells and ships bulls to practically every country in the world. Without a doubt he'd be a competent, maybe even ferocious, deliberator of political and social issues, and under other circumstances I might look forward to such a debate. But I'm not geared up for it on this trip. I feel vulnerable, searching for points of connection with humans along the way, feeling the need to avoid contention. But mostly I don't want to discuss politics with Dave because despite the fact that I disagree with plenty of his views, he's a damn nice guy and I like him.

At one point, Dave brings the pickup truck to a sliding stop and orders me out of the truck to stand in front of a field for a picture. Because he is like a big kid teeming with a secret, I oblige, but I've seen plenty of Iowa farmland and don't think the picture will be of any significance. As I climb back in the truck, Dave explains that I've just had my picture taken in front of the latest crop of low-grade marijuana that grows wild along Iowa back roads, which he thinks might be a good photo to send to my father.

At dinner, Dave and Phyllis feed me on Iowa beef and corn, both grown by Nichols Farms, and we sit for a while in the television/reading room—a room apparently designed by and for Dave. A recliner directly faces the television with numerous remote controls within reach. Around the chair—and in fact, around the entire room—are stacks and more stacks of books, newspapers, and magazines. What looks like chaos apparently is not; Dave speaks of this article he'd read or this book he'd just finished and produces it from the middle of a stack within minutes.

While we sit talking, I remember a guy I met in Nauvoo who said he was originally from I-o-way before moving to Missoura, so I ask Dave what part of the state a person who pronounces it "I-o-way" might come from.

"Wisconsin," he says.

Then he tells me I should go call my mother and tell her I'm here and safe and she doesn't need to worry about me. I get up to do as I'm told. Phyllis leads to me the nearest phone, chuckling, and says, "You know you don't have to do whatever Dave says."

"Oh," I respond, realizing at that moment that I am feeling about thirty years younger than my forty-five years. "I guess I kind of like the fact that he cares and seems to worry about me almost like a daughter."

"Then why don't you stay here and I'll ride off on your motorcycle," she says, still laughing quietly.

I lie in bed under the noses of the deer and antelope watching flashes of light in the dark expansive sky and listening to rain fall on the grass outside my window, feeling completely safe for the first time since I left Nauvoo.

# 16

ABOUT 7:45 A.M., DAVE AND I FINISH OUR BACON AND eggs, slip into the seats of his pickup truck, and slide down the muddy road between the house and the farm, talking about cows and religion over the top of faint voices coming from the truck's radio. With a great show of grandiosity, the sun breaks through a cloud and spreads over an Iowa cornfield. In New York City, American Airlines Flight 11, carrying ninety-two people, hits the north tower of the World Trade Center and flies apart, setting everything on fire. I remark on the serenity of the Iowa morning. Dave responds that in all the mornings through all the years he's watched the sun roll over his farmland, the wonder is never diminished. I roll down the truck window and stick my head out, draw the untouched morning through my nostrils into my lungs, and let the rest bounce off my face. Dave reaches out to turn up the sound on the radio. As the reporter's voice enters the truck cab, we look at each other but don't speak, unable to fully comprehend the words we're hearing.

Around 7:55, we arrive in the farm office, where Phyllis, Lillian, and others are gathered in the conference room around the television. A few minutes later we watch United Airlines Flight 175, carrying sixty-five people, shatter the south tower of the World Trade Center and explode. We stand in silence for a few seconds, unsure of what we've seen, as the ruptured towers billow flames and black smoke, before the gasping and questioning and conjecturing begin. We have not moved beyond this when American Airlines Flight 77, carrying sixty-four people, crashes into the Pentagon, shredding everything in its path—concrete, steel, paper, and flesh. We are still standing when the south tower of the World Trade Center collapses, killing most everyone left inside. And we still stand as United Airlines Flight 93, carrying forty-five people, slams down in Somerset County, Pennsylvania, flinging debris and bodies for miles. And we still stand as the north tower of the World Trade Center collapses, killing still more people. Once we begin to comprehend the magnitude of what has happened, no one knows the right thing to do, no one knows what is expected of us. Should we call people? Should we continue to stand by the television? Should we feed the lowing cattle unmoved by the morning's events? Should we haul the loads from the fields? Should we do the work that seemed imperative yesterday and trivial today?

Dave has arranged for me to talk to Beverly Pote about the wagon ruts in her field. He has planned to show me additional wagon ruts in another pasture in the next town over. I had hoped to find a forgotten Mormon cemetery rumored to be in the "corner of Lockery's cow pasture" and talk to Beth Christensen, the local historian. But now I stand in the Nichols Farms conference room, unable to formulate any sort of plan that makes sense. At once it seems ungracious not to speak to those who have arranged their time for me and insensitive to intrude upon them today. My important project, my search for understanding through the acts of my ancestors, suddenly feels not only trivial but self-indulgent.

Incapable of making a decision, I wait, and the town of Bridgewater, Iowa, shows me the way. In Bridgewater, nothing else makes sense but to confront the atrocious with the ordinary. Not that the folks of Bridgewater are unaware of the enormity and gravity of the events; they, like everyone else in the nation, are devastated. But the work of farmers is not determined by the farmers themselves—it is set by the time of day, the season, the temperature, the darkness of the sky, the needs of the cattle, and a bunch of other factors that pay no heed to human crises.

The skies cloud up again as Gary Antisdel, who has offered to be my tour guide this morning, pulls up in front of the farm office in his pickup. Dave introduces us, and we acknowledge the disturbing events of the morning because we are obliged to do so, feeling guilty for speaking or thinking of anything else. We quietly walk to his truck and start out. Gary wears a flannel jacket, jeans, and a ball cap. He was born in Bridgewater and has spent all of his sixty or so years here, and speaks of it, as we slip around on the muddy roads, in a soft, country-modulated voice laced with tender passion for the land. I'm not sure if it's the morning's events, the drizzle that soaks us as we wander through tall grass, or the gentle nature of Gary himself, but I find myself talking easily to him about faith and God and indirectly about millions of people who collectively and individually find themselves stunned to their cores today.

My first response to the terrorist attacks in relation to faith is that they offer proof of the nonexistence of God. How could a just God let such a thing happen? But that's an emotional, knee-jerk reaction. I'm not willing to believe in a God who orchestrates every human deed—good or evil. I'm not ready to blame God for every vile act, just as I'm not ready to give God credit for every kind deed, every charitable undertaking. I'm not willing to believe in a God who jerks us around like marionettes in a Punch-and-Judy show, handing us a crisis to deal with one day and a gift the next—the great micromanager in the sky. If human beings are not responsible for human actions, if God is to blame for our aggregate sins or to be given credit for our aggregate goodness, then the things that distinguish us as human, that determine the worth of our character—will, honor, integrity, courage, fortitude—are nothing more than a hoax. The design can't possibly be that simple.

My sister tells me she's been "saved" and I think how nice for her, how comfortable and safe that must feel to believe your bases are covered. Life must become very sweet at that point. When I started this trip, I might have been looking for my own version of being saved, something to calm my days and soothe my confused and questioning mind. But that simple aspiration has been obliterated, and I'm questioning my motives, which now feel small and self-serving.

Chittister writes, "Private piety is what we so often seek in order to justify our lack of raw, clear . . . commitment, the kind of commitment that puts a person on a cross."

And very often private piety is exactly what religion offers, a series of symbolic gestures to be performed—attending church, taking the sacrament, confessing, performing temple rituals—all intended to make us feel righteous, ready, and safe or "saved." My sister scoffs at such rituals as those performed in the Mormon temples, implying that performing "tasks" to get ourselves to heaven is not only unnecessary but profane. She tells me the only requirement to get to heaven is accepting Jesus Christ because "he died for our sins," as if his torture and murder were all part of God's great plan. What kind of demented plan is that? I suspect that then, as now, humans were to blame for their own atrocious acts.

But if God does not have the power to save us from ourselves, praying seems useless—at least the kind of praying I've heard people do. Why ask God to keep us safe on a trip, for example? My gut feeling is that most praying we perform is not really a conversation with God so much as it is a conversation with our larger selves, with our spiritual selves—the part of ourselves we don't tap in to on a regular basis, the part of ourselves that is enlarged by our beliefs, by our faith, by our questioning, by our searching. What we are tapping in to through prayer is obviously not a direct line with a supreme being who will keep a car from crossing the yellow line and smashing into a motorcycle. What we are tapping in to is the mystery of life, the mystery we hold in ourselves.

Gary believes the lack of faith and religion today has left people fluttering, untethered to anything larger than themselves, and I'm in no position to argue. For this very reason I now find myself behind the dashboard of his pickup truck, talking about family and kids and disappearing farms and corporate cornfields with a stranger who immediately feels like a friend.

We stop at the intersection of one muddy road with another—they all look the same to me but I know each one is distinct to Gary—climb a small incline, and crawl through the second and third wires of a barbwire fence. Gary wanders for a moment with his eyes to the ground before finding what he's looking for, a small scattering of ten or so crumbling headstones detached from the ground. I remark that they seem to be scattered arbitrarily and hit a sore spot with him. The owner of the cow pasture dug out and gathered up the headstones, stacking them in his machine shed with the apparent intent of plowing up the pasture. But the townsfolk of Bridgewater preserve history with an intensity that is at once disconcerting and unusually moving, especially when it is your history—not theirs—they are protecting. Apparently Mr. Lockery was persuaded to put the stones back where they belonged and leave the dead in peace. Without knowing for sure where they belong, they are now scattered in the general vicinity among a few cow pies.

"How would he like it if someone plowed over the top of his dead relatives?" Gary says. On another day, I might have been more cynical about his near fanatical sense of duty to the undisturbed rest of the dead. But today the preservation of that little cemetery, holding the disintegrated tiny bones of a three-year-old Mormon girl and her mother buried more than 150 years ago, means more to me than Gary could fathom. I feel as if the townspeople of Bridgewater, Iowa, have reached in and gently stroked the rawness of my soul. The rain camouflages my tears, and I suppress an urge to hug Gary there in the corner of that cow pasture, not wanting to embarrass a tough old cowboy, but there's a softness to him that makes me think I could have gotten away with it.

We stop at the Potes' farmhouse, tiptoe our way through the mud, and go in through the backdoor. Jake Pote, a small man of few words, welcomes us into the kitchen. At the table, Beverly Pote has laid out a stack of papers about the Mormon Trail and in a clear, loud voice that fits her sturdy stature apologizes for receiving company when "the house is such a mess." The only dirt in sight is what I've brought in on the bottom of my shoes—Gary slipped his boots off at the door.

We soberly acknowledge the morning's news, knowing we must. She talks of her grandmother, who used to tell stories about the Mormon women trading recipes with the Iowa settlers as they passed through, and behind her Peter Jennings talks of the morning's death toll somewhere in the thousands. Gary tells the Potes we've just been to the little cemetery in the Lockery cow pasture and Beverly says, "Oh? It's still there, huh?" They talk about the near loss of it and the gall of someone who couldn't recognize the duty to preserve it.

"He finally done the right thing and put them back," Gary says, referring to the headstones. "But he's still got cows walking all over them. How would they like it if we turned cows loose in all these cemeteries around here? That's just not right."

The four of us sit uneasily, all of us wondering if it is somehow wrong to go on with our conversation about the Mormon Trail. We stop in the middle of a discussion about a Mormon gentleman from Salt Lake City who found his ancestors in the corner of Lockery's cow pasture—the first confirmation that those buried in the cemetery were Mormon—and turn our attention to Peter Jennings. We again acknowledge the events with small statements of disbelief and shock that don't come anywhere close to measuring the atrocity. It's all we know to do. With small glances and bodies half-twisted between the television and the kitchen table, we give one another permission to turn back to the materials spread out before us, and with quiet voices we tentatively bring the conversation back to rumors of a Mormon baby buried under a stand of trees a couple miles west of the old Johnson place or at the bend in the river that goes through another farm.

The sense of relief to be talking about anything other than the obvious quickly spreads around the room, and the conversation leaps from wagon rut visitors to Beverly's Great-aunt Caroline, who once served dinner to Jesse James, to Beverly's quirky hobby that has produced a recipe file box holding names, dates, and circumstances of every death in Bridgewater for the last fifty or so years, drowning out Peter Jennings and giving us all a moment to breathe. Gary and Beverly spend a few minutes talking antiques—Beverly has several cabinets full, and she can tell you not only the year and the worth but the story behind each piece, who owned it, where they kept it in their house, and what they used it for.

When we leave the Potes', Gary drops me at the Bridgewater Oil Company—two gas pumps and a garage—to pick up Phyllis's car, which was in need of a tire repair. My intention is to pack the bike and leave this afternoon, but when I get back to the farm office Dave insists I stay another day, and I have no desire to argue. I've never felt more incapable of getting on that bike and riding than I do today.

There are a couple of sites in the next county I want to see, and Dave offers to take me. We bounce over the gravel roads at Dave's usual speed—about sixty miles per hour—as if we are on a paved highway. We soon arrive at the Nishnabotna Ferry House in Lewis, Iowa, which once stood on the Nishnabotna River at the location the Mormons crossed the river. We next stop at the Hitchcock House, part of the underground railroad, a historical site unrelated to the Mormon Trail but located nearby.

Dave and I enter and a woman, thrilled to have two devoted listeners, takes us through the house, painstakingly explaining a myriad of old kitchen utensils. I get the feeling she has been in the Hitchcock House all day without television or radio, un-aware of what's happened this morning; she is utterly cheerful from the moment we walk in the door. I find solace in not hav-ing to exchange proclamations of shock and horror, and al-though I had heard more explanations of old kitchen utensils in Nauvoo than I ever want to hear again, I'm content to trail her around the house until she shows us what we really came to see—the basement, where slaves were given temporary refuge on their way north. I'm not paying much attention when she picks up a utensil and makes us guess its use. When neither of us can—neither trying very hard—she seems thrilled to have stumped us and, with glee, informs us it is a sauerkraut masher. I appropriately offer a set of raised eyebrows and a slight "Ah," and Dave nods and grunts.

"Sauerkraut masher!" Dave says with a guffaw when we get back in the truck. "That wasn't a sauerkraut masher! Who mashes sauerkraut? Cabbage is sliced or chopped to make sauerkraut. That was a potato masher!" I just laugh and look out the window. I'm sure Dave is right.

Dave knows of another set of Mormon Trail wagon ruts in another pasture in Cass County but is unsure of the exact location. He makes a call on his cell phone, and the owner of the land agrees to meet us and take us there. Kenny Cousins shows up looking like a pinup poster for Iowa corn-grown farm boys with tousled blond hair, a square jaw outlining a tan, slightly weathered face, sparkling blue eyes, and the body of a man who spends few hours in front of a television set. Dave had taken to introducing me as Jana Richman, daughter of Reese Richman, and a famous writer or university professor or whatever fits the moment. I explain to Kenny that all details beyond my name and my father's name are fiction, and he nods and flashes a perfect smile as we pile into Dave's pickup and drive out to his pasture.

I stand in the deepness of the ruts wishing for a moment alone, wishing actually to sit down in the very spot my ancestors had tread and seek some clarity of the incomprehensible day now coming to an end. Instead, we snap a few pictures and bounce over the roads, conjecturing the path of my ancestors, pointing at landmarks, bluffs, and ridges that only Dave and Kenny can see.

• • •

I PULL MYSELF out of bed at 6:30 A.M. on September 12 after wandering the room all night, unable to sleep. Dave and Phyllis are already up, breakfast already on the table. We're all quiet this morning, physically exhausted simply by going on with life in the midst of madness. Dave has arranged for me to speak to Beth Christensen, the local expert on the Bridgewater section of the Mormon Trail, and I feel obliged to do so, although speaking at all seems a rather large undertaking this morning.

Beth, a short, stout woman, answers the door and leads me into her kitchen through the living room, where her wiry husband sits in farmer overalls speaking loudly on the phone to be heard over the even louder television—continued reporting of dead, missing, destroyed, burned, and it makes me think of a World War II Ernie Pyle quote I'd once read and could never get out of my mind, something found on a piece of paper in his pocket when his body was recovered after being shot by a sniper on Ie Shima in 1945: "Those who are gone would not wish themselves to be a millstone of gloom around our necks. But there are many of the living who have had burned into their brains forever the unnatural sight of cold dead men . . . Dead men by mass production . . . Dead men in such familiar promiscuity that they become monotonous. Dead men in such monstrous infinity that you come almost to hate them."

I feel a little light-headed and sick to my stomach and quickly sit down on the chair Beth offers me.

"Get off the phone or shut off the television," Beth tells her husband, nudging him on the arm. She brings out an even larger stack of Mormon Trail information than Beverly Pote presented. I begin to finger through it while I tell her what I'm

working on, speaking loudly to be heard over the phone conversation and the television reporting.

"Wilbur! Get off the phone or shut off the television," she
says again, more insistently this time. Wilbur shuts off the television, then hangs up the phone. He sticks a hand out to me
and I take it.

"Hi, I'm the boyfriend. You look a little skinny. Maybe you
should stick around and have some taters."

I laugh and decline his offer but feel immediately better—as
if life just came back into focus. He saunters out the door. A
moment later he returns and presents me with a small tomato
from his garden, apologizing for its puny stature. I take it and
thank him for the simple gesture that seems monumental in its
goodness.

Beth spends two hours of her time telling me what she
knows about the trail through Adair County, Iowa, and the efforts to map and preserve what little is left of it. As I rise to
leave she takes my hand in both of hers and says, "Thank you
for stopping; I'm so glad you did." I drive down the road a ways
in Phyllis's car and pull over, Beth's words echoing in my
head—"Thank you for stopping; I'm so glad you did"—and I
begin to cry. Beth, Dave, Phyllis, Gary, Kenny, the Potes—all
acting as if I had done them a favor by interrupting their days,
intruding on their time, tracking mud through their homes, eating their food, borrowing their cars. I am struck dumb by their
kindness toward me, a complete stranger. I cry as hard as I've
ever cried before on that country road in Bridgewater, Iowa,
feeling entirely free to do so.

# 17

LEAVING BRIDGEWATER FEELS MUCH LIKE LEAVING Nauvoo, as if I'm foolishly riding away from a narrow margin of safety. Dave, Phyllis, and Lillian follow me out of the farm office to the motorcycle to say good-bye. We snap a few pictures, give a few hugs, and they perceptively leave me alone to pack the bike, which takes longer than is comfortable to have people standing around waiting for the moment of departure. My stomach churns as I tighten straps and check tire pressure. I'm uneasy about everything—getting myself down off this grade, stopping at the bottom if necessary, not stopping and getting flattened by one of Dave's farm trucks, finding my way through Council Bluffs and Omaha on a crowded freeway, the loss of reason in the world.

Once the bike is packed, face shield cleaned, and decisions made—jacket liner or not, winter gloves or summer gloves—I try five or six times in vain to get the bike off the double stand. The idea of walking back into the farm office for help after good-byes have been said, expressions of gratitude made, doesn't sit well with me. I get off the bike to take a look and realize that it has sunk into the rain-drenched lawn and the tires now rest on the grass. I'm lucky the bike isn't lying on its side. I climb back on, start the bike, and gently drive it off the double stand. I baby it down off the steep grade as much as possible, but the combination of mud and gravel doesn't allow much braking. Stopping at the bottom on two wheels will be near impossible. I glance up the road, quickly hoping for a clear path, and fortunately have it. As I pull out on the road and head for the highway, a farm truck coming toward me pulls over to let me pass. Too late to stop, I realize it's Gary; he rolls down the window and hollers something as I go by. I have no idea what he says, but the act itself calms my stomach.

I don't get away until afternoon, and the sun leads me through the last few towns of Iowa, through the last few cornfields. Shades of green turn to shades of brown as the West approaches. According to my map, I will be forced onto a freeway three times during this trip: once near Omaha, again in Wyoming, and last through Salt Lake City. The Salt Lake City freeways are as familiar to me as Utah back roads and the Wyoming freeways will be devoid of urban traffic, so the most dreaded freeway lies ten minutes to the west. Although I antic-ipate it, I am embroiled in traffic and road construction at Council Bluffs, Iowa, so suddenly it rattles me.

I hope to find my way to Winter Quarters, the Mormon site in Nebraska where Brigham Young and all who could reach it before the snow fell spent the winter during the first year of travel. But once on the freeway, I need every bit of focus I can muster just to keep myself alive on a road that squeezes from four lanes to two and back again in a matter of seconds due to road construction. Although the signs read forty-five miles per hour through the two-lane, winding construction zone, which suits me fine, the traffic darts at about seventy-five miles per hour. I move through the last construction zone on frazzled nerves, sandwiched between a temporary cement abutment and the tire of a semitruck bouncing halfway into my lane as it speeds through.

I quickly give up on finding Winter Quarters and head for the safety of a friend in Lincoln. I'll have to go back; Winter Quarters is one of the most consequential Mormon sites on the trail. But right now I'm out of the swirling mess of freeways and construction on a four-lane divided highway with minimal truck traffic and breathing more steadily. I've ridden in horrible freeway traffic before, but everything feels different now. I feel as if people are cavalierly playing with my life in a mean-spirited way. The truck driver who squeezed me against the cement wall knew I was there—he'd come from behind me—but my life was expendable to him, secondary to his schedule. The mother with her kids in the minivan who tailgated me in exasperation because I wasn't moving fast enough through the construction zone seemingly would have preferred me dead to slowing her life down in the smallest way. The newscasters were talking about the coming together and compassion of Americans, but I see none of that on this road.

I have known Pat less than six months. We were thrown together in a college dorm as roommates at a conference, and I knew immediately we would be friends. She makes dinner for me, and I sleep soundly under her care for the first time in many nights. The next morning I rent a car for the day and drive to Omaha, unwilling to give the mother in the minivan another shot at me on the bike. The sky clouds over as I drive, and when I step from the car in the parking lot of the Winter Quarters visitors center, the breeze is cooler than I anticipate. I reach for my sweater but I've forgotten it, and I'm more upset by this than I need to be.

The Winter Quarters visitors center is done in grand Mormon style—life-size oxen, authentic replicas of handcarts for visitors to pull, great stories of struggle and survival told in Hollywood style—and I hate it immediately. Inside, two smiling missionaries greet me. Very often the missionaries in visitors centers are retired folks, leaving the young and strong to knock on doors and sleep in shacks in third world countries. But in this case, the two older missionaries step aside for a young woman who looks to be about fourteen but is obviously eighteen or nineteen, directly out of high school and on a mission for her church. She is assigned to take me on the "tour." She smiles from beginning to end. They don't like to ask, "Are you a member of the Church?" because they don't want people to get defensive right off the bat, but she is smart enough to try to determine my level of knowledge so she won't over- or under-explain things. I appreciate her effort but do nothing to aid her. And she smiles. She smiles through stories of persecution; she smiles through stories of starvation, malaria, and scurvy; she smiles through abysmal stories of the freezing and suffering of the handcart pioneers. She smiles as if six thousand Mormons had not been buried along the trail. She smiles as if some still undetermined thousands of people had not been murdered two days ago. She is sweet and earnest, and I want to slap her.


BY JUNE OF 1846, Brigham Young had devout followers strung out across Iowa—some in the settlements of Garden Grove or Mount Pisgah, others still battling heat and rattlesnakes as they crawled across prairies, still more converts arriving from Great Britain—all in varying degrees of ill health, a good many near death from malnutrition or disease, and others bogged down by poverty and lack of provisions. It had taken four months for the lead party to slog through the Iowa mud from the Mississippi River to the Missouri River, far longer than Brother Brigham had anticipated, and he began to realize that his envisioned well-ordered, steady march from Nauvoo to the Rocky Mountains was unlikely. He needed to find a place to hold out for the winter, and, although he knew the Saints were capable of building an entire town in a few weeks, he needed to find it quickly if they were to get crops in the ground and a harvest before the snow fell.

After some diplomatic dealings with the leaders of the Pottawattamie Indians, who had temporary land rights along the east side of the Missouri River in Iowa and who found empathy with the Mormons, having been driven from their homes also, the Mormons set up camp to wait out the winter in what is now known as Council Bluffs, Iowa, and was then called Kanesville, after Thomas Kane, a friend of the Mormons. Later, Brigham would insist on setting up another camp on Indian lands on the west side of the river—known as Winter Quarters—in a controversial deal made between Brigham and Captain James Allen, sent by the federal government to enlist Mormon men in the United States' fight against Mexico. The Mormons spread themselves in camps up and down both sides of the Missouri, but most gathered either in Kanesville, which at one time had as many as seven thousand people living there, or in Winter Quarters, populated with as many as four thousand people, some living in houses, some in huts, and some on the soon-to-be-frozen ground in tents.

Thomas Kane, Philadelphia aristocrat, son of the attorney general of Pennsylvania and brother of Arctic explorer Elisha Kane, befriended the Mormons after hearing of their unjust treatment at the hands of what he referred to as "border scum" and the refusal of the U.S. government to come to their aid. A non-Mormon who lived among them, shared their illnesses, and nearly died among them, he worked some diplomacy on their behalf with the federal government through his father's connections with President James Polk. It is hard to say now how much his influence helped the Mormons, but Mormon history has deified him, as it is wont to do.

Kane's major contribution, however, is his detailed observance of and poetic writing about the Saints' situation. Although he was in no way an impartial observer—his love for the Mormons was apparent—it is impossible to exaggerate the dire conditions along the Missouri River in 1846. Kane reported plague-level illnesses through the Saints camps on both sides of the river, more needing burying than there were people to do the digging, mass burials in trenches, and women sitting in doorways shooing flies from the faces of their dead, decaying children. As the earliest of the Saints dropped into camps in June and July, many were already down with malaria and dysentery, and malnutrition and exposure across the wet and muddy trails of Iowa had left them susceptible to death from almost anything, including a common cold. As malaria waned with the end of summer, scurvy and pneumonia set in with winter.

By the time Brigham rallied his apostles and started out from the Missouri River for the Rocky Mountains in the spring of 1847, six hundred or so people had been buried on the hill in Winter Quarters and many more scarcely accounted for buried in makeshift graves up one side of the Missouri and down the other.

HERE, TOO, TEN years after Brother Brigham first set up camp at Winter Quarters, begins the agonizing tale of great-great-grandmother Hannah's travel to the Salt Lake Valley, for it was here that in August of 1856 they discussed wintering before making the fateful decision to continue on to join the gathering of Zion in the Great Basin, believing in their hearts it was the Lord's plan. Franklin Richards, in charge of the Liverpool Mission and instrumental in bringing the handcart pioneers this far, wrote: ". . . we confidently look for the blessing of God to crown our humble efforts with success, and for the safe arrival of our brethren the poor Saints in Utah, though they may experience some cold." To this Stegner adds about Richards, "If he had been God's worst Enemy, instead of the essentially good man that he was, God could not have denied his expectations more harshly."

At the age of thirty-three, Hannah had been a member of the Mormon Church for nearly a decade, and she ached to join the gathering of Zion, but the means to do so were scarce for a widowed mother of three. When she saw a notice in the *Millennial Star* that she could go for $45 under the new "handcart program," a scheme thought up by Brigham Young to gather converts more cheaply after the Church found itself short on cash following a crop devastation by a grasshopper infestation, Hannah gathered her skirts and her three children and went to the docks of Liverpool to catch the *Horizon* along with 852 others, setting sail on May 25, 1856, and arriving in Boston Harbor six weeks later. From there they were herded onto cattle cars and dumped at the end of the Rock Island Railroad in Iowa City. Hannah kept the two little girls, Margaret, who had just turned five, and Hannah, three, tucked in close to her skirts, and relied on her stepson, fourteen-year-old James, to help her with the small amount of luggage and supplies they brought. Bewildered maybe, but she was filled to the brim with faith not only in God but in the capabilities of the men running this operation, led by the prophet of God himself, Brother Brigham.

The expectation, the plan that Brigham laid out, was that the Saints would be delivered in waves to Iowa City and pick up their waiting handcarts. The handcarts were basically a wood box on a set of wheels with two handles about three feet long and a yoke joining the handles so one or two people could step inside and push against the yoke, basically pulling the handcart as a set of oxen would. The cart was built to exact specification so the wheelbase would match that of a wagon and fit easily into the well-worn wagon ruts that ten years of travel over the Mormon Trail had left behind. After picking up their waiting handcarts, the Saints would step out merrily into the Iowa sun, becoming stronger and faster as they pulled, before the next wave arrived. Because the Mormons had in the past decade managed to move mass quantities of people as if they were widgets on an assembly line, they had no reason to expect this would be any different. But in this case, at every station along the line, a cog was knocked loose in the machinery and the assembly line was momentarily halted.

To begin with, high winds prevented the ships from leaving Liverpool as early as they should have. The first set sail on March 23, the second on April 19, the third on May 4, and the last, carrying Hannah and her children, on May 25. The line came to a halt again when they arrived in Iowa City to pick up their handcarts and found instead a shortage of seasoned lumber and qualified labor to build them, resulting in one shipload of immigrants being dumped on top of another and leaving them to scare up lumber and labor enough to help build their own handcarts. This set them back a good four weeks and, in their zest to be on their way, caused some lapses in judgment, such as building handcarts from green wood that would dry and split as soon as it was rolled in the golden Iowa sunshine.

The line was further slowed by the fact that a good many of the handcart pioneers were people like Hannah—widows with small children. Men were scarce; children under fifteen plentiful. The trail struggles of the Nauvoo pioneers—a fairly rugged group of Saints used to pitching tents, plowing fields, building bridges and homes, then pulling up stakes and moving on—would look like playtime to this ragtag gathering, most of whom lacked even the basic skill of building a campfire.

What they shared with their Nauvoo brothers and sisters, however, was that unique Mormon defiance of the impossible, that inner galvanization that tore them away from families and homes and sent them across stormy seas, over snowy mountains, and through icy rivers. For a people used to relying on heavy doses of divine intervention, none of the obstacles were enough to squelch the burning in their hearts, the fervor of being Zion-bound. That Mormon willfulness in the beginning would be their undoing; in the end, that alone would save them.

# 18

ACROSS THE STREET FROM THE VISITORS CENTER, I wander through the cemetery that holds the remains of those who wouldn't make it to the Land of Zion, shivering in my T-shirt and sandals under dark skies and a stiff breeze. A marker remembers the Mormons, although their graves are now gone and the sight taken over by the more recent dead. Dead on top of dead. I walk in the cold and I weep—again. A new Mormon temple sits next to the cemetery, looking warm and safe. I want to go in, but I'm not allowed. I want to tell them how much it means to me at that moment to have them nearby, to know I can present myself and be taken in. I will only be taken in so far, but it's enough.

Down the block and several worlds away from the Winter Quarters visitors center I sit in a torn vinyl booth just inside the door of Harold's Koffee House sucking in secondhand cigarette smoke. Harold's sits on the main drag of what is referred to as Historic Florence, Nebraska, really the northeast part of Omaha. Spelling Koffee with a "K" must have been clever at one point in American history and for some stupid reason it now brings me a little comfort. The smell of cigarette smoke has not quite smothered the smell of fried food, and that also brings me a little comfort. I order one of the few things appropriate for such a place—cheeseburger, French fries, and a Coke—and I rub my arms trying to warm up while I wait for my food. I wish for the feel of intense sunlight on my arms, and I remember the glorious sight of gold spreading over Iowa cornfields Tuesday morning.

The conviction of the Mormons buried across the street, my ancestors who lived through a winter here on gruel, is ever more staggering and confounding to me today. The radio on the trip up from Lincoln said millions of Americans were now turning to God and to prayer. Is that faith or despair?

I'm on the edge of despair myself, fighting like hell not to give myself over to it entirely. I'm just plain scared. Simply afraid I'm not going to make it back to Arizona alive. Nebraska feels like nowhere to me. People seem cold and mean ' here. They seem petty talking about their bad knees and their bad relatives and their bad spouses, all the while smoking their bad cigarettes. But they aren't bad. They laugh and joke and call one another by name—Joe and Betty and Sharon and Bud. No one calls me by name. I want to get back on the bike and ride straight for Utah. No more stops. No more visitors centers. No more cemeteries. No more death. I lack the resolve of my ancestors.

The waitress brings my cheeseburger and fries and puts a large Coke in one of those skinny-at-the-bottom, fat-at-the-top Coke glasses down in front of the plate. She smiles and says, "Do you need anything else?" I wait for her to finish that sentence with "hon"—"Do you need anything else, hon?"—but she doesn't. She's too young; she's the wrong kind of waitress for Harold's Koffee House. I smile back at her and shake my head and the tears start to fall again. She notices but turns away, either out of politeness or embarrassment. Why am I crying again? Because the people of Historic Florence won't call me by name and tell me about their recent bout with kidney stones? Because several thousand people died this week and I can't hug my husband or my mother? Because I'm walking on the graves of six hundred dead Mormons who had something in their lives worth dying for—a notion I can barely grasp?

I eat my all-American meal through tears and the folks of Florence are kind enough to ignore me. Seeing people crying over a cheeseburger might not be a strange sight this week. Harold's sign advertises "fine foods," and sure enough this is a fine cheeseburger.

In the Florence Library, a woman signs me in and kindly points me to a vacant computer. I need to connect with *my* world. I scroll through job-related e-mails without opening them until I get to a familiar sender—a friend from Tucson. The date of the e-mail is September 12. The e-mail is three words long: "Are you alright?" I collapse into the chair, hit the reply button, and stare at the screen through what has become a steady flow of tears, not knowing what to type. I take a few inhaling sobs and finally type "Yes," sit for a bit longer, type "Thank you," and hit the send button. Young girls practicing cheers in the library corridor bounce to either side to let me pass through the middle on my way out the door.

In my rental car, I blast the heater and sit in the parking lot. Stories of thousands dead along the Mormon Trail spin in my head with stories of thousands dead in New York City, and I'm no longer clear about the precise reason my tears continue to fall. A little more than twenty-four hours after the World Trade Center crumbled to form a mass crematorium, I watched a truck driver put his semitruck within three feet of the bumper of a small car driven by an elderly man who was frightened and desperate to move into the steady stream of traffic whizzing by him on the right. The well-being of our fellow human beings means so little to us.

I find my way back across the Missouri River and into Iowa once again to visit the Kanesville Tabernacle, and leave the warmth of the car for a cold drizzle. As usual, two cheerful Mormon missionaries—a retired married couple—greet me inside a small, surprisingly modest visitors center. I am their only visitor, and I'm glad they have each other to spend the day with. They welcome me warmly as usual and act as if they are genuinely glad to see me. They ask where I'm from and I tell them, then they ask if I'm traveling alone and I tell them yes.

"Oh, my," the woman responds. "Well . . . are you Mormon?"

"No," I tell her, "but I come from a Mormon family."

"Did you have any relatives in the Mormon Battalion?" the man asks.

"Yes," I say. "My great-great-grandfather Orin Hatch."

"Oh, yes," the woman says. "Orin Hatch was one of the youngest to go, he was only sixteen. He went with his brother."

"Yes, Meltiar," I say.

She takes me to a wall with a list of five hundred or so names—every person in the Mormon Battalion. "Would you like to have a picture with you in front of your relative's name?" she asks, and I think that sounds like a fine idea. I strike a tourist pose and point to Orin's name on the wall. She snaps the picture.

"Would you like to see the film about the Mormon Battalion?" she asks, and I nod.

"Oh, yes! You have to see the film; it's a wonderful film!" she says, as if she's been hurt too many times by too many tourists scurrying through, never taking time to view the film. I do want to see the film, but I would sit through it just to please her regardless. In the empty room, I pick a front-row seat from about twenty chairs. She leaves me, closing the door quietly.

WHEN, ALMOST PRECISELY two years from the day of Joseph Smith's murder, President Polk sent amiable young Captain Allen to recruit five hundred Mormon men to fight for the United States in a war against Mexico, the general reaction among Mormons was one of incredulity. A government that had, in effect, invited their exodus from the United States by refusing to protect them from murder, torture, and loss of property was now asking for their help. It was almost comical. Needless to say, few initially volunteered for that reason alone. In addition, stirring up five hundred men healthy enough to march to California among the pitiful camps of diseased Saints wouldn't be easy. Many of the healthy young men were already spread out, hiding their Mormonism and seeking work among Gentiles to provision themselves for the trip west. Those left in camps were needed to care for the ill and bury the dead.

But for good reason Brigham Young emerged as a clear leader of the Church after Joseph's death, and he didn't for a moment see the request as either comical or impossible. He saw it for what it was, an ironic twist of fate—maybe even divine intervention—that had the capacity to feed the hungry, supply the impoverished, turn the gaunt and graying racks of flesh-draped bones back into the resolute Saints who had built the city of Nauvoo, and get them moving toward the Rocky Mountains the following spring. Not only would the government outfit and feed five hundred Saints on their way west, but they would be paid in cash, which would be sent back to Brigham and his counselors and used like a direct deposit from

God to get ten times as many Saints through the winter. In addition, as part of the deal, Brigham got Captain Allen to agree to let him set up a camp on the west side of the Missouri, which would stand for two years while the federal government argued about Captain Allen's authority to grant such a wish. However, even among men willing to follow Brigham through sleet, ice, mud, rain, and surging rivers to an unknown destination on nothing but a promise, sacrificing wives and children along the way, persuading the Saints of their patriotic duty toward a country that had in essence left them wounded and bleeding would not be easy. According to some Church accounts, it took Brigham three days to recruit just over five hundred men for the job, but the reality is that it took him closer to three weeks of roaring like the lion of God he was known as, and still men did not shuffle forward until he threatened to draft old men and women if the young men didn't step up to the task.

One of those five hundred was my great-great-grandfather Orin Hatch. Orin had traveled from Nauvoo in Brigham Young's company with his father, his stepmother, five brothers, and one sister, after burying their mother in Nauvoo. According to the family records, Meltiar had served as a third lieutenant in the Nauvoo Legion under Joseph Smith, so at the age of twenty-one he was immediately recruited. Meltiar had made a promise at his mother's deathbed to keep Orin in his care, so Orin enlisted also, although at sixteen he was younger than most.

The battalion marched from camp on the Missouri River to Fort Leavenworth, Kansas, before marching on to Santa Fe and then California. Orin came down with scurvy in Fort Leavenworth. His condition became so serious that he was unable to walk, and Meltiar was ordered by his commanding officer to leave him by the side of the road to die. Meltiar left his canteen with Orin and marched on until they stopped for camp at night. From there, Meltiar and a friend went back for Orin and carried him into camp. They did this for several nights. To this point, the family stories agree. After this point, however, the commanding officer either turns into an angel or a monster, depending on which version of the family story you believe. The compassionate officer loans Meltiar a horse to collect his brother each night. The monstrous officer insists once again that Orin be left to die and Meltiar, remembering the deathbed promise to his mother, saves him with the help of some friendly Indians, the probability of those Indians being sent by God, of course, duly noted in the family history. Regardless, Orin and Meltiar make it to California, work for a while in Sutter's Mill during the gold rush after their discharge from the U.S. Army, and save enough money to return to the Missouri River and collect the family waiting for them there. On their way back to Winter Quarters, they pass through the Mormon settlement then in Salt Lake City and stake a claim on some land in what is now Bountiful, Utah. The entire family travels west and arrives in Utah in October of 1849, three years and eight months after being forced from Nauvoo.

THE FILM LASTS about twenty minutes and portrays a stalwart Mormon wife who searches the horizon each day waiting for her soldier to return. He never does. I cry much of the way through it. When the credits start to roll the woman missionary opens the door, flips on the light switch, sits in a chair next to mine, and begins to cry herself, as if we've just watched the movie together.

"Oh!" she says. "When I think of how those men and boys did what they did . . . well, it just makes me proud to be a descendant of one of those men." I nod. She dries her tears and simultaneously says, "Now! Would you like to see the tabernacle?" in such a cheerful tone it jars me out of my seat. I nod again.

The husband takes over once we reach the well-lit lobby and leads me to the tabernacle, a replica of the original, a large rectangular log structure that looks more like a mess hall than a religious building. The Kanesville Tabernacle's significance was formed when it became the spot where Brigham Young was *officially* voted in as leader of the Church, although there was no question of his leadership up to that point, the Saints knowing they had been blessed by the Lord to have someone with Brigham's logistical genius and authority to galvanize the suffering ranks again and again.

The missionary couple thanks me for stopping and tells me to be extra careful on my travels. I promise to do so.


I CALL WILL in the middle of my struggle to find a reason to continue this journey, seeking his clear thinking and wanting to hear his sure voice. I tell him I'm thinking about leaving the bike at Pat's and flying home, that this is no longer important. I tell him I need to see him, need to feel his hands on my face, need to sit on my couch with a cat on my lap. I tell him the obvious—that I can't stop crying. I tell him I feel alone, isolated, vulnerable, and quite frankly scared to death. I tell him I heard on the radio on the way back from Omaha that lots of people are experiencing fear and vulnerability, but lots of people aren't on a motorcycle fighting for road space with semitrucks and construction barriers. Lots of people aren't in the middle of nowhere familiar, depending upon the kindness of strangers. He listens quietly without interruption. I stop speaking and wait for him to tell me the same, to tell me he needs to have me there, to smell my hair, to hear my silly banter with the cats. But he breaks my heart, as he has done so many times before, by understanding me far better than I understand myself. He tells me not to come home. He tells me my journey has more significance now than it had three days ago, that I need to finish it. He tells me not to close off the beauty in the world, he tells me not to lose my way, he tells me not to give up on things that matter to me. He assures me he's safe and I'm capable, and he'll meet me in Flagstaff in a couple of weeks as planned.

I started this trip because my life had become narrow. Through my twenties and thirties, I had cast off my religion, my culture, the traditions of my family, the geography most dear to me, not only with ease but with zest. I had moved to New York City to work on Wall Street—severing my rural Utah roots as deeply as possible—part of the unleashed generation, the generation not tethered to family farms and family dinners and family burial plots. I felt as if I had escaped from something, something that would keep my life from being full and rich. When I left the town of my youth and others stayed, I thought nothing but apathy and fear kept them there.

I had dismissed Mormon pioneer stories as just more of those "in my day . . ." stories meant to make kids feel guilty and grateful for the excesses we enjoyed. Every Mormon kid had pretty much the same history, the same stories, so the importance of them was lost on us. We simply weren't interested.

What started this trip was a sense of unease, a sense of having shrugged off my fittings too nonchalantly without really discerning what it was I was throwing aside, a sense of something precious and possibly essential being lost with the rituals so carelessly tossed away. What I also didn't understand in my twenties and thirties—what started dawning on me in my forties—was that leaving the physical place and refusing to participate in the religion didn't leave me free of it. I had a sense, but no real comprehension, that the devoutly Mormon men and women of my family, particularly the women—my mother, my grandmothers, and on back to Hannah, Maria, Anna Maria, and the others who walked this trail—had formed everything I knew to be individually mine: my values, my perceptions of the world, the meanderings of my mind, and, without a doubt, the shape of my heart and soul. This was what I had felt as I stood in the rain in the corner of Lockery's cow pasture among the scattered headstones of that tiny Mormon burial site, almost as if one of my own great-great-grandmothers reached out and gently nudged me onward, showing me the importance of making the connection between the generations, trying to make me understand how useful her faith can be to me. Will is right, this is no small thing. I need to finish this trip.

# 19

CLOUDS KINDLY PROVIDE A COVER AS I MAKE MY WAY through Lincoln. At a gas station, I strip off only my gloves to enable me to pull money out of my wallet. When I go inside to pay, the clerk turns to another customer and says, "Let me take care of him first." I am the *him* he refers to. He hands me a receipt and says, "Thank you, sir." I correct him and inadvertently embarrass him, but nine times out of ten he would have been accurate.

I don't entirely understand why men continue to dominate the world of motorcycling, why so few women respond to the allure of a bike. Alone on a bike, on a country road with no traffic in sight, no safety handles to reach for, no backup plan, is as close as I've ever come to knowing my fears, my capabilities, my weaknesses, my desires. As close as I've ever come to understanding the choices I've made, as close as I'll ever get to that elusive and fleeting state of clarity. An hour's ride offers more introspection than a year's worth of expensive therapy.

Men who ride must have known this for years and have kept it a secret in a seemingly conspiratorial fashion. Maybe they did try to tell us, but we weren't equipped to hear it. We've been led to believe riding requires masculinity, some sort of brute strength. Or maybe it's something that can't be told. I've tried myself to explain it to nonriders and have failed. Maybe one cannot perceive this level of consciousness through the telling; you have to discover it for yourself.

A steady rain begins to fall on Highway 34. I pull over to the side of the road, drop both feet to the ground, leave the bike idling, exchange my light leather gloves for a pair of winter gauntlet gloves out of my tank bag, and start out again. The rain falls harder and I begin to shiver. I pull over again, this time shutting off the bike and leaning it onto the side stand. I dismount and dig my jacket liner out of my saddlebag, pull my gloves off, tear my jacket off, zip in the liner as fast as possible before getting soaked, and pull the jacket back on. I close all airflow zippers, then dig a pair of glove liners out of my tank bag before starting out again. The gamble in all of this is that the rain will stop, the clouds will disappear, and the sun will bake me like chicken in tinfoil. But today it gets consistently colder the farther west I go; my bet on the extra layers pays off.

My hands have started to cramp, partially because I am un-wittingly squeezing the grips as if I'm dangling over a cliff, and partially because I have the hands of the Hatch women— my mother and her three sisters. I slap my left hand on my thigh to get the circulation going, turn the cruise control knob near the throttle, and alternately slap the right hand in the same manner.

> *I have two little hands so soft and white*
> *This is the left and this is the right.*
> *Five little fingers standing on each*
> *So they can hold a plum or a peach.*

*When I get as big as you*
*Lots of things these little hands can do.*

My grandmother used to recite this poem. I have no knowledge of its origin, but its irony was never lost on me. I first noticed the curled hands of the Hatch women as if they were spring-loaded and tripped overnight. By age sixty, all four women had them, the curling fingers of my grandmother, Ethel Gooch Hatch. The Hatch women blame the Gooch women, but it is a Hatch trait now and I will unfortunately but proudly carry it forward through another generation.

The Hatch women don't hide their curled fingers; they aren't ashamed. They display them as proudly as they would any other component of their heritage. They decorate them with splendid rings of silver and gold holding stones of amethyst and garnet. They offer them out to greet people and extend them to push others away. They wave them and point them and wring them and fold them softly in their laps. They hold a book in one hand and dab the index finger of the other first on the tongue, then on the page. They no longer attempt to turn the pages by slipping a finger between.

I know the feel of my mother's curled hand in mine. I've run my fingers over the top of hers, feeling bumps of loose skin, protruding veins, and bulging knuckles. Most of my childhood I drove my mother crazy by trailing her around the house, watching busy hands at eye level scribble out grocery lists, swipe dust off tabletops, and polish houseplant leaves. She does less of that now as her hands have become more crippled with two different types of arthritis.

She's likely sitting now at her kitchen table preparing for Sunday school class. Her left hand will brush along the pages of an open Book of Mormon—only the tips of her fingers and the base of her wrist making contact with the delicate paper. Her right hand will curl around a pen, and she will slowly and painfully make notes. The stones of her rings will glitter incongruously on the bent claw.

At one point in my mid-twenties, I attempted to copy her style with rings of my own, but I couldn't pull it off. The heavy stones twisted awkwardly, lodging between two bony, nail-bitten fingers. After a few months I abandoned the practice; my hands have remained undecorated since. Many of my friends and relatives are appalled that my wedding ring has remained in a small box on my dresser almost since the day of my wedding, but Will has never questioned it.

I try in vain to visualize how my mother's hands must have looked when I was young, but I cannot conjure up a visual image, only a sense of touch. I can vividly feel the cool smoothness of my mother's fingers on the side of my face when she kissed me goodnight; I can feel the strength of my mother's hands in my hair as she pulled it back from my face and twisted it into a ponytail; and I can feel the heat of her hands on my back when she pulled me toward her time after time to let me know that my father's wrath could not penetrate that hold. But when I try to *see* her hands, I can only see my own.

I never saw my grandmother's hands before they began to curl. They fascinated me, all the things they could do in that condition. I saw them black with dirt from digging potatoes, I saw them red and raw from scrubbing pots, and later I saw them resigned and lifeless, hanging over the arms of her wheelchair, jeweled with a single gold band, but I never saw them straight.

When my grandmother became a widow at the age of forty-four, she put her capable hands to work cooking and cleaning, and tending to the sick and aged. By day she peeled pound after pound of potatoes as she prepared meals for the Sigma Chi fraternity at Utah State University. After washing and drying the last of the pots each day, she went to the home of Mrs. Nebeker, where she would gently pull the pins from the old woman's thin, gray hair, allowing it to drop down her back. Ethel would wrap a red and chapped hand around the bone handle of a hairbrush and gently stroke Mrs. Nebeker's hair one hundred times before helping her into bed.

Her mother, Mary Ann Gooch, put her hands to use sewing burial clothes and laying out the dead—her assigned duty as a member of the Relief Society of the Rich, Idaho, ward of the Mormon Church.

With the body stretched out on the dining room table, Mary Ann ordered a bowl of warm, soapy water and one of cold water, sent the family out of the room, and stripped the corpse naked. She placed a cold, wet cloth over the face, then stepped down to take a look at the toes. She returned to the head, placed a small bundle on the table next to the right ear, tugged at the string, and unrolled the pouch. She chose a pair of sewing scissors kept sharp by her husband, Belton Gooch, to clip the hard, yellow overgrown toenails. Mary Ann dropped her hands into the basin of warm, soapy water and paused for a moment before pulling them out and wringing the wet rag between her fingers. She scrubbed between the toes and then moved up the body, unfolding skin and swabbing crevices. She paused midway to replace the facecloth with a fresh one so the face would not darken to the color of a blueberry stain. With the tip of the scissors, she dug dirt from under the nails, polished them with a wire brush, and cut them close to the finger. Mary Ann dressed the body, bundled up her tools, and stepped out quietly past the family as she massaged the palm of one aching hand with the fingers of the other.

Mary Ann was the daughter of Anna Maria, who, pregnant with a child who would be stillborn, walked the trail I now travel. My grandmother's voice—unheard since 1981—plays in my head. "Idle hands are Satan's workshop," she'd tell me. "The devil and idle hands work together." The stories she told are lodged with a certain discomfort in my memory like a piece of wood in the sludge of a drying riverbed. I hold an image of an unbroken chain of never-idle hands in the service of God and the Mormon Church, but I stand alone, unattached, my hands dangling uselessly by my sides.

IN A MCDONALD'S bathroom in Aurora, I run warm water over my hands and hold them under the drier for a good five minutes to get them moving again. As I walk out pulling my gloves back on, a gray-haired, heavyset woman stops me and asks if I'm from Arizona and if I'm traveling alone. I tell her yes to both questions, and she gazes out the window at the bike as if she were remembering something.

"Best to travel alone," she says, "no better way to travel."

"Yeah, I think so," I say, and for the first time in days believe my own words.

"I motorcycled through Arizona once myself," she says wistfully. She appears to be making her adult son nervous, and he jumps in immediately to jar her out of her nostalgia.

"You headed west?" he asks, and I tell him I am. "Gonna get colder the farther west you go. This storm is coming from the west; they're getting snow in Wyoming. You going through Wyoming?"

I nod.

"Well, you better expect snow."

I thank him for the weather report and tell her it was nice to meet her.

"You have a real good ride," she says to me. And then, as if speaking to no one but herself: "No better way to travel."

I feel their eyes watching me through the window as they sip coffee while I slowly readjust jacket, liners, gloves, helmet, and glasses, already shivering from the cold. For a while, the son is wrong; the sun comes out and offers just enough warmth to make the ride comfortable, but when it disappears a short time later, the frigid air finds even the smallest access to my bare skin.

The amiable Iowa farming towns and wandering roads through them arc behind me. Iowa had a feel of county fairs, 4-H projects, and Sunday dinners; rural Nebraska has a feel of farming co-ops, corporate feedlots, and stray dogs. On my left the Union Pacific Railroad runs a steady line of trains past numerous small towns—some smaller than others—most with several large grain silos and a mishmash of shiny and rusty industrial-looking buildings and other contraptions that likely play some important part in the world's food chain. Some towns offer nothing more than a house or two, others host a thriving little main street and a local café filled with tall tales of better days. The railroad industry also brings more traffic— pickup trucks and semitrucks—most heading toward the nearest access to I-80, which runs parallel to Highway 34 just a few miles to the south.

By the time I reach Kearney, the weather has made a drastic shift. The sun shines hot and traffic thickens to a crawl. I'm dressed for speed and cold, and sweat begins to trickle in numerous places. At a stoplight, I pop my face shield and suck in car exhaust while I unzip every zipper I can find for airflow. Overheated and light-headed, I find the turn for Fort Kearny State Historical Park—and by the time I get there, less than ten minutes later, the skies are cloudy and cool again.

Fort Kearny was established in 1848, and became a resting point for some Mormon pioneers. Most of the Mormons, however, stayed on the north side of the Platte River to avoid going over the same grasslands as those headed to Oregon and California. I wander for a few minutes, but decide to move on when it begins to rain. By the time I stop for gas, the drizzle has turned to a downpour and the streets are quickly becoming flooded. I duck into one of the few nonchain hotels, the Western Inn, and the woman behind the desk greets me with a big smile and a room key.

"Getting a little nasty out there," she says. I nod, rain running off my shoulders and onto her carpet, but she doesn't seem worried about it. "I'm going to put you on the first floor so you don't have to drag all your gear upstairs," she says, as if she's been in my situation before.

Inside the motel room, I feel flat and uninspired. The street odors of gasoline and grease float from the soles of my boots, and I suddenly want to leave Kearney, Nebraska. A sore throat and a cough make me realize that I haven't eaten a green vegetable in probably two weeks, so I set out to find some.

The smiling woman at the front desk points me to "the best restaurant in town," and I enter with high hopes. I ask the hostess if they have a nonsmoking section, and she looks at me like I've asked her to serve my dinner out of coconut shells while wearing a hula skirt. She seats me at a table by the door that offers a blast of cold air every time someone walks in or out but also offers the only breath of fresh air in an otherwise smoky room.

People twist in their chairs to get a look at me. Either they overheard my nonsmoking request, or I've sprouted horns like those once rumored to adorn the heads of Mormons, or women don't eat in "the best restaurant in town" by themselves in Kearney, Nebraska.

I order a big slab of meat—prime rib—and a bunch of broccoli. They bring me a salad—iceberg lettuce—and a little basket of crackers. I bide my time and try to look busy to those who seem interested by arranging the crackers in alphabetical order: breadstick, club, saltine, and wheat. Then I remove all the club crackers and stick them in my fanny pack. The waitress smells of flowers, lavender or rose I think, and every time she whooshes by I think about funerals. She brings my beef—not a pink spot left on it—and my broccoli—cooked to green mush. She offers to drown my broccoli mush in cheese sauce, but I decline.

On my way through the front office, the desk clerk once again reminds me to visit the Archway Museum, which spans six lanes of I-80 in Kearney. Supposedly it is the most technologically advanced historical museum in the country, with "21st Century interactive displays." She's been awfully nice to me and I don't want to disappoint her or give the long explanation why I'm not going there, so I assure her I'll go first thing in the morning, but I have no desire to see one more life-size ox or one more twenty-first-century pioneer film. My story lies in the tall grasses of the Nebraska prairie, not in an interactive display case.

# 20

AS I PACK THE BIKE A DENVER BUSINESSMAN INFORMS me that Highway 30 west of here is closed for road construction. Graded asphalt and uneven lanes are fine for cars—going slowly from a lower lane over a three-inch differential to an upper lane in a parallel motion is nothing for a car at a slow speed. On a bike, it's near impossible and could be deadly. He tells me the detour will take me to I-80, and I consider heading there from here, but I find freeway travel as unpleasant as road construction, so I stick with my original plan.

"My neighbor is a BMW motorcycle nut!" the guy tells me, looking at my bike. "He owns five of them!"

I just nod, say something inane, and smile. I don't tell him that owning five bikes doesn't qualify his neighbor as a nut—just a normal male motorcyclist. My husband tells me the optimal number of bikes to own is five. He owns three, one of which is in pieces and stored in various places throughout the garage and house like it's part of an Easter-egg hunt. From what I've seen, this also appears to be a common trait among male motorcyclists, the desire to tear a bike down into small bits, then slowly and obsessively put it back together again. When I first met my husband, pieces of a 1981 Honda Gold-Wing adorned his apartment like furniture or artwork—saddlebag end tables, a fairing sculpture—and occupied staggering amounts of his free time and thoughts. I own one bike, fully assembled. Seems adequate.

Ten miles west of Kearney the skies turn dark again—very dark—and cold. I stop without getting off the bike and pull my glove liners out of the tank bag. I debate zipping in my jacket liner, which requires shutting off the bike and rummaging through a saddlebag. It also requires taking off my jacket and right now I'm too cold to do it. I rationalize it by thinking the sun will pop out again soon, but it does not. Ten minutes down the road I stop again to get the job done.

Rails and grain silos continue on my left. I ride along lost in thoughts of great-great-grandmother Hannah pulling a handcart through the wet green grass here, skirts weighed down with the dampness that crept halfway up to her waist, two tiny girls bouncing on top or trailing alongside, and a nearly worn-out stepson pushing the cart from behind. Suddenly a train sneaks up alongside me, blows a whistle at a tiny little crossing, and jolts me out of my seat. Even when I see them coming toward me, even when I anticipate the blast, it awakens every organ in my body, and they vibrate in unison like a cartoon alarm clock.

Along Highway 30, I travel several miles next to some astonishingly large feedlots. Although I like the smell of cow manure for purely sentimental reasons, the intensity of feedlot cow manure is too great for pleasure. The first whiff or so evokes a momentary twinge of nostalgia, but one mile, two miles in, it just stinks to high heaven.

In North Platte, I stop for gas and remove my helmet to take a few moments' rest.

"I'll pay for your gas if you'll pay for mine, young lady," says an old farmer stepping out of his half-ton, extended-cab pickup truck.

"No thanks," I say smiling.

"Well, that's a heck of an attitude. How far can you go on that thing?"

"About two hundred miles or so. It gets about fifty miles to the gallon."

"No, I don't mean gas. I mean how far can you ride that thing before your back starts to give out?"

"It doesn't. My back never bothers me. My knees start to hurt a little, but it's very comfortable to ride."

"I can't imagine that! Seems like your back would hurt all the time." I explain to him the ergonomics of a bike like mine, which spreads your weight pretty evenly through your legs, hips, back, shoulders, and arms, unlike a cruiser-type bike that puts all your weight on your butt and lower back. I tell him it's probably more comfortable on the back than his truck seats. He seems unconvinced and changes the subject.

"What did you bring all this cold weather with you for?" he asks.

I smile and agree that he's probably a lot warmer in that truck than I am on this bike. I start to put my helmet back on and he climbs back in his truck, rolls the window down, and sticks his head out.

"You have a good trip, young lady."

The impact of small moments of human geniality is immense.

THROUGH THE YEARS, my father never gave up on his commitment to purge me of what he perceived as my fear of horses. He was sure I had natural ability, and he was not going to let that go to waste. I stood my ground as often and as long as I dared—usually not often and not long.

My mother's preference for peace and quiet usually took her down the path of least resistance, but when it came to his battle with me, she was subtly persistent in my defense. She saw my father's stubbornness in me, and she knew that the conflict that had been going on since my first horseback ride would never end unless he ended it.

As I entered my teenage years, most likely at the urging of my mother, my father gradually backed off on his quest to make me ride. During hot summer days when he was off ranching, I would walk out to the horse corral and put my arms around the neck of a horse named Little Goldsmoke— Goldie—as she stood off balance with one relaxed knee bent, swatting flies with her tail. I rested my head against her warm neck, breathed in her musky scent, and apologized for her life in this Western household. She stood calmly, eyes half closed, and sometimes nuzzled my back pocket as if she were trying to comfort me.

Once the pressure to ride was gone, I threw a halter on her and rode bareback almost every day in the fields behind our house. My father was right. Riding came naturally to me; then, as now, the motion was part of me. Goldie loved to run without the pull of a bit in her mouth and the weight of a saddle on her back. She was smooth and easy. In the summertime, when we got back to the corral, she'd roll on her back to cool off, and I'd quickly strip off the pants covered with her hair and sweat. In the wintertime, she got used to me riding bent over with my arms around her neck to keep warm.

When I left home at eighteen, I was afraid my father would take Goldie to auction and sell her "for hamburger," the phrase I'd always heard growing up. She was old and no longer of use as to him as a cattle horse. I went to my father with a shaking

voice and fear in my guts and asked him to keep Goldie until
she died. My father simply nodded, picked up the pitchfork,
and threw hay over the fence to her, acknowledging the horse
that was able to accomplish what he could not.

THE CLOUDS HANGING low on Highway 30 sedate me,
and the buzz of my tires on wet pavement lulls me into a peaceful trance. I want badly to abandon the rules and turn myself
over to it, to let it appease my body and pacify my mind, to
wrap myself in the hush and let it smother the tiny cautions
that perpetually float through my head. I verbally remind myself to stay focused. I run through my classroom motorcycling
training—SIPDE, SIPDE, I repeat to myself. Scan, identify,
predict, decide, execute. Head up, eyes level with the horizon.
And therein lies my problem. I see no horizon. I see a pearly
white cocoon inviting me into its womb; I see a silky promise of
serenity; I see snatches of cotton reaching for me, tips dabbed
with fluorescent orange. Orange. Why orange? Springing out
of the whiteness as if I'm somehow invoking them by riding
over a hidden trigger, screaming at me rudely, are construction
cones and warning signs. I roll off the throttle.

The construction signs put me first on graded pavement
running next to a lane of freshly laid asphalt two inches higher
than the lane I'm currently in. I run in fear of being asked to
cross over to the higher lane, but it never happens. Instead, the
road closes entirely, and I'm shot down an access road to the
cold, swirling world of I-80. I stay to the right, traveling around
sixty-five miles per hour. Semitrucks and RVs flash by on my
left, drenching me with muddy spray as they pass. The same
clouds hang low around me but now take on a menacing
demeanor, and I'm happy to see the orange detour sign sending me back to Highway 30. The detour has taken me around

the turnoff for the Sandhill wagon ruts, so I turn east on 30 to see if I can get to it before I hit the road closure from this side. I turn left on Pioneer Trace Road and travel about four miles to an unmarked location, but no one needs to tell me I'm in the right place.

The lead party of Mormons upon leaving Winter Quarters in April of 1847 consisted of a small scouting party, including 9 of the Quorum of the Twelve and 150 or so others—all but 5 of them men—handpicked and led by Brother Brigham. All advice the Mormons received told them they should travel up the Platte Valley on the south side of the Platte River where companies making their way to Oregon and California had packed a hard, good road and reported good feed for the cattle. In addition, crossing the Missouri River put them into what was known as the Permanent Indian Frontier, and the Indian threats and prairie fires were said to be fewer on the south side of the Platte.

But Brigham had more to consider than getting this small group to some still-unknown destination in the West. They were road-making for thousands of Saints following them who were justifiably paranoid about mixing with the Gentiles travel-ing to Oregon and California, and Lord knows the Mormons had never been hesitant to separate themselves from the pre-vailing ideas of those around them. With the odor of prairie-fire smoke in his nostrils and already one skirmish with the Pawnees behind him, Brigham Young made the decision to take his Saints up the north bank of the Platte River, pretty much the same route Highway 30 takes today.

In the next few years, cholera would dash up the south bank of the Platte faster than Oregon- and California-bound wagons could outrun it, leaving the bones of hundreds to be picked clean by wolves and bleached white in the Nebraska prairie sun. The separatist Saints, left mostly untouched by the cholera epidemic, noted in journals, with a hint of smug self-righteousness, the divine delivery of retribution on the "scum and mobocrats" who persecuted them, as many of the wagon trains hit hardest by the cholera epidemic were traveling from Illinois and Missouri.

As if just for me, alone on this country road, the rain subsides and the clouds lift slightly. On the right side of the road, coming over a hill, in the soft and easily eroded Sandhill terrain, a prominent indentation in the soil marks the road Brigham Young and his boys built up the north side of the Platte River in 1847. Six of my great-great-grandmothers walked where I now stand. The first to trudge through the sand and top this hill was Maria Thompson, twelve years old, in 1851. The last was Anna Maria Larsen, twenty-nine years old, who came over the hill pregnant and weary in 1866. Between them came Mary Jane Atkinson, fourteen years old, traveling in 1853 from Canada with her parents and eight siblings, one of whom they buried in Keokuk, Iowa; Hannah Middleton Hawkey, by handcart with her small family in 1856; and Elizabeth Lallis Thomas and Sarah Ann Stephensen Richman, who immigrated with their husbands in 1862. Another great-great-grandmother, Martha Shelton, who traveled with her two brothers, five sisters, and their families from New Brunswick, Canada, had the misfortune of being wealthy enough to buy teams and wagons in St. Louis and consequently traveled the Oregon Trail on the south side of the Platte River. She lost six nieces and nephews and two sisters to cholera before arriving in Salt Lake City in 1854. And still another great-great-grandmother, Ann Birkenshaw Gooch, traveled from Liverpool by ship and rail to Ogden, Utah, in 1873.

My mother travels with me on this trail. In my mind, we stand along this country road and I point out the wagon ruts to her, but she has a hard time seeing them. She's heard the story of the trail so often it persists fresh in her mind the way it looked 150 years ago. The persecutions, the trail, the movement west all remain such a sacred piece of her history, she would have difficulty imagining that even nature would tread upon such consecrated ground, left unplowed and untouched by man.

As if she were physically here now, I stretch one strand of barbwire down with my foot and pull the other up with my aching hands to allow her arthritis-riddled body passage through the fence. As I walk slowly to the top of the hill, I feel the weight of her arm through mine. I sit in wet grass that grows lush in the wagon ruts; she would insist on standing. Been sitting all day, she'd say.

I'd remind her which of her great-grandmothers came this way—Maria, Anna Maria, and Mary Jane—the years and how old they were at the time. Her tears would fall softly; at every stop along the trail her tears would fall. This propensity to cry easily, I inherited from the Hatch women. At the Hatch family reunion held every year, the ritual calls for each of the brothers and sisters to stand and update the group on their children, grandchildren, great-grandchildren. As my mother and each of my aunts stand to speak, before a word is uttered, the tears start to flow. When my grandmother was alive, she would do the same. And I now find myself seizing almost any opportunity to let the tears flow.

I speak my end of the conversation with my mother aloud, send the words out into the prairie wind. Hoping, I guess, they will somehow reach her, somehow get to the spot where she sits praying for the physical and spiritual well-being of a daughter who can't ever seem to find the obvious path. During each con-versation, I end with a promise to my mother that if I make it home alive, I'll take her to Nauvoo and back home to Utah along the Mormon Trail.

In this spot, I'm taken with such a mixture of emotions they are difficult to separate and identify. I certainly feel a sense of sadness, of grief, that so much was demanded of those who walked this trail. But the grief gives way to pride for exactly the same reason—that so much was demanded of those who walked this trail. And they gave it—freely and willingly—knowing that an untested covenant is really no covenant at all.

# 21

I LEAVE BEHIND CORNFIELDS, TRUCKS, AND TRAINS when I turn off Highway 30 and head northwest on Highway 26. The treeless, tall-grass prairie closes in on me from both sides, but is soon interrupted on my left by a field of giant sunflowers, drooping heads exhausted by a long summer. After traveling next to them for several miles, I'm nodding also, as if I've entered the sleeping poppy field in *The Wizard of Oz*. I find their surrender to the change of seasons irresistible, a clear and obvious choice.

At Ash Hollow, the trail ruts have turned themselves into a gorge, accommodating water runoff with no consideration for historical preservation. I am alone again, and I breathe the mild, moist air deeply and marvel at a sudden stand of ash trees in the treeless prairie. The ruts come down off the slope—supposedly so steep that wagons had to lock their wheels and be eased down with ropes—and fade into the adjacent field but can be picked up again at the crest of the next hill. I skip the visitors center that lies across and up the road and instead make a ten-minute climb to the top of the hill. This is what I need—to stand in the trail with my hair whipping my face, to hear the dry grass shuffle in the wind, to see the endless trail disappear over the next hill.

I sit in the tall grass, dig in my pocket for my temple rock, and pass it back and forth from one hand to the other. I've been searching for faith, hoping to understand it and possess it with the same certainty and clarity my ancestors seemed to have, but it remains out of reach.

The Mormon missionaries used to knock on my door on a regular basis. They were typically young—teenagers—and so earnest in their desire to share the *true gospel*, any person with a heart would do at least as much as my husband and I did: take them in out of the desert heat and offer them a glass of water or lemonade. Once they discovered we already knew the basic tenets of the Mormon Church but that we lacked the knowledge of its truth, they would outline for us the simple process of gaining that knowledge: pray to God, asking him to tell you that the Mormon Church is the only true church on earth, and have faith that your prayers will be answered. To prove that faith conquers all, they would tell us the story of Job, a story that shows God at his absolute worst, baited by the devil and subsequently torturing a man to prove a point and win a bet. A story most unlikely to stir my faith in God.

But by "faith," the missionaries seemed to be talking about the power of positive thinking found in an abundance of American self-help books, the stuff that claims you can create your own reality, the stuff that leads people like me to believe they can be the next Whitney Houston in spite of shrill singing voices. Anything is possible if you believe it to be so. If you fail, it isn't because you caw like a crow, it's because you didn't believe enough.

When I told them I had no faith they were at first incredulous, insistent that prayer without faith wouldn't yield the proper results. They kept repeating "You must have faith" as if it were something that could be *had* as easily as buying bananas at the grocery store, as if I could opt to have it and instead choose to be difficult like an obstinate child.

I've been thinking of faith that way, as something *out there*, a product that can be acquired. And I've been searching for it that way, as if I might find it nestled in the Nebraska prairie grass or tucked behind a bluff. But I wonder if faith might not be something a person *has* but instead something a person does, a particular way of being in life. Faith, I think, might not offer certainty that the rituals of a particular religion will guarantee salvation, might not offer certainty that God sits ready to respond to every prayer we utter, might not offer certainty of the superiority of one religion over another, but perhaps the opposite.

When I was a child I was encouraged, as all Mormon children are, to stand in church on the first Sunday of the month—when Sacrament Meeting was turned over to the congregation—to bear my testimony. It went something like this: "I know The Church of Jesus Christ of Latter-day Saints is the only true church on earth and I know Joseph Smith was a true prophet of God." Adults would go on to tell their own personal stories of what struggles they might currently be working through, but us kids would just quickly end with "I say this in the name of Jesus Christ, amen."

At the time, I had no reason to believe the words coming from my mouth and no reason to doubt them. I concerned myself only with the horrifying idea of speaking in public. But I'm now intrigued by my many childhood friends who continued to say those words year after year right up into adulthood and say them today without a flicker of doubt. How did they arrive at that certainty, and how did I miss it? It is that certainty that I've always defined as "faith" and that type of "faith" that I've been

seeking. But it now seems possible to make a distinction between "faith" and "belief."

I'm beginning now to think of faith as a practice, a practice
that allows acceptance of uncertainty and allows for the unex-
plainable. The practice of faith, I think, might ask us to snuggle
up next to the mysteries of life and remain quiet, without seeking reason and resolution. The practice of faith may make the
elusiveness of clarity not only OK but necessary.

Most of us—including those of us who choose not to con-
gregate and claim not to believe—want to know what it is we
need to do now to guarantee the safety of our souls later.
Churches can falter under their human constraints without
shaking the beliefs of their members. Priests can be arrested for
raping children, men can exclude women from the ranks of
power, but if religious leaders can't offer certainty and promise,
if Mormons can't offer up temple rituals as steps to salvation, if
Catholics can't offer up confession and penance and Commu-
nion, if instead they shrug their shoulders and say, "Embrace
uncertainty, we don't have a clue what will get you into heaven
or if there even is such a place," their congregations will drift
away at best, revolt at worst. My gut feeling, though, is that this
embrace of mystery is exactly what faith demands.

The lure of certainty is a powerful and comforting one in a
world where hope is as elusive as clarity. Recently in Tucson,
two teenage boys skinned a puppy and set it out—still alive—
in the desert sun to roast. A seventy-year-old woman was
raped and beaten to death in her home. Corporate executives
continue to knowingly dump death-producing toxins into
ground water. Forests are being clear-cut, the desert around
my home is being swept clean of saguaro cactus. And five days
ago a few men killed a few thousand people to make some sort
of point.

"Hope," writes Joan Chittister, "leads us around dark corners looking for the grace of the moment, confident that God's will for us is good . . . Hope whispers within us like a soft, steady draft of daylight . . . Hope in a world that has the capacity to destroy itself is an egg on the edge of a cliff. Someone, everyone, is responsible, together and alone, for hope's surety. Each of us bears the burden of its future."

When hope can't be found in the world around us, when we hit block walls as we try to round that dark corner, when the draft of daylight narrows into an imperceptible sliver, the practice of faith might be the power we need to live by.

Faith might demand more of us than choosing a particular package of religion off the shelf and shaping our lives according to the directions on the side panel. Faith insists that we do more than settle down into our personal paths to salvation. Faith, I believe, insists that we reach not only upward but outward, that for it to thrive in the first direction requires practice in the second. Faith asks for more than private piety, for more than personal spirituality; it asks for public commitment.

William James describes the central state of faith as one of peace and harmony, "the *willingness to be,* even though the outer conditions should remain the same." The certainty of salvation, says James, does not necessarily accompany such a state. In many people who claim faith today, I find the opposite to be true. I find the certainty of salvation without peace and harmony.

I'm caught up and wholly complicit in a society that has lost all boundaries between needs and wants. We need bigger houses, two or three cars, more oil to run those cars, more money to buy more stuff. It flows out of my mouth just as naturally as the words of a well-memorized song. When our television recently went silent, I declared, "We need a new television."

In fact, my needs are quite small. What I have taken, accumulated, and consumed thus far in my life exceeds my needs by
embarrassing proportions. My wants are largely out of control
and almost unconscious, unlikely ever to reach a point of satisfaction. Peace and harmony are reduced to political buzzwords
in such a society.

I've heard some religious leaders blame this hunger for excess on our barren souls, on the fact that we've taken God out
of our schools and out of our daily lives and we're all going to
hell in a handbasket. I think they are partially right, but praying in school or attending church or choosing a particular path
to salvation obviously does not satiate the hunger—we have
plenty of examples to prove that point. The hunger, I believe, is
not for the next world. The next world is, in fact, quite tidily
taken care of by religion. The hunger is for this world, for
earth, for humanity, for understanding and hope that exist beyond our grasp—if they exist at all. In a society saturated by
the self-help notion that every emotion experienced, every instinct felt, every action taken, and every small miracle observed
can be dissected, analyzed, explained, and resolved, we hunger
for the quiet practice of faith, a practice that allows uncertainty
without resolution and mystery without explanation; a practice
that in the heart of excess and greed asks that we each bear the
weight of our own indulgences; a practice that in the face of in-
equity and oppression asks that we each bear the responsibility
of justice and compassion; a practice that in the midst of military might, chaos, and despair asks that we each bear the burden of hope.


I DROP MY temple stone in the tall grass and search frantically, holding my hair from my eyes with one hand and lightly

sweeping the grass with the other. I find it, caught in the place where a blade of grass shoots and separates into three blades. I breathe a sigh of relief and tuck it back into my pocket.

Some days, when the Saints came through this area, if the weather was nice like it is today, mild with a cloud cover, there may have been singing among the children and chatting among the young mothers. Even the handcart pioneers, enduring the harshest possible travel of this trail, had a marching song to help them on their way, although it seems ridiculously cheerful now:

> *For some must push and some must pull*
> *As we go marching up the hill,*
> *And merrily on our way we go*
> *Until we reach the valley-o.*
>
> *And then with music and with song*
> *How cheerfully we'll march along.*
> *And thank the day we made a start*
> *To cross the plains in our handcart.*

I stand at my bike facing the wind and try twice to get all my hair tucked under my helmet liner, which happens to be the most unattractive but necessary piece of gear I own, and finally succeed on the third attempt. I never start my engine until I'm certain all errant strands of hair that could float inside a face shield, tickling a jawbone or brushing against a cheek, are secure. Imagine trying to operate heavy equipment while someone brushes a feather across your face, under your nose, and you get the picture. I'll stop anywhere on any road and remove gloves, helmet, and liner to start the process over again if even one hair works itself free and up to my face to torture me.

The formations that fill Mormon journals—Courthouse Rock, Jail Rock, and Chimney Rock—jump awkwardly out of the Nebraska prairie. I feel the same elation at the sight of them that the journals describe, a relief to find my way out of the infinite, treeless prairies, as if the jutting steeple of Chimney Rock marks the beginning of the end of my journey, the entry into the West. I stop at the Chimney Rock visitors center just long enough to use the restroom; standing in an air-conditioned room reading about and trying to visualize the passing string of suffering Saints seems absurd at this point.

Just outside Scottsbluff, I circle a small industrial area several times and finally find the gravesite of Rebecca Winters, a Mormon woman who left Nauvoo with the Saints and died on this spot. Her grave marker, an iron rim of a wagon wheel engraved "Rebecca Winters, age 50," was one of the few hastily built markers of the six thousand or so victims of this trail that survived more than a couple of years. Burlington Railroad surveyors discovered the marker buried in the weeds and grass when they were laying railroad track along here. They kindly diverted the track to the south of the grave, and Rebecca remains today in this odd location, a small sacred spot in the midst of restlessness. Sandwiched between the railroad and the highway at a busy intersection, the site refuses its visitors reverence or reflection.

WHISKEY RIVER RESTAURANT sounds like one of those horrible restaurants designed around a gimmick that we all flock to like a movie with a good chase scene and crashing cars. They will feed us food and entertainment simultaneously; heaven forbid we be left in silence with nothing to occupy us but our own thoughts or the conversation of our companions. I detest the idea of it, but in a steady line of tractor dealerships and car sales it seems to be the only restaurant within walking distance of the Super 8 Motel I've just checked into.

The gimmick, I soon find out, is peanuts. Upon being seated, each patron is given a small silver pail of peanuts and, like a bad child, you are allowed to throw your peanut shells on the floor. The accumulation of peanut shells on the wood floors, in addition to ceiling-mounted televisions hanging every ten feet or so blaring country music videos, builds an expectation that a cowboy and cowgirl will be two-stepping past the table at any moment. It's a backslapping, yee-hawing sort of place you go to with your friends on a Saturday night, and by the looks I'm getting, I apparently stick out like a grandmother at a strip club. Unlike the patrons at other tables, I'm offered no peanuts. Maybe it is too pathetically sad, too upsetting to the other customers, to see a woman alone eating peanuts from a pail on a Saturday night. Or maybe they think I'll want to order quickly, eat quickly, and get out quickly so as to not cause myself undue embarrassment by lingering alone over a peanut pail. A young woman in a foursome with her back to me, as if by instinct, turns to look just as I lift a forkful of iceberg lettuce to my mouth, then turns back to comment to her companions, and I am just able to shove it mostly in before all four twist and crane to have a look. I glare at them defiantly, causing them to turn back embarrassed by their indiscretion, then wipe the ranch dressing from my chin.


THE SOUND OF more rain awakens me in a stale-smelling motel room around 6 A.M. My hair sticks to my head, the sheets stick to my body as if I've been sleeping in a steam bath. Horrendous images of last night's dream linger in my mind: torsos and limbs lying in wagon ruts. I feel responsible, as if my viewing of the wagon ruts is the reason for the deaths, as if they gave their lives specifically to make wagon ruts for me to ponder. I feel as if I'm missing something, some symbolic message that will change my life in an instant like a hypnotist snapping his fingers in front of my face. If I could wake up and see it, it would explain everything, soothe my world, show me the greatest gifts life has to offer.

I went to bed last night exhausted in every possible way—body, mind, and soul—bereft of all emotions, deprived of my capacity to feel. This morning I feel the opposite, hypersensitive in a disconcerting way. My gear is strewn around the room as if I've been here not merely ten hours, but ten days. It takes me three hours to eat a bagel, repack everything, and strap it to the bike.

Scottsbluff, Nebraska, is cast in tones of gray like a black-and-white television town—foreboding and lonely. But as always, the movement of the ride changes everything. The picture fast-forwards and color begins to emerge. From under shrouds of mist, fantastic bluffs fall silently from sky to ground without even a thud.

I park in the empty lot of Scotts Bluff National Monument and go in to the visitors center to pay the fee.

"Are you riding a motorcycle or just wearing funny pants?" the woman collecting the fee asks.

"Riding a motorcycle."

Her eyebrows go up in an attractive fashion. "I thought so! Where did you come from and where are you going? Tell me everything!"

I don't tell her everything; I just tell her that I started in Nauvoo and I'm following the Mormon Trail to Salt Lake City.

"Fantastic!" she says. "Well, the Mormons didn't see what you're seeing here. But they would have seen the bluffs from the other side, and they would have been just as spectacular as they are here this morning."

I agree with her that they really are spectacular this morning, sporting their white sheets.

"Can I tell you something," she says, more like a statement than a question, and without waiting for my reply she tells me, "I think you are a very brave woman."

I tell her there have been times on this trip I've felt more foolish than brave, but she stops me short with the wave of her fingers. "Don't you let yourself feel that way. Nothing foolish about it," she says unequivocally, as if she knows my entire story.

The mist begins to lift as I walk among the bluffs in solitude. The beauty of them is so pure, it seems as if the mist plays an essential role, exposing them slowly to prevent stupefying a person seeing them for the first time. It's a sight sure to make non-believers stop and think for a moment. It must have been sheer inspiration and affirmation for the Saints. The skies are white this morning—they remind me of the winter skies of my child-hood—only the warm temperature keeps me from believing they might release snow.

The bluffs mark the end of the prairie, the beginning of the mountains. My stomach flutters a little with the thought, an even mix of dread and joy, which is exactly what many keepers of Mormon diaries experienced here. The mountains present unpredictable road conditions and weather patterns, high winds and a possibility of an early snow. But the mountains represent the West; I'm going home.

# 22

ACCORDING TO GEOGRAPHER ROBERT HAY, THE DEPTH of one's bond to a place is affected by one's ancestral and cultural sense of place. Generations of family on certain land and spiritual connections to that land create a deeper bond with a place than can be created simply by length of residence. Hay finds that developing a sense of place is a basic need common to humanity. "Without connections that are lasting, as in a rooted sense of place," writes Hay, "we may find it difficult to integrate memories and feelings in later life for the mosaic of places . . . we have known, that there is little continuity to our own life stories. Without individual continuity," he writes, "community and societal cohesion are themselves at risk."

In the winter of 1981, I packed as much as I could into a beat-up Oldsmobile Ninety-Eight and left my hometown. I left behind two parents, one brother, one sister-in-law, two nieces, many friends, and one husband. I left behind a job at Tooele Army Depot and two weeks of paid vacation. I left a stifling expectation that I would raise children, join the Relief Society, and retire from the depot. But all the years leading up to that would not crystallize in my mind. I panicked and left. I went only forty-five miles to Salt Lake City, but it felt like a zillion miles to me.

Four years later, I left again. I felt proud of myself as I drove across the country from Salt Lake City to New York City, headed for my new job on Wall Street. I had beaten the small-town rap. I had escaped. I weep now when I think of leaving my rosebush-surrounded home in the Sugarhouse area of Salt Lake City with its strip of green grass running down the center of the driveway. It was the first and only home I've ever owned completely by myself. But I didn't cry then.

New York City exhilarated me. For three years I buzzed with energy. But the passion stirred in me by the city was similar to the passion I feel in the first few days of a vacation in a strange land as I scurry to take in every sight, every taste. I was a visitor in New York, a long-term tourist. Subconsciously, I must have known I would never stay there.

After I met Will, a New Jersey native, I was surprised to hear myself singing the praises of the West. I must have been convincing, because before long we were packing our belongings into a forty-foot Ryder rental truck and driving west, not to Utah, but only one state away. If anyone were to ask me if I've ever known true euphoria, I would have to say yes, during a five-day road trip from east to west. I was giddy with joy, playing license plate games and dining on chicken-fried steak. I'm a Western girl. The region has a line on me; if I stray too far, it reels me back in.

I'll never find contentment in my hometown—it has changed too much and it hasn't changed enough. The changes sadden me: A gate has been put across the road to Settlement Canyon because vandals have carved their names in trees, started fires, and dumped beer cans in the streams. Settlement

Canyon holds the memories of my first hike, my first overnight camping trip, my first taste of beer, and my first kiss. It holds the memories of the late sixties and early seventies, when we thought we understood peace and love.

The town's population has almost doubled since I left more than twenty years ago, and it has traded its rural status for that of commuter town. I'm no longer guaranteed to know the name of the pharmacist filling my prescription or the produce manager at the grocery store. The empty fields that filled my time with discovery and adventure are now filled with cookie-cutter houses, and the pussy willow–lined irrigation ditches that used to flow freely through town carrying my newspaper boats have gone underground. The hamburger joints sure to have local favorites such as fry sauce—that sickly sweet concoction known only to small towns in Utah and Idaho—have been shut down in favor of generic and tasteless food served up by McDonald's and Carl's Jr.

The things that have not changed break my heart: high teen birth rates, suicides, poverty. The federal government still has some remaining stockpiles of the original 12.5 million pounds of blister agent, 12 million pounds of GB nerve agent, and 2.7 million pounds of VX nerve agent, which it buried in the county starting around the 1940s. Since 1996 our government has been sending those chemicals up an incinerator smokestack, which sits about twenty miles from my childhood home.

But my hometown friends' children now attend the same schools and churches we attended and eat roast beef with their grandparents every Sunday. My friends sit on the town council, fill the mayor's office, and teach in the classrooms. Some say they intended to leave, they just never got around to it—there were gardens to be tended, animals to be fed, and graves to be visited. There were softball games in the park and cookouts in the canyon. Then that little piece of land they used to play on as a kid came up for sale. Their contentment, their community, and their ability to stay in one place touch me. I am impressed by their rootedness. Home is not easily transported. Those of us who left can attest to that. They are impressed by my severed roots, by my ability to leave, by my experiences outside of their world. We all do our best to show the others that our lives are full, well lived. And we all wonder about the things we have given up by making the opposite choice.

In his essay "The Sense of Place," Wallace Stegner writes, "No place is a place until things that have happened in it are re-membered in history, ballads, yarns, legends, or monuments." To put that on an individual level, I'd say no place can be my place until my own things have happened in it—big things such as births, deaths, love, and tragedies, and little things such as dog bites, a special limb of an apple tree that holds secrets of little girls, turning forty, and planting a garden in the backyard of a first home. I now live in a place where I am awakened each morning by a cat that thinks my eyebrows need to be groomed. I am in a place where my partner understands the fine line be-tween companionship and mutual dependence. Every day, one more memory is created in the place where I now reside, and eventually it may feel like home.

I have lived in Tucson more than fourteen years now. It is a place of extremes—monsoon rains immediately absorbed into a dry, cracked earth; dizzying, intense heat that will eventually give way to at least one annual freeze; clear, black nights that open up to blinding sunrises. Its fervor fits my senses. But at times Tucson feels like a noncaring, unemotional system, a col-orless maze of scurrying individuals pulling in and out of strip malls. At other times it feels like a community of friends, a place of compassion and knowledge. The shrinking surrounding desert always draws me with its warmth, with its acute sense of survival; it offers a place of comfort and encouragement.

Not long ago, I went hiking with a friend in the Santa Catalina Mountains north of Tucson. We sat on the summit of Mount Kimball, 7,255 feet in the air, ate bagels and carrots, and talked about the consequential and the inconsequential. The sun hit my back; the cold wind hit my face. I leaned back and let the sharp rocks jab at me while I looked down upon peaks of smaller mountains. Restlessness began to seep from my body. I've shaped a place in Tucson. I've committed acts and created memories. Tucson holds the memories of a man and fourteen years of love. And it holds the attitudes of the West.

But even after being gone more than seventeen years, Utah is the only home I've ever claimed. Something far greater than nostalgia draws me; it is my place of optimal flow. For me, all things come together there: the Oquirrh Mountains that watched over me as a child, five generations of ancestors who molded and formed me, a web of aunts and uncles who track and support me in the most subtle way, the tish-tish-tish of irrigation sprinklers on a summer night, a mother who comes to life wandering the streets of Salt Lake City, a father who finds rare peaceful moments on a two-lane Utah back road, and the portentousness caused by the sound of the Great Salt Lake slapping at the lonely east shore of Stansbury Island on a cold, foggy day. I belong to Utah. It holds the continuity of my life story; it is the incarnation of my existence.

FROM SCOTTSBLUFF, NEBRASKA, to Lingle, Wyoming, an unsettling number of dead raccoons litter the road, their little masked faces turned up toward the sky, toward me, looking surprised and innocent, attached to mashed and mangled bodies. I dodge around them, struck at the same time by a disproportionate number of anti-choice billboards. Both feel like warning signs, as if I'm entering hostile territory. But cows now graze on brown grasses instead of green and mountains fill my vision, signifying my entry into the West. The day is perfect for riding—sunny and cool.

The welcome sign claims Fort Laramie is home to "250 good people and 6 soreheads." When the first party of Saints passed through here, they found Fort John, built by the American Fur Company. It became Fort Laramie in 1849, a military post that served as a supply station for the Pony Express, the Butterfield Overland Stage, the transcontinental telegraph system, and as an operations base for the Plains Indian Wars. It is now operated by the National Park Service, all the old stores and homes furnished with period pieces and Park Service employees in period garb to act out the parts. Fortunately, they are "partially closed" for the winter, which means most of the actors have gone home but the buildings are still open to the public.

In the "general store," however, one lone, enthusiastic employee stands ready to play his part dressed up in cowboy duds and a handlebar mustache. He starts his spiel in a drawl set somewhere between Texas and Alabama, and my eyes apparently glaze over. He cuts it short.

Then he takes a look at my pants and asks if I'm traveling by motorcycle. Once I tell him I am, he launches into the gory details of a motorcycle accident that damn near killed him and ended his riding days. I glare at him. I expect this from nonriders. They love to tell about every motorcycle accident they've seen, heard, or read about and how the rider ended up in multiple pieces or now eats dinner through a straw while staring blankly at a fuzzy television as if I obviously haven't heard about such things and need to. But this guy should know better.

IN THE SMALL town of Guernsey sits a benign-looking National Guard Center very much like the one in my hometown—the kind normally used more for dances, weddings, and basketball games than guarding things—with both entrances to the parking lot blocked by two trucks and four guards packing rifles.

On the south side of Guernsey signs lead me to a sandstone cliff about three miles out of town. Register Cliff became a site of declaration for both the Mormon pioneers and those traveling the Oregon and California Trails. Brigham and his boys, finding the north route of the Platte impassable, crossed the Platte just east of here and traveled the Oregon Trail until they separated again near Big Sandy, Wyoming.

As the Saints passed this point, some left messages for friends or family who would follow, but most carved only their names and the date into the smooth sandstone as if doing so could crystallize a moment in time, letting such a moment live beyond its earthly constraints.

Placing a hand against the smooth dusty surface and scratching with a small, sharp rock alongside—or over the top of—a Gentile name must have provided a moment of refreshed resolve in addition to irreverent triumph among the pious Saints, who looked upon their western migration in the name of God and Joseph as honorable compared to those rushing off to Oregon and California in search of land and gold. Leaving a name and a date on the rock for all who might come later was, in fact, an act of self-preservation, a confirmation of life itself, when death loitered so closely.

I circle the huge rock in solitude—the "signature" trail ruts up the road stop and satisfy most tourists—with a small hope that I might find a familiar name, a direct link, but the possibility quickly slips away. Although a few readable names remain from the 1800s, most have been scrubbed away by local kids eager to declare their own existence and somehow capture their fleeting love for one another. On the side of the rock nearest the parking area, a new entry catches my attention: "September 11, 2001—USA."

The signature trail ruts near Guernsey, where all westward migration trails came together, cut deeply into the Wyoming sandstone outcropping. The erosion of a century and a half has not had much impact on the ruts that are several feet deep in some places. Scrapings of wheel hubs against rut walls are still apparent. The skies to the west, which are turning a beautiful but ominous bluish black, and a good many children hopping in and out of the ruts and screaming to be heard above the wind, attribute to the briefness of my stop.

For the first time since leaving Illinois, I pass two motorcycles packed for touring heading east. The riders wave and I wave back. For no apparent reason at all—they are headed in the opposite direction and can be of absolutely no use to me if I need help in what looks to be a huge storm coming my way—the wave is momentarily comforting. Thunder, lightning, rain, wind, freeway traffic, and road construction converge at the entrance to I-25, which will take me directly north for a while. I immediately wish I had stopped prior to the freeway and switched my light leather gloves, which will be quickly saturated, for the winter gauntlet gloves, but the opportunity has passed.

If all my attention weren't needed just to keep the bike moving down the graded road between cement construction abutments with wind and slanting rain coming from both east and west alternatively and throwing me dangerously close to one cement block, then the other, I might find this moment inevitably Mormon—a perfect opportunity to prove my mettle, to "gird my loins" and live up to my legacy, a harsh testing of my character and faith. But as with so many tests of American modern-day faith, this one is short and easy to skirt. About thirty miles into the storm, signs for the Douglas Best Western Inn begin to appear and my fortitude begins to wane. In a most nonpioneering sort of way, I slap down $60 for a room—$20 more than I've spent any night so far—draw myself a bubble bath, order grilled halibut and cheesecake from room service, and spend two hours with Gregory Peck and Audrey Hepburn in *Roman Holiday*, then sleep like a baby.

THE WIND BLOWS ceaselessly in Wyoming; I know this. But this fact seeps from my memory immediately upon leaving the state to surprise me each time I return. Now heading directly west again, I pass the first eleven miles of the day leaning to my left into a steady wind. The road is scattered with "tar snakes," those annoying squiggles that look like a road-repair kit. In the Arizona sun, they become disconcertingly mushy to a person on two tires, and on a curve, when the very narrow portion of your tires in contact with the road demands and expects solidity, they can be deadly. In the Wyoming wind, they stay firm but still make me dizzy. I spot a sign for Ayres Natural Bridge and wobble down a damaged paved road splashed with chunks of mud fallen from the undersides of trucks and tractors, which in ten minutes' time delivers me to a small spot of paradise.

Each morning of my travels, it seems, I'm handed a gift, a reminder that the journey matters, that the destination can wait. Today I drop out of the wind suddenly and find myself in a lovely small park that seems to have been forgotten by anyone but its devoted caretaker. Sun scatters through trees onto green grass and water rushes along the edge of the grass, tumbling through a hole in red rock that forms Ayers Natural Bridge. The wind blows through the trees above my head in a rush but leaves me untouched. An empty swing beckons; I sit, get a tight grip on the ropes, lift my feet, and tilt my head back toward the damp earth.

The smell is that of the canyons of my youth, some combination of wet leaves, damp dirt, tree bark, and grass. It has a calming effect but also elicits a note of sadness. When I close my eyes I can feel rhythmic movement under me, hear the squeak of leather against leather mixed with the clacking of horseshoes in a shallow creek bed. I can smell the scent of a hardworking horse rising up among the trees.

I fought my father's idea of the West my entire life. I would have loved to embrace it, wanted to love it, but that would have meant loving him, pleasing him, and very early in my life, we had set up an undefined opposition to each other. Still, we came together on horseback in the mountains of Utah, a place that spoke to both of us in such a way as to render our antagonism impossible. My father became a person I seldom saw and barely recognized when, after tightening my cinch and adjusting my stirrups, he swung a leg over the muscled rump of his horse, naturally and quickly threaded a pair of split reins under his first three fingers and over the little finger and thumb of his left hand, and settled into his stirrups and saddle as his horse stepped out on a narrow trail with my horse close behind. The transformation was immediate and significant. He joked, he laughed, he became patient and tolerant of a tired horse's stumble on a high rock in the trail. He also became patient and tolerant of me and surprised me by asking, "How are you doing, sweetheart; are you ready to stop for lunch yet?" I threaded my reins through my left hand the same way he did and relaxed into my saddle.

Late one afternoon, we picked our way through the trees without a trail to follow and came upon a steep and gravelly slope off the side of the mountain. Darkness would be upon us soon, so my father dismounted and told me to do the same. He then tied the reins loosely around the saddle horns, leaving enough room for the horses to put their noses to the ground. They started picking their way down the slope, and we did the same a short ways behind them. But the large sorrel I was riding stumbled and fell, stirrups and straps flopping about wildly, the yellow rain slicker attached to the back of the saddle alternately flashing and disappearing. He finally came to rest on his side at the bottom of the slope, lifted his head for a moment, then dropped it again.

Terrified that the horse was dead, I looked to my father, ready to blame him for the accident, but the look on his face—a mix of fear and compassion—pulled me up short. My father traveled down the slope in great leaps and slides, and I did my best to follow. As we reached the bottom of the slope, the sorrel lifted his head again, scrambled to his feet, shook himself off, and stood ready for me to remount. "Big-footed, clumsy son of a bitch," mumbled my father as he ran his hands down the legs and under the belly of the sorrel, straightened the saddle, tightened the cinch, and held the stirrup for me.

# 23

THE SERENITY FROM AYRES NATURAL BRIDGE PARK
carries me through the mess of traffic and road construction in
Casper, and when I'm spit out the other end of town on Highway 220, everything changes. Dropping down out of Casper, I
feel like a piece of lint on a stream of air. Open space runs free
until it's stopped short by mountains. It soon finds its way
around them and runs free again until it juts up against another. This game goes on indefinitely. The beauty of the mountains force clichés to roll off the tongue. Majestic. Glorious.
Splendid. Grand. They all fit. I've never felt so small in all my
life and that feels remarkably good. Here I don't have to understand the world; here I can just be a tiny part of it.

A few miles outside of Casper on Bessemer Bend Road, I
find the Saints' last crossing of the North Platte River. Today
the river bends quietly through tall swaying grasses in what
seems almost an apologetic manner. But in spite of the gentle
beauty here, the place also holds something of the severity of
so much faith answered by so much suffering. I feel it immediately as I walk through the grass to the river's edge. Near here,

Hannah laid the body of her stepson, James, in the snow with little ceremony.

The day after Hannah walked away from the son she had raised since he was three years old, she reached the place I now stand: Bessemer Bend. I stoop on the bank of the gentle river and drop my hand into the cold water; an early fall breeze tosses my hair over my eyes. Hannah stood on the opposite bank in a flurry of sleet and snow. She dropped the yoke of the handcart and stepped out of the shafts long enough to make sure the girls were tucked safely in to the load. She told them to hang on tight, stepped back inside the shafts, picked up her load, and took a deep breath before plunging into the frigid river amid floats of slushy ice.

The handcart Mormons chose this crossing because the river was shallow here—two feet deep most of the way, a little more in some spots. A toll bridge had been established by Gentiles upriver shortly after 1847, but Hannah's party passed it by, having no means to pay the toll. Hannah may have known this was the last crossing of the Platte River, and she may have taken heart in that. But she likely didn't know, and it's just as well, that she would soon reach the first of many crossings of the even colder Sweetwater River fifty miles from here.

BACK IN IOWA city twelve weeks before, Hannah and her children had finally been able to secure a handcart, and on July 28 they'd departed in the company of 572 other Saints under the supervision of Edward Martin. This ragtag group would henceforth be known as the Martin Handcart Company. I know the date and location of her son's death. I know the ages of her children. I know the magnitude and force of her desire. The rest of her story I have pieced together from a few details she left behind and journals of other women traveling alongside her.

According to Brigham's plan, each adult was allowed a mere seventeen pounds of luggage and each child, ten. Upon leaving Iowa City, however, most of them had loads strapped high and wide, and many were pulling as much as five hundred pounds, unwilling to part with beloved books, dishes, and furniture after already parting with home, family, and all else dear and familiar.

Pulling across the Iowa prairie presented few problems, except for one or two hints that the hastily thrown together carts would not serve them well on the trail ahead. In Florence, Nebraska, the leaders of the Church debated whether to send the Martin Company and the Willie Handcart Company, which had left Iowa City about a week in front of the Martin Company, on to Salt Lake City or hold them over until spring. The majority of Church leaders were eager to prove Brother Brigham's plan a success by getting the Saints to the Salt Lake Valley quickly and cheaply. Holding them over in Florence would require supplies not readily available. The lone dissenter, at least the only one willing to speak up, was a man by the name of Levi Savage. According to the writings of Emma James, who traveled with her father, mother, and six siblings:

> *Brother Savage said with tears streaming down his face, "Brothers and sisters, wait until spring to make this journey. Some of the strong may get through in case of bad weather, but the bones of the weak and the old will strew the way." I remember that when he finished there was a long time of silence. I was frightened. Father looked pale and sick. I turned to mother to see what she was thinking and all I saw was her old determined look . . . "We must put our trust in the Lord as we have always done," said mother and that was that.*

Emma's father would die on the trail shortly after the first snowfall.

With the Martin Company, Hannah left Florence on August 25, a warm Nebraska day offering wildflowers and assurance. Little three-year-old Hannah and five-year-old Margaret ran and played along the way, picking flowers and colored rocks, then climbed on top of the stack of belongings when they got tired, as Hannah and James pulled and pushed. As they trudged through the deep and endless Platte Valley sand, many of the company began to understand Brigham's weight limitations. The loads got smaller and lighter as the Saints forced themselves to part with cherished belongings, placing them carefully beside the trail as if there were some hope of retrieving them later. Once they were in the arid West, the green wood on the carts dried and split apart like kindling. The continual need to stop and rebuild handcarts slowed the pace to a torturous crawl up the Platte Valley, delay on top of delay.

Toward the end of September, somewhere near the Nebraska-Wyoming border, Hannah found it difficult to walk on the frozen ground, now covered with slippery frost each morning. The girls had lost their gaiety and their ability to skip along beside the handcart. The slow creep across the Platte Valley had diminished their food, and each adult was now rationed one pound of flour per day, which they usually mixed with a little water and ate as gruel. Hannah likely gave part of hers to keep her children well, as was common. When her stomach snarled with hunger, she simply replaced thoughts of food with thoughts of God and marched toward Zion. They were hungry enough then, but the ration would soon be cut to three-quarters of a pound, again to half a pound, then ounce by ounce until they were scraping flour off burlap sacks along with the lint and making a meal of that.

By the time they reached Fort Laramie on October 8, James staggered behind the handcart, pushing as best he could, trying not to hold on to the cart and put an extra burden on his mother up front. As they started the steep climb into the mountains, Hannah paused in the tracks for a moment when she felt a delicate touch on her head, once, then again. Her empty stomach clutched as snow fell gently around her. Then she picked up the yoke, possibly whispered a small prayer, and continued on.

Snow gathered on the frozen ground, at first a few inches, providing a temporary cushion for her steps. But the snow continued to fall day after miserable day, and soon Hannah plodded along the splotched red, snowy path, stained by the bleeding feet of those she followed, pulling the cart deeper into the mountains. On October 18, saved from the last icy crossing of the Platte River, James dropped into the snow for the last time. Hannah helped cover his pale, emaciated body in snow with several others; by this time there were no single burials. The Martin Company started with a shortage of men, causing an excess burden on those they had, who at this point had given their all. Many of the deaths were men who were simply dropping from exhaustion.

"The Lord took away the sting of death," Hannah would later say when asked about the day she lost James. By this time on the trail, the dead were considered the blessed ones. Hannah was stoical about the dead, relieved "that they were being taken from this extreme trial and suffering."

The horrific irony of the handcart pioneers is that before they reached the frozen Rocky Mountains, they were too weak from starvation and exhaustion to pull heavy loads. Two days before reaching the last crossing of the Platte, they were forced to lighten their loads by casting off extra clothing and bedding if they had any hope of dragging their remaining possessions and their wretched bodies through knee-deep snow up steep mountain grades. Consequently, few had dry clothing to change into after crossing at Bessemer Bend, and their clothing quickly froze to their skeletal frames. In this state, they marched onward.

I read somewhere that those who love Christ want to suffer in imitation of his suffering. If that's true, then the love for Christ must have been deeper than the Wyoming snow among this pathetic party of believers in October of 1856. When I first read about Hannah and her little girls, I assumed they must have had someone to help them after James's death. But they did not, and the raw truth is that Hannah was no worse off than the person ahead or behind her on the trail; there were simply far more who needed help than there were people to offer it. Hannah was on her own. The most anyone could offer now would be to gather her body and lay it to rest if need be.

The group set up camp that night several miles from the river crossing. Her skirts frozen to her body, Hannah pulled her cart into camp close to dark and, with hands beyond any feeling at all, fumbled among her belongings for a tin plate. With this, she cleared a place in the snow large enough to gather her daughters and lie down for the night. With the ground too frozen to pitch a tent and the tent too frozen to unravel, Hannah took what meager bedding she had left, propped herself against a rock with a daughter in each arm, and waited for morning.

Elizabeth Sermon, traveling alongside Hannah in the Martin Company, would bury her husband in these snowy mountains and be forced to commit unspeakable acts to get her four children—John, nine; Henry, seven; Robert, five; and Marian, three—to Zion. Years later she would describe those acts in a letter to her son Henry:

*I had to take a portion of poor Robert's feet off which pierced my very sould [sic]. I had to sever the leaders with a pair of scissors.*

*Little did I think when I bought them in old England that they would be used for such a purpose. Every day some portion was decaying until the poor boy's feet were all gone. Then John's began to freeze; then after a while my own . . . I was terribly put to for clothes to wrap my poor boy's legs in, his feet all gone. I got all I could from the camp, then I used my underclothing until I had but two skirts left on my body, and as such I finished up my journey for my wardrobe would not be replenished where I was . . . A severe storm came up. I think it was on the Sweet Water, but I was so troubled I forget all about the names of places. My eldest boy John's feet decaying, my boys both of them losing their limbs, their father dead, my own feet very painful, I thought, "Why can't I die?"*

Patience Loader, in her early twenties, also traveled in the Martin Company with her father, who died on the trail before reaching the mountains, her mother, three sisters, and two brothers. The experiences described in her journal entries are unbearably typical throughout the Martin Company:

*One morning as we was getting ready to leave camp I saw . . . two dear boys. The eldest was eleven years old I believe and youngest not more than four or five years. The eldest was crawling along on his hands and knees. His poor feet was so frozen the blood running from them in the snow as the poor thing was making his way to the sick wagon. The other dear child crying by his brother side his poor little arms and hands all scabs with chilblains and scarcely anything on to cover his body.*

From Jane Griffiths, also in the Martin Company, as told to Ella Campbell:

*The night that my oldest brother died there were 19 deaths in camp. In the morning we would find their starved and frozen bod-*

*ies right by the side of us; not knowing when they died until day-*
*light revealed the ghastly sight to us. I remember two women that*
*died which sitting by me. My mother was cooking some cakes of*
*bread for one of them. When she had passed one to her she acted*
*so queer then tossed it in the fire and dropped over dead.*

The journal entry that touches me most deeply doesn't deal
at all with the horrors incurred; it deals with the immeasurabil-
ity of love. Elizabeth Horrocks Kingsford, who traveled in the
Martin Company with her husband, who died on October 25
lying next to her on the bank of the Sweetwater River, and
three small children, wrote this description of the last crossing
of the Sweetwater:

*It was a severe operation to many of the company. It was the last*
*ford the company waded over. The water was not less than two*
*feet deep, perhaps a little more in the deepest parts but it was in-*
*tensely cold. The ice was three or four inches thick and the bottom*
*of the river muddy and sandy . . . When the handcarts arrived at*
*the bank of the river one poor fellow who was greatly worn down*
*with travel exclaimed: have we got to cross here? Being answered*
*yes he again exclaimed: oh dear, I can't go through that. His heart*
*sank within him and he burst into tears. But his heroic wife came*
*to his aid, and in a sympathetic tone said, "don't cry Jimmie,*
*I'll pull the handcart for you."*

"Now abideth faith, hope, and love these three; but the
greatest of these is love," says 1 Corinthians 13:13.

The last crossing of the Platte River is marked only by a Bu-
reau of Land Management interpretive panel—no visitors
center, no earnest missionaries to recite their memorized
lines—for that I am grateful. Here in the stiff grass along the
river, I come as close to Hannah as I'll ever be. I feel sad here

but calm. I've read and reread these journals and many more with similar stories. I've read about men eating the flesh off their own fingers to stay alive and women frozen to the ground by their hair, mistaken for dead in the early light of morning when they were unable to rise. I've had my heart tugged in every direction by them. I've railed in anger over the arrogance of the men who urged them, ragged and wretched, into those frozen mountains. I've wept in despair of their suffering. I've wallowed in confusion of the zealousness that made them believe they could survive such a reckless plan. But I realize, here alone on the spot at which Hannah somehow steeled her backbone and walked into the icy river on that blustery October day, that it wasn't about survival. Whether they arrived in Salt Lake Valley or returned to God along the way wasn't the issue. What mattered was the act, the movement; what mattered was faith. To me, an elusive, abstract notion I'm still trying to work out; to Hannah and the others who walked the same path, a concept as solid as the frozen ground they slept on. The most staggering of all journal entries are those such as this one from Patience Loader: "I can truthfully say that we never felt to murmer at the hardships we was passing through. I can say we put our trust in god and he heard and answered our prayers and brought us through to the valley."

And my great-great-grandmother's resounding "No, never!" when asked if she regretted leaving England and enduring the sacrifices of the trail, including that of her son's life. How many modern-day believers, I wonder, can proclaim a faith so deep, so profound.

There were a few who dropped off along the way, who found the test too harsh, who felt God and the Church had asked too much of them, but not many. Proclamations of faith from survivors of the Martin Handcart Company, such as those above, are plentiful. The cynical part of me might think the faith stems from a reflection ten or twenty years later, an easier time when wounds have healed and a fireplace warms the damaged feet. But I'd be wrong. I feel that as sure as I feel the grass under my feet and the wind blowing off the Platte River into my face.

I know that as Hannah put one bloody foot into the snow in front of the other, she walked in faith. She expected God to take care of her and her children, and when she arrived in Salt Lake City with toes burst open and bleeding, with half-starved and half-frozen, shrunken daughters, with the body of her son lying in the snow behind her, she felt God had done just that. God had delivered on his promise. Still believing, Hannah died among the Saints in the Kingdom of Zion at Paradise, Utah, forty-seven years later at the age of eighty-one.

# 24

INDEPENDENCE ROCK RESEMBLES THE REMAINS OF A prehistoric creature that took a rest along the Sweetwater River and never got up again. Like Register Cliff, the dome-shaped piece of granite served the purpose of noting passersby. Most early Mormon journals mention it in a celebratory mode, a milestone reached, signifying a good portion of their journey behind them. The handcart Saints, following a decade after the first wave of Saints, hardly mention it at all, not finding much reason to celebrate and by then barely having the energy to lift a rare cracker to their mouths, let alone chisel their names on a rock. At one point in time when travel to Oregon and California was at its peak, never ones to miss a business opportunity, the Mormons stationed a couple of professional stonecutters at Independence Rock to charge the Gentiles $1 to $5 a name, depending on the length, for engraving.

The rare Wyoming roadside bathroom makes Independence Rock a popular stop today; however, few people journey farther than one hundred feet from their cars, so as I make the quarter-mile walk to the rock, I leave the sound of car doors slamming and kids screaming behind. The scratchings of those who once passed here are faint and barely readable, but I pause on the far side of the rock, away from the parking lot, where a few names remain and place my hand against the smooth granite. I understand the compunction to scrawl a name on a rock, very much feeling the need myself to proclaim my own existence, to confirm my reality here in this vast landscape, feeling as if that act alone might prevent the land from quietly devouring me.

Six miles down the road from Independence Rock, a wretched group of Saints huddled in a cove to wait for a release from suffering in whatever form it might take. The place is now known as Martin's Cove. After the last crossing of the Platte River on October 19, the Martin Handcart Company traveled one day, then took refuge to wait out a blizzard. It is probable they dug in to wait for death also, and there likely wasn't one among them who didn't know it. More than a week later, on October 28, they were found by two men on horseback sent by Brigham from Salt Lake City, part of a rescue party that was snowed in about thirty miles up the trail. With hundreds needing help and only two men to give it, little could be done, but the encounter gave the dismal bunch enough hope to set them moving again through the snow toward the rescue wagons. Had the two men not kept riding through the snow to satisfy their own curiosity as to whether any human could survive such conditions, it is unlikely a single member of the Martin Company ever would have moved again.

Halfway between the last crossing of the Platte and the rescuers who arrived like angels on horseback, Hannah, living now only for the purpose of keeping her two little girls from a snowbank burial, turned thirty-four on October 25. I have no pictures of Hannah at that age and few details of her as that young woman. Still my great-great-grandmother is vivid in my mind, physically unremarkable but spiritually stunning. She doesn't think of herself that way, sees no reason at all to entertain thoughts about her own resolve, simply does whatever is before her to be done. She would be surprised to know that her magnitude shames and inspires me every mile of this trip.

By November 2, Hannah and her fellow travelers had all straggled into Martin's Cove, where they were again snowed in for days and quickly ran through the rescuers' supplies. Another group of rescuers coming up the trail from Salt Lake City—seasoned men who had by now been over this trail several times—were so daunted by the amount of snow that they gave the Martin Company up for dead and turned back. But again, a few of the toughest rode on, found the hangers-on still alive on nothing but the grace of God, and sent back for the wagons.

A few years back, the Mormon Church bought some of this land from the private owners of the Sun Ranch. I was told, although I don't know the truth of it, that the land was once strewn with the remains of handcarts. Less noticeable would have been the remains of close to 60 people who died after the last crossing of the Platte. By the time the survivors of the Martin Company reached Salt Lake City, most of them in rescue wagons but a few still walking on their own tattered feet and pulling in shafts, close to 150 of their relatives lay dead on the trail, and many of those who survived would make a sacrifice of feet, legs, and hands.

The doomed handcart operation may be the only dark smudge on an otherwise brilliant and unique orchestration of mass migration conducted by Brigham Young over two decades. He certainly must take some blame for working the emigrating Saints into a zealous froth to reach Zion with his speeches full of grit and promise. To begin with, his judgment had been proven sound over the first ten-year testing period, but even more important, he spoke as the Prophet of the Lord, and if the Prophet says, "Let them gird up their loins and walk through and nothing shall hinder or stay them," who's to say otherwise? But there was plenty of blame to go around, and Brigham was more than willing to share it. He placed the majority of the blame squarely on the head of Franklin Richards, his loyal follower and leader of the British mission, for not holding the Martin and Willie Companies in Florence, Nebraska, over the winter, and it came down on Richards like the falling walls of Sodom.

Much like his predecessor, Brigham didn't take criticism well. Whereas Joseph would simply cast the malcontent out of his circle and out of his church through excommunication, Brigham's style was much more flamboyant. He favored public humiliation through colorful and explosive speeches as a reminder to others who might be in a position to inadvertently cast doubt upon him. On November 2, about a week before the survivors of the Willie Company would begin staggering into the valley, and no doubt knowing what he would see when they did, Brigham delivered a fiery speech in the tabernacle to unequivocally let his Saints know precisely where the blame could and could not be placed: "If any man, or woman, complains of me or my Counselors, in regard to the lateness of some of this season's immigration, let the curse of God be on them and blast their substance with mildew and destruction, until their names are forgotten from the earth." Eager to prove that the faultiness resided in the execution, not in the plan itself, Brigham continued the handcart operation after the Martin and Willie disasters for three more years without further calamity.

AS EXPECTED, THE Mormon Church has placed a visitors center at the Martin Handcart site. As I pull into the parking lot, I note that the missionary-to-visitor ratio is about four to one. I have more interest in walking into the cove itself than spending a half hour in the visitors center, but the missionaries—all older folks—look upon me so eagerly as I remove gloves and helmet that I'm loath to disappoint them. At least that's what I tell myself. The real story is that I haven't been in the company of Mormons now since I left Winter Quarters, and I'm just as eager to fold myself into the familiar comfort of their fellowship as they are to have me.

I'm assigned to a tall, big-shouldered, big-bellied, gray-haired Wyoming cowboy–looking missionary wearing a bolo tie and cowboy boots who gruffly retells the stories of the Martin Handcart Company. When he gets to the part where the rescuers arrive from Salt Lake City, I'm surprised to hear a quiver in his voice. He asks me if I had any relatives with the Martin Company, then helps me find Hannah's and her children's names on the wall of company members—the name of James in gold along with the others entombed in the snow along the trail. I tell my missionary I want to skip the film, that I just want to walk out to the cove instead, and he tells me he understands.

"Hold on," he says. "I can get somebody to give you a ride out there and drop you off if you don't mind walking back. That way you can have some time alone in the cove."

I thank him and accept his offer. Another missionary pulls up in a golf cart and tells me he's waiting for some people who want to go out also. He whispers a piece of advice to sit up front if I don't want to be bounced out on the road along the way. He reads my mind about the others and says, "Don't worry, I'm not dropping them off. They just want to ride out, snap a picture, and come right back."

Two couples in their sixties come out of the bathrooms and get in the back. One of the men takes a look at my pants and asks if I'm traveling by motorcycle.

"I used to ride," he says, "but had to give it up."

"You aren't going to tell me an accident story, are you?" I ask.

"Had to get my hip replaced after my accident."

His wife elbows him and says, "I think she just told you she didn't want to hear about it."

"I was too old to be riding anyway," he says, and I'm just about to tell him I don't think there's an age limit when his wife breaks in.

"Where are you from?" she asks, trying to change the subject. I tell her the whole thing—where I live now, where I'm from originally, and so on. She tells me they are from Cache Valley, and I tell her my parents are from there also. She says they are originally from Brigham City, so I tell her I have an aunt and uncle in Brigham City and tell her their names.

"Oh, for heaven's sake," she says. "Don and Edna are your aunt and uncle? We know them real well; we used to be in their ward." She again elbows her husband. "Don and Edna Nelson are her aunt and uncle," she says as if he weren't there for the conversation. He grunts, apparently still smarting over not being able to tell his accident story. And so it goes with Mormons from Utah. If you talk long enough, chances are you'll find a connection.

At the top of the hill near the trail that leads to the cove, the missionary gives me directions for walking back to the visitors center and tells me to keep an eye out for rattlesnakes. I thank him, bid good-bye to the others, and watch them bounce away before I walk down off the hill.

As I enter the cove, located around a small rise and tucked in neatly against the mountains, the incessant Wyoming wind quiets as if out of reverence. In spite of the snake warning, I feel the need to wander down off the trail into the brown grasses and sagebrush, feeling pretty sure these pants and boots would be hard to penetrate anyway, and find a rock to sit on. The hush that drops over the cove is haunting, and when a short burst of wind blows through, it provides a moment of relief, a moment to take a breath, but sends a chill up both arms and along the back of my neck.

One woman, distraught over the idea of leaving her husband's body to be torn apart by the ever-circling wolves and unable to bury him in the frozen ground, managed to hang his body in a tree before leaving here. The last thing she saw from the back of a rescue wagon as it moved slowly out of the cove was her husband's body poised in that tree, as if an angel of God would retrieve it as soon as they were out of sight. Here in the heavy stillness, the shadow of death lingers. But so also do the testimonies of the devoted. And if anyone ever deserved a deliverance from God, it would have been that wife. Sitting in the cove that simultaneously witnessed despair and hope, acquiescence and resolution, affliction and comfort, it's not impossible to believe that her last prayer for him may have been answered.

When I arrive back at the center almost two hours after I left it, the driver who dropped me off declares, "You made it; we've been watching for you," and tears immediately well up in my eyes. He hands me his handkerchief without embarrassment. "I go up there to sit myself sometimes," he says.

THE SUN HANGS low in the sky by the time I leave Martin's Cove. I haven't seen a gas station since Casper, but according to my map, there are three possibilities between here and Lander, where I'll stop for the night: Muddy Gap, Jeffrey City, and Sweetwater Station. The turnoff I want to Highway 220 meets up with 287 just before reaching Muddy Gap, so I continue on to Jeffrey City.

Jeffrey City—inappropriately named—has two gas stations, one that looks as if it's been closed for years and one that seems only temporarily closed, but I'm unable to determine if temporary means fifteen minutes or a few weeks. Between Jeffrey City and Sweetwater Station sits another small Mormon visitors center called Sixth Crossing, which tells the story of the Willie Handcart Company. I consider stopping to ask the missionaries for help, and I know without a doubt they would rush around to find a gallon of gas for the bike or drive me to the nearest gas station with a gas can. But I hesitate. I hesitate because it feels like the act of a hysterical woman. Chances are I can fill up with gas in Sweetwater, and if not, I can likely make it all the way to Lander. No reason to panic here and rush back to the safety of the Mormons.

At Sweetwater Station, nothing more than a smattering of houses, my odometer tells me I've gone about 160 miles on this tank, and Lander is 39 miles from Sweetwater. I have no gas gauge but figure I can travel about 200 miles on a tank. I don't include in my calculation the fact that I've driven head-on into a wind much of the morning and up steep mountain grades with a heavily loaded bike, but it matters not. I'm as low on options as I am on gas. I start toward Lander.

Dark blue and gray clouds roll into the sky and the temperature drops a good ten degrees, making the gas situation feel a little more ominous. Cars are scarce out here; wind, sagebrush, and clusters of rigid yellow and gold grasses plentiful. They run unfettered from the road to the foot of the mountains, then stop abruptly and turn the land over to rock. I once heard someone describe this area as desolate and ugly, and I was shocked by the description. It was my first exposure to the East Coast idea of beauty residing in the color green. I love this unforgiving land—at once tough and fragile—and the expectations it holds of whoever wants to dwell here.

I once met a Sweetwater rancher well into his nineties living alone out here, with only a horse for company, as he had done the better part of seventy years. He had never married and had no children, but friends had convinced him when he turned ninety that he should move to town and make his life easier. He sold his ranch to the Mormon Church—it was where the members of the Willie Handcart Company were camped and dying when the rescuers found them—and moved into Lander. He stayed close to six months, then called Church officials and asked if he could move back into his old ranch house. They welcomed him back and told him to stay as long as he liked. He said he was thinking he might like to spend the rest of his life out here where absolutely nothing can stop the wind and snow from blowing across his wrinkled face. As far as I know, he's still here.

In spite of my near-panicky mood, I can't help but notice the desert smells like rain, a smell hard to describe to a person who grew up around lush green grasses and dense forests. The dampness hangs in the air and, because it is such a rare treat, the dry sage and crackling grasses and alkali-encrusted soil reach up to meet it, unable to contain their anticipation for its arrival. They converge at the level of your nostrils in a musky bouquet that can make the toughest Wyoming cowboy well up.

I try to drive "sensibly" as if that's going to help, keep the bike around sixty miles per hour, a nice steady pace. And I start to make plans, start to look for places along the road to stash the bike if I need to. But like I said, this is unforgiving land, and it provides no such shelter. A narrow shoulder—less than two feet wide—runs alongside me then drops off at a fairly steep grade into brown, thorny weeds. My only option would be to leave the bike on the narrow shoulder and hitch a ride into town. There's a chance that a bike could be left alone untouched for days out here. There's an equally good chance I might return to find my clothing and gear spread all over the road. The most likely possibility is that a hefty gust of wind will send the bike tumbling down off the road and into the weeds. And what forty-five-year-old woman in her right mind hitches a ride in the middle of Nowhere, Wyoming, in the rain and the dark?

My odometer reads 183 when I hear the first cough and feel the first hesitation in the engine. My stomach clutches. No, no, no, not yet! This can't be right! My speed drops suddenly although my hand is steady on the throttle. As I coast to a stop, I hear a wheezing, gasping sound, and I search frantically for whatever might be slowly dying nearby, horrified at the possibility of what I might see. But as I do this, I realize that what's gasping is my bike, in a horribly animalistic way, like a pig being slaughtered. I immediately shut it off and sit for a moment to compose myself. The wind shoves me from one side to the other. My legs shake and I feel as if I might drop the bike, so I put the side stand down for support and lean a little to the left.

I know from one other unfortunate experience on a mountain road in New Mexico that my bike does some sort of vapor-lock thing when the gas in the tank gets too low. I don't know the mechanics behind it, I just know that opening the gas tank and releasing the vapor lock might get me down the road a few more miles. "Please, please, please," I find myself saying out loud, without concerning myself about the entity I might be addressing.

The key drops from my shaking hand as I pull it from the ignition. Squatting by the bike not only allows me to locate my key but quells the shaking in my legs, so remaining there for a moment makes sense to me. A car zooms by like a threat, barely moving over enough to avoid me, so I straddle the bike again, tip it upright, tug my tank bag toward me enough to uncover my gas cap, and open it, expecting to hear a sigh of relief from the bike—but I hear nothing. I jiggle the bike back and forth while peering into the tank, hoping to see some liquid sloshing, but I see only darkness. The cap closes with the thud of my gloved palm while I utter one more pathetic plea of "Please" and hit the starter button. Nothing. I breathe deeply to hold the panic at bay and look across the scrubby desert to the mountains. Both are inexplicably part of this situation, always testing me to see if I belong. The bike should at least sound like it's trying to start and I'm getting nothing at all. Then I recall a safety feature on this bike, which prevents me from driving away with my side stand still down and killing myself on a left-hand turn. I kick the side stand up and push the starter button again. The engine purrs.

I ride as if on a temperamental horse, gently coaxing it up to around fifty-five miles per hour. It takes me another ten miles, close enough to Lander to see billboards for motels and restaurants, then the jerking begins again, the coughing, the dreadful gasping. I pull over quickly and shut it off, certain that I'm inflicting permanent damage.

The late-afternoon sun has broken through the clouds and Lander lies six miles over a few hills, an easy walk. After tugging my tank bag toward me one more time and opening the gas cap again, I reposition my tank bag awkwardly around it to leave it open. The bike starts again and takes me about two more miles before it begins wheezing in the most horrific manner yet, but a roadside sign makes promises of fuel ahead so I keep going. Choking, gasping, wheezing, coughing, we heave forward a bit at a time. I feel like I'm torturing a thirsting cow, poking it with a stick as it staggers toward its watering hole. As I top the hill, it sucks in its last gasp and dies. But just down the hill, on my right so I don't have to cross traffic, a gorgeous shiny-red station with six pumps! We float off the hill to the nearest pump; the black hoses reach out to welcome us with fuel for the tortured beast.

I start it up again on another prayer that I haven't done any permanent damage and we run smoothly into town and into the parking lot of the Lander Best Western Hotel. After checking in, I pull the bike around the back, sneak a fluffy white towel out, and wipe the bike down gently in an attempt to make amends.

I WANDER THE streets of Lander for two days unnoticed, eating alone in restaurants without turning a single head. Apparently, I look as if I belong in this town where the old West—ranchers and cowboys—butts up against the new West— environmentalists and outdoor guides. I shop at the corner drugstore, check my e-mail at the library, and sit on the lawn outside the city building. I relax into the West.

Over a burger at an outdoor picnic table along Lander's main street, I make the mistake of reading a local newspaper— eight college boys killed by a drunk driver, a young local kid. I've never been afraid of death, although I've always had what I assume is the common sentiment about death: now wouldn't be a good time. But from time to time as a motorcyclist, I've been overwhelmed—almost paralyzed—by the level of violence that nice, normal human beings willingly inflict on one another. A teenage girl willing to play loosely with my life if she's in a hurry to meet her friends; a businessman on a cell phone and drinking coffee willing to gamble with her life for one more business deal. After reading the article, I feel doubtful that I'll make it back to Tucson alive. But I've made it back to the West, and for now that's just enough.

My father lingers in my consciousness when I'm in this sort of small Western town. He's been drawn to them his entire life, knowing what I never understood until many years later—that this is what every Western town should look like, sparse and small and miles away from the next Western town. Places like Salt Lake City and Phoenix and Tucson and Denver and Las Vegas (not to mention almost every city in California) simply make no sense in the arid West.

Lander, now, would be too big for my father, and the infusion of environmentalists—a group he sees not as the children and grandchildren of Western ranchers, which many of them are, but instead a "bunch of Easterners" who know nothing about the West, don't belong here, and have no right to be here—would keep him emitting a steady stream of obscenities. My father never cared much for the town I grew up in— too large, population about 14,000, and too close to Salt Lake City. When he bought the ranch, when I was about ten years old, he bought a piece of land 150 miles from our home between the towns of Ferron, population 1,600, and Clawson, population 150.

While I tried my best at my young age to be contrary to everything my father pursued in his quest of the Western life, I loved the ranch itself—not the lifestyle, but the land, the farming side of ranching. I loved walking through the alfalfa on a summer morning, stumbling over irrigation rows when the hay was just high enough to be cut, leaving the front of my Levi's soaked with dew. I loved pulling off a shoe and making a footprint an inch deep in alkali soil, like I was stepping into newly fallen snow.

My father loved being a cowboy; this better fit his dream of what the Western man should be. Ranchers/cowboys in the West have always looked down their noses a bit at farmers; nothing nearly heroic enough about digging in the dirt. Tough to make a good movie out of that. The fact is, the Western cowboy exists mostly only in movies, books, and in the minds and dreams of people like my father and brother. There are some who make their living as "real cowboys," if you will, ranch hands who make just enough money to keep themselves fed and clothed, but seldom enough to actually own a piece of the land they work. Most are like my brother—weekend cowboys. Holding down eight-to-five federal government jobs and counting their vacation hours in the hopes they can make it to the rodeo two states away by Saturday night. Or my father, who continued to teach school until the age of retirement so he could be a weekend and summertime rancher.

Nevertheless, my father and brother were in heaven at branding time—grabbing a calf by front leg and flank, lifting it into the air and slamming it to the ground with enough force to knock the fight out of it; a hot fire holding several irons; the sizzle and smell of burning hair and skin; the tortured bawling of the calf; the dust blowing under the calf's snorting nostrils; the wild eyes of its mother pacing close by; a vivid red stream of blood from a fresh castration; the bloody testicles scattered around the dirt. With this part of ranching, I found my defiant stance easy to hold.

At the hotel, I do what I've always done when my father overwhelms me: run to the safety of my mother. She answers the phone hopefully, waiting to hear my voice, needing to know I'm OK and one more day closer to home.

I ask my mother if she remembers the two years before I started kindergarten, before my grandfather died and my father's ranching mission began. My brother and sister were safely tucked away in school each day, and for those two years I was my mother's only child. Once a week, we drove to Tooele Bowl for the Wednesday morning ladies' league, and on Thursday afternoons we had a standing appointment at the Ritz Beauty Salon to have Mom's hair done. Every night I helped her wrap her head with toilet paper to preserve her beautiful hairdo until the next Thursday.

I know she's smiling as I talk; I can feel it. Maybe that was the last time we both felt truly safe, thinking that life would hold for us nothing more stressful than growing daffodils in the built-in planter box under the living room window. I remember her laughter from those days, a sound that faded in later years. She must have still believed at that time that she'd find her way back to the Mormon Church with her husband at her side and her children in tow.

"How's the praying going?" I ask her.

"You're still alive, aren't you?" she says.

# 25

THERE'S A BITE IN THE AIR AS I PACK THE BIKE TO LEAVE Lander; it feels like an autumn morning. When I pulled the bike around the back side of the hotel to a gravel lot two days ago, it was the only vehicle there. Now cars are tight against it—a firefighters' convention began last night—and I barely have enough room to fasten the saddlebags into place. When straps are tightened, tires and lights checked, zippers zipped, everything in order, I straddle the bike to back out from my narrow parking slot. The bike won't budge. I'm on flat ground, but the rear tire sits in a hole left from the last rain and I don't have enough strength to push it out. I have two choices—unload the bike and try again or get off the bike and try walking it back. The second choice makes the most sense, but it puts me at the greatest risk for dropping the bike.

I dismount, place my helmet on the grass, and sit down next to it. A big guy with muscles bulging out of a firefigher T-shirt walks toward me with a nod and pulls something out of the trunk of the car next to me. I hate to look like a helpless woman, but at the moment I fit the bill and he's my knight.

"Could you give me a push?" I ask, and he smiles. I know he rides because he knows to push me slowly and gently so I don't lose control of the bike. He pushes until the bike clears the cars and is turned toward the exit, then he strides back, picks my helmet up off the grass, and brings it to me.

"Thanks a lot," I say.

"Keep the shiny side up," he says smiling and disappears into the building.

From a pullout a short way out of Lander, I look down on a sweep of red rock plateaus dropping off to meet rolling brown hills decorated every so often by a splotch of green near a trickle of water. On car trips, my father used to stop at such places, stand outside the car, and shake his head in awe. We frustrated him—us kids and my mother—by refusing to see what he saw, by refusing to let the land roll over us in waves of melancholy the way it did him. Most times we refused to even step out of the car unless our stiffened joints needed stretching.

It took me years to recognize the longing that washed over my father's face in those moments, and I'm not sure I entirely understood it until now. The geography of the West belongs to another day, it belongs to the contemporaries of Brigham Young and Hannah Middleton Hawkey. It tolerates the great-great-grandchildren of that era, but we are not allowed to reside comfortably until we acknowledge the true spirit of the place, and those of us who have not done so can never shake the feeling that the fit is not quite right. It's a nagging feeling, as if you just can't get close enough to the land no matter what you do. It makes you want to roll in the dirt; it makes you want to lie down on a plateau and offer yourself up in sacrifice; but about all you can really figure out to do is sit down among the sagebrush and cry.

This unidentified longing, this need to be taken in by the land and be connected to the past, drove my father to purchase those 250 acres of alkali-crusted soil broken up by a 70-acre patch of alfalfa and an irrigation pond in central Utah, opening up a financial drain on the family that would practically suck the life out of my mother. For this, I hated my father. I hated him for the tears my mother would shed over unpaid bills, over never-purchased Christmas gifts for her children, over bedroom drapes filled with holes that would eventually rot right off the curtain rods. But mostly I hated him for the yearning that sank low in my stomach every time I walked through the high, damp alfalfa, for that persistent ache that arose whenever I wedged myself between two bales in the haystack, whenever I chewed on a stiff piece of clean, green hay. Often I would find my mother in the same spot. She would quickly swipe at her eyes, give me a big smile, pull me into her warmth, and point out the beauty in the barren, purplish hills that surrounded us—and the ache would fade.

My mother can't understand the longing my father and I share and never will because she never lost the connection. Standing in the place I'm standing now, she would simply nod her head and move on, the same way her great-grandmother Anna Maria likely did when she passed this spot in 1866, certain that this is where God intended her to be.

My father and I still stand at odds, an opposite stance strangely driven by the exact same yearning. He calls me a "radical environmentalist" and a "nutso animal rights activist" and sees both as a direct threat to the Western way of life. The fact is, I'm not as radical in either of those areas as I ought to be. The sheer scale of the West—mountains and plateaus jutting a mile or two into the sky, canyons cutting equally deep and wide, desert dirt floor running endlessly—makes us believe the West is tough and strong and indestructible. It digs at that American part of us that needs to attack, conquer, and control anything that seems bigger and stronger than we are. And we have done just that to the West—we dammed and killed the rivers; we mined the guts out of many mountains and left them ravaged and defeated, others we stripped and left naked; we created alkali flats from overirrigation and dust bowls from overgrazing. We have proven that the West is not as tough and strong as it appears to be. And it is certainly not indestructible.

The damage done to the West does not rest solely with agribusiness, mining companies, and timber companies. We are all complicit. Those of us who live in dry states still do so with the expectation that the place will adapt to us instead of expecting that we should adapt to it, that it will soothe our Eastern sensibilities (even those of us who grew up in the West still have them) with greenery and water. One of Arizona's largest industries is tourism, and much of that tourism is based on the idea of "resort living." One of the most absurd, not to mention heartbreaking, things to watch is the conversion of the most beautiful desert in the world into golf courses and gated communities. Second to that absurdity is the significant number of Arizona homes with backyard pools, once considered a luxury in one of the driest states in the nation, now considered almost a necessity. How else would one survive in this desert? In the seventh year of a drought here, I've yet to see one golf green turn brown or one swimming pool drained dry. We simply list such things among the basic American rights in our pursuit of happiness.

In the state of Utah, my ancestors have done their own share of damage to the home they love so obsessively. The Mormons take quite seriously the Lord's directive to be fruitful and multiply and replenish the earth, and the Lord's promise that the desert will blossom like the rose for his chosen people. They've kept up both ends of that agreement to the point of straining their beloved home far beyond its arid capacities, and they show no signs of reversing this trend.

I know my father harbors the same love for the West that I do. The closest either of us can get to feeling at home on this earth is when we have our feet firmly sunk into chalky, alkali-crusted Western soil and our noses in the wind inhaling the sweet aroma of cow manure. But something in him—maybe that "rugged individualism" myth built so solidly by Western movies—won't let him recognize the damage we've done here. The acknowledgment is not easy. The pain of it keeps me from being a better activist on behalf of this land. Facing it every day, reading about it, writing about it, observing it, is like watching a seeping, infected wound that won't heal. Eventually it makes you sick to your stomach and you just want to turn away. I'm as guilty of this as my father.

WIDE, SWEEPING CURVES take me over the summit and down the other side. The bike and I sway smoothly from side to side in a slow dance, our rhythm perfectly matched. I relax onto the tank, drawn in by the scent of musky sage, by the music of the engine. We are alone and safe with each other, momentarily forgetting the possibility of interruption, letting the wind tear away all remnants of caution. Giving the practice of faith a try.

Too soon, the signs for South Pass City loom into view, and I'm jarringly dumped onto a gravel road as if shaken from a dream. I stop in the middle of the road to peer into the clear plastic cover of my tank bag for the directions to the Willie Handcart Company rescue site.

Now a pleasant little meadow cut through by the gurgling Rock Creek, here Captain James Willie gathered what was left of his ragged group of Saints and prayed with them. I can't imagine what a person might ask of God in such a prayer at such a point in time, knowing that God thus far had not seen fit to soften the extremes of agony and ordeal for this small sub-section of his chosen people. I close my eyes to picture them here in the meadow, skin barely covered by tattered clothing hanging on skeletal frames, such an easy mark for the biting wind and deepening snow. Of course they would gather to pray, and the prayer likely started the way all Mormon prayers start, by thanking the Lord for their many blessings, and likely ended with a testimony of faith in the Lord and belief in his two prophets: Joseph Smith and Brigham Young. What came in between barely matters—the only other option to praying being to lie down in the snow and die.

After the prayer, James Willie took one of the strongest men—having few to choose from—and they rode out on two skinny mules in search of help, knowing they had a very small window of time to get it. They rode hard through a blizzard for one full day and, by luck or God's hand, straight into the camp of the rescue team they didn't know had been sent from Salt Lake City. The rescue team members had stopped to wait out a blizzard they thought too severe for travel. Captain Willie told the rescuers there wouldn't be anyone left to rescue if they didn't go now, and they broke camp before daybreak.

Close to seventy members of the Willie Handcart Company are buried here and back along the trail. I sit for a bit in the small cemetery and listen to the shallow water tumble past me over its rocky creek bed. This gift of the West—solitude in the purest form I've ever known—always touches me. At times I barely know what to do with it, and this is one of those times.

From the moment I walk into the meadow along the creek, I feel a strong pull—or push—toward home, as if the hands of those who were left behind gently but persistently nudge me toward the valley—toward the religion—they died for.

AT THE SOLE gas station in the tiny town of Farson, Wyoming, I chat for a while with a familiar-looking cowboy about the best possible routes to Evanston. He looks like someone from my past, but I'm sure we've never met. He's simply the embodiment of my Western memories, all wrapped up in a pair of well-fit Wranglers and worn-out boots, leaning against his truck and watching hay leaves swirling in the breeze around the bed of his pickup.

Kitty-corner from the gas station sits a monument to mark the spot where Brigham Young and his boys met up with Jim Bridger and camped with him for a night. By this point, Brigham's group had been gathering information from trappers and mountain men they encountered on the trail, and they were vaguely considering the valley around the Great Salt Lake as a good spot for the promised land, mostly because it was so desolate no one else wanted to settle there—a perfect spot to build up the Kingdom of God in peace. About six miles back, most of the Gentile wagons had continued west to Oregon and California, but Brigham and his boys made a left turn and headed south, following the Hastings Cutoff, the trail that got the Donner Party into so much trouble.

According to Mormon folklore, Jim Bridger thought the Great Salt Lake Valley so uninhabitable he offered a thousand dollars for the first bushel of corn grown there. True or not, it's doubtful such a dare would have swayed the tenacious Mormons, except maybe to raise their dander just enough to prove him wrong. Bridger suggested the area farther south of the Great Salt Lake, known as Utah Valley, but it was the domain of the Ute Indians, and the Mormons had no desire to set down homes they'd be forced to fight for or flee yet again. (Several years later, having regrouped and feeling the strength of their numbers, the Mormons under Brigham's leadership—a man historian Bernard DeVoto called "the foremost American colonizer"—would settle without regard to prior domain throughout what is now Utah, Idaho, and parts of Arizona and Nevada. As DeVoto put it, "He [Brigham] was not gifted at seeing into the mysteries of heaven . . . but he saw into the making of society . . . the state of Utah is his monument.")

Although the Mormons took fastidious notes of the meeting between Bridger and Brigham—as they always did whenever their prophet held court—they left the next morning more bewildered than enlightened. Apparently Jim drank and talked in such quantities they had trouble distilling his wandering oration on his travels in the West down to useful information. So they went ahead to see for themselves.


HIGHWAY 28 CUTS through open range, a rarer and rarer sight in the West. Cattle meander along and across the road as if they barely notice the big tanker trucks barreling through, the drivers of which return the favor by paying equally scant attention to the cows. I cannot afford such luxuries. If I tangle with a cow, neither of us will fare well. I'm also on that part of the range where deer and antelope play—at least antelope—in big, easily spotted herds and not so easily spotted singles that dart across the road just as I reach them. I slow down to a speed that suits me and the animals but badly annoys the truck drivers, who careen around me recklessly as if I'm road debris.

The Green River floats under Highway 28 at the historical site of the Lombard Ferry crossing. Near here, Brigham's party camped—most of them sick with something they were calling mountain fever—for three days while they built a ferry to get themselves across the river, which at the time measured 264 feet wide. Brigham left a few men behind to operate a ferry business, which they did from that day in 1847 until 1856, the year Hannah would have been ferried across in the back of a rescue wagon.

I feel detached from this spot where I now stand in the grass on the bank of the slow-moving river, pausing in an obligatory sort of way as any tourist would because the place is listed on the things-to-see map. I'm unable to conjure up either the images or the spirit of the place, and I wonder at the possibility that my great-great-grandmothers passed this spot in the same way: numbed from the miles they had covered, tugged by the closeness of their final stopping place.

In an effort to avoid Interstate 80 for as long as possible, I find myself on a frontage road that dead-ends in the parking lot of the Little America hotel/restaurant/truck stop/gas station. After lunch, I take my ten-cent ice cream cone—the same price they were when I was ten—to a spot of lawn in front of my bike and pull my Wyoming and Utah maps from my tank bag. The wind carries strands of hair across my face and into the ice cream to be sucked into my mouth while I comedically tear at my face to pull them out. I keep adjusting myself on the lawn, stuffing maps under my knees, and expecting I will eventually get to a spot where I'm facing into the wind. I never do. Regardless, I manage to get tens cents' worth out of the ice cream, and from the maps figure it will take me about five good hours of riding to get home—home being my parents' house in Tooele, Utah. I could be there in time for dinner.

There's no folding the maps in the wind and I don't need them anyway—haven't really needed them since I crossed the Nebraska-Wyoming border, the line that in my mind and heart clearly delineates the West from the rest of the nation—so I crumple them and cram them into my tank bag, then struggle to catch all of my hair into a ponytail and secure it under my helmet liner. As I reach for my helmet, the liner blows off, forcing me to chase it across the parking lot. After three repeats of this, I step inside the nearby gift shop to accomplish the task in front of curious shoppers.

For some reason—probably my mind has clutched on to the thought of home at the expense of all else or is sopped down with nostalgic memories of ice cream and country-and-western music—this little bout with the wind prepares me not at all for what's to come. As I top the on-ramp to I-80 at around sixty miles per hour in an effort to squeeze myself between a semi-truck and RV, I'm hit with a blast of wind from the south and in a split second I find myself four feet to my right on the shoulder of the freeway. I carefully make my way back into the right lane and lean to my left, steeling myself for another blow. The next one hits me from the opposite side and I jump the white line into the left lane, which is fortunately empty. I pull back to the right in time to allow a trucker to barrel past me on a down-grade without ever having to hit his brakes. I squeeze the grips tightly, knowing the gust will hit hard as the truck passes, but in spite of my preparation, I'm again blown onto the shoulder. I feel disoriented and out of control, much like a piece of litter that gets picked up in a gust of wind and dropped down again in a different spot.

As I pull back onto the road, trying to maintain a speed around sixty miles per hour to keep myself from being killed in heavy truck traffic averaging around seventy-five miles per hour, my magnetic tank bag, which hasn't budged in more than fifteen hundred miles of travel, flies up and hits me in the chest. I bring my body down over it and treacherously let go of my left grip in an attempt to pull the magnetic panels back into place around the tank. The heavy magnets flip up and waver in the wind like they're made of Styrofoam.

As I hunker down over my tank bag to keep from losing it altogether, semitrucks roar by me on the downgrades, coming so close I hear chains clanking on their undersides and feel the pounding of the load bouncing atop the tires. I take gusts of wind from both directions, trying to give the bike enough freedom to jump back and forth within my lane but fighting to keep it from being blown and dragged into the underbelly of the truck. Those same trucks slow to a forty-miles-per-hour crawl on the upgrades, forcing me to go out around them, and in this game of leapfrog, we move down the freeway fifty or so miles to Evanston.

On the far end of town, wanting to be as close to the Utah border as possible before stopping, I pull into a gas station to regroup. As I come in next to the pump and drop my right leg to the ground, I realize quickly that my shaking leg is not going to hold the weight of the bike. I throw my hand up against the gas pump and catch the falling bike just in time. The gas spills out over the top of the tank while I'm gazing down the road at a motel sign, figuring that's about as far as I'm going on these nerves.

"Please tell me you have a room," I say to the desk clerk when I reach the motel. "I need to wait out this windstorm."

"Oh, honey," she says to me in a cigarette-induced raspy voice, looking as if she wants to reach out and put my face between her hands. "Did you just come west on I-80?"

I tell her I did.

"Oh, sweetie," she says with a chuckle and a look of pure pity. "There's no waiting out this storm. The wind's been blowing like that through here for one hundred years, maybe more." She apparently sees the look on my face and figures I might be near tears or worse. "Which way you headed from here?"

"South, down to Salt Lake City."

"I'll tell you what," she says cheerfully. "It ain't going to be quite as bad going down that way and the calmest it ever gets around here is first thing in the morning. You can leave the bike right there under the cover out of the wind if you want, and get an early start in the morning."

When I was in my early twenties, I worked at the Tooele Army Depot, another place where the wind blew steadily. We'd get out of the car with our big 1970s hairdos—moussed and sprayed—and by the time we reached the building the wind had reduced it down to the size of our scalps. We had a saying about the Tooele Army Depot, a place where the only thing more prevalent than the wind was apathy: "It's not that the wind blows out here; it's just that the whole place sucks." Right now, I feel that way about Evanston, Wyoming, with the exception of one very kind hotel clerk.

AT 6 A.M., the wind blows ice cold but, as promised, much lighter. I pack up quickly, debating whether to dress for cold— jacket liner, glove liners, winter gloves—or heat, which I'll get as soon as the sun gets high. I opt to go without liners, ride out the morning cold, and avoid having to stop an hour from now to strip off gear.

By 6:15, I'm shivering inside my jacket and berating myself for not putting in liners when I pass a sign welcoming me to Utah, and I'm immediately content to be exactly where I am:

sandwiched between two semitrucks—the one on my rear tire a little too close for comfort—in a one-lane construction zone on I-80 with numb, frozen fingers. I'm home.

THE OLD HIGHWAY 30 does not appear on my map but exists in my mind. The two-lane road I find off the next exit doesn't match the memory. It is narrower than I remember and suffering from neglect, filled with potholes and road debris. But as I ride through Echo Canyon, the sandstone canyon walls draw the cold and tension from my body.

Every morning of my trip soon after I start riding—as if to gently jostle me awake, as if to whisper in my ear, "Pay attention now"—I reach a place that touches me with unbearable tenderness. The Nauvoo temple bidding me farewell across the Mississippi River, the sun sliding over the Iowa cornfields, the mist-shrouded bluffs of Nebraska, the sweeping valleys butting up against the majestic mountains of Wyoming, and here, the narrow, welcoming canyons of my home.

I've come to expect it now. I start each morning with the warnings of motorcycling running through my head, reminding myself to be aware, to scan for potential hazards, to keep my head in the ride, to make sound decisions. Then I reach the place that drains all anxiety from my body and replaces it with something soft and generous. And there in that place all comes together; the requirements of motorcycling coalesce with the needs of the spirit. It flows naturally, subconsciously. The sun bounces from the canyon walls to flood my body with warmth, the bike purrs, and we glide among potholes effortlessly, not unaware of the danger but willing to trust the flow, willing to trust the generosity we've been offered. I believe it was the same for the women of my family who traveled this trail before me—each morning, a small practice of faith in the beauty of a single day, a single moment in a long journey.

The steep and narrow canyons of Utah—the last fifty or so miles of the two-thousand-mile trip—would prove to be the most severe for Brigham Young's lead party. Having split off entirely now from all Oregon- and California-bound wagon trains, they were on their own to pick a trail through the canyons, rivers, and willows that grew as thick and lush as Joseph Smith's hair. The Donner-Reed party had come down these canyons but hadn't left much of a trail. It was yet to be discovered that choosing this particular path had been the reason for their fatal late-season disaster in the Sierra Nevada. For Brigham's party, it would start out bad here in Echo Canyon and get considerably worse the closer they got to the Salt Lake Valley, as if God were demanding one final test, making sure his chosen people were still capable and worthy, before offering up the sacred place in which to build his kingdom.

By the time Hannah came through here packed into the back of a rescue wagon ten years later, a young daughter under each arm and kept warm by the bodies of her fellow travelers, the Mormons had moved so many wagons and Saints through these canyons that although the going was still very steep and rough, the worst part of her journey was behind her. Even though Hannah's passage through here was two months later in the year than mine, I like to think she felt the warmth of these canyon walls the way I do now.

The small town of Henefer, Utah, is just waking up as I roll through. On the other side of town, I share a narrow two-lane road with a few sheep and a herd of cows. Creeks cut through green pastures and the cows all walk slowly south—I'm sure to an expected feeding location—but they appear to be joining me on the last leg of my trip.

This stretch of thirty-six miles—from Henefer to the Salt Lake Valley—would take the Donner Party sixteen days; Brigham's lead party, six days. From Echo Canyon, I ride briefly into Weber Canyon, then into East Canyon and Main Canyon. The summit of Main Canyon, now called the Hogsback, was dubbed by early Saints as Heartbreak Ridge, a place where the road-weary travelers would get their first look at the massive Wasatch Range of the Rocky Mountains and understand that the harshest mountain crossing lay ahead, not behind them. They had no way of knowing what I know, that those mountains will reach around to meet up with the Oquirrhs and other ranges, and although the crossing may be harsh, once you are inside of them they will enclose and hold you like a mother's arms.

I climb into stands of spruce intermixed with aspen trees dressed in fall colors. Their vibrancy is dulled by years of drought, yet they hang on, as tenacious as the Saints settled in the valley below. The road begins to turn back on itself sharply but the flow stays with me. I slip through the switchbacks quietly, effortlessly. These are my roads, my canyons. I can't stop smiling.

From the summit, the drop to the Salt Lake Valley below is magnificent and must have looked near impossible to anyone intent on coming off it in wagons. But near impossible to the Mormons was only a minor inconvenience at this point. A story about a woman in the Martin Handcart Company, one of the few well enough to still be pulling a cart at this juncture, tells of her reaching a point such as this one, possibly even this exact spot, taking her cart full of belongings to the very edge, and giving it a little shove to send it crashing to the bottom of the canyon. She then strode on into the Salt Lake Valley to begin her new life unencumbered by the old.

At a pullout, I remove gloves and helmet, walk down off the west side of the gravel parking area into the grass, and find myself a rock in the sun to sit on. Tears flow freely. I feel overwhelming gratitude to some still-incomprehensible God for carrying me home.

# 26

A NARROW ROAD LINED WITH MAPLE AND BOX ELDER trees takes me down through Emigration Canyon and past Ruth's Diner, an old hangout of mine, to the turnoff that leads to a larger-than-life bronze sculpture of Brigham Young. He's flanked on either side by his counselors, Heber C. Kimball and Wilford Woodruff, and they stand atop a sixty-foot-high granite shaft overlooking the valley of Zion.

"THIS IS THE PLACE," say the words engraved in the granite below Brigham's feet. The story we heard as kids was that Brigham Young stood tall and strong upon this very spot above the valley and, after a moment with head bowed in consultation with his leader, loudly and proudly proclaimed, "This is the place." The real story is much less dramatic. In fact, Brigham was sick in the back of a wagon upon arriving here two days behind many of his counselors, and instead of standing and roaring like the lion of the Lord he was known as, he struggled to rise up on one elbow and gaze down at the valley below. The original record says only that he expressed his satisfaction with the valley as a resting place, but the retelling of the story to generations of Mormon children is a good and proper ending to the Mormon Trail, accurate or not.

I sit in Brigham's shadow on the grass surrounding the monument and dig the Nauvoo temple rock from my pocket to roll in my hands while I gaze down at Salt Lake City. The years since 1847 have seen an influx of non-Mormons into the valley, but the Mormons hang on to the city with a fierce grip. Temple Square, surrounded by several blocks of Church-owned buildings, remains the city's center, and Mormons reside here among the new Gentiles with the same disconcerting mix of smugness and meekness they've been carrying since Joseph's day.

Even during my most anti-Mormon phase, the Mormon propriety of Salt Lake City never bothered me as it did many of my non-Mormon friends. It always seemed right to me that the Mormons should hold sway over the city they built from the desert floor.

"This is the place," writes Stegner, "Mormons go away from and return to." A more accurate statement has never been placed in print, and in this way, I am undeniably Mormon. This is the place that lies at the core of my soul. Every thought I think, every choice I make, everything I am or hope to be can be traced back to this place, to these people. I am proud to find my essence here among the Saints. I belong here in this valley, here among the descendants of the fellow travelers of my great-great-grandmothers, but not within their fold. I don't have the faith of the modern Mormon woman who finds love and beauty here in spite of the Church leadership's disrespect for her intelligence and dismissal of her capabilities, the kind of faith that allows her to transcend the limitations of men. And I don't have the strength of the modern Mormon woman who toils tirelessly and against magnificent odds to create change, to

right the Church, to bring it back into a balance of partnership I believe early Church leaders once understood and respected in spite of the power they held.

I pull myself up from the grass and walk all the way around the eighty-four-foot-wide monument—typical in its pallid portrayal of the women involved in this trek—before kneeling at its base. I rub the temple stone between my hands and utter the words "Thank you" to the pioneering women of my family, especially those who stayed close by me on this trip—Maria, Anna Maria, and Hannah. The words seem too small for the enormous debt I feel toward them, but they would understand that; the words are altogether unnecessary. I let the temple stone slip from my fingers and it disappears, indistinguishable from the rest.

Here at the end of my journey, I feel as if I've done right by these women. I still can't claim to know much about God. I have not discovered how people gain an understanding and sustain a belief in God. However, I have been talking to God on a fairly regular basis since somewhere in Iowa. Call it prayer if you wish, but I'm not entirely sure it fits the definition. I've not "found God" in the way I've heard some describe it, no moment of joyous recognition where the answer to the large questions in my mind comes miraculously into focus. But I have put the remarkable gifts of my grandmothers to use and followed the clearly trodden path they made for me—one of exploration, of self-determination—a path each of them willingly risked their lives to go down. In return, they have changed me in subtle but profound ways. They have smoothed my edges and opened me up to a perceptible sliver of hope. They have taught me to live in peace with uncertainty, to stop demanding clarification, to embrace my own contradictions and just let them be. They have made the practice of faith possible.

• • •

THE ANGEL MORONI appears to me as if in a vision. Against the late-morning sky he hovers above the city from his perch atop the center spire of the Salt Lake temple, 210 feet in the air, horn at the ready to notify the Saints of the Second Coming of Christ. He stands 12 feet tall above the spire, made of copper dressed up in twenty-two-karat gold leaf, swaying slightly in the wind by weights attached to his feet and suspended inside the spire. I've always thought of the weights as keeping him not from tumbling to the ground but from ascending to heaven.

The temple was intended to be the very heart of Salt Lake City, and in spite of city sprawl and a more ecumenical population today it steadfastly holds that position. Built to be around during Christ's next visit regardless of when that might be, the solid granite walls are nine feet thick at the base, tapering off to six feet near the top. Six spires reach heavenward above 170 rooms that take up about 253,000 square feet of floor space. The architectural masterpiece of the ten-acre temple grounds took the Saints forty years to build.

West of the temple, the road spits me onto I-80 and past the Great Salt Lake. I long for the old two-lane cement road with its rhythmic cracks that once skirted the edge of the lake from the city to the west side of the Oquirrh Mountains, allowing a person to look across the water to infinity. Now on the safe and convenient freeway, I get only dissatisfyingly short glimpses of my childhood memories, but modern improvements have not been able to suppress the lake's fetidness, caused by decaying plant and animal remains along its shallow shores, and I suck in the familiar rotten-egg aroma as if I'm smelling daffodils.

The valley on the west side of the Oquirrhs, like an aging movie star, fights to keep its beauty, marred by one more housing development, one more superstore. As I enter my hometown, I'm immediately bombarded by a town I never knew and refuse to accept—Wal-Mart, Wendy's, McDonald's, Taco Bell, Kentucky Fried Chicken, Pizza Hut, Carl's Jr., Applebee's, Blockbuster, and others—clustered and growing like mold on the north end of Main Street. The town I know begins a few blocks south with a somewhat forlorn Main Street sporting a few shops and a few boarded-up windows. I turn right on Vine Street, past the park, my high school, and junior high school and on down to the end of Vine.

Splotches of grass nine or ten inches thick have taken advantage of the cracked concrete in the driveway of my white-brick childhood home, pushing the concrete up and over as if it were made of paper and a blade of grass made of muscle and brawn. My father now mows the driveway when he mows the rest of the grass, content to let the lawn and the driveway fight it out on their own terms. I bounce over the grassy veins and bring the bike to a stop in front of the closed garage door.

I expect any moment now, as I strip off glasses, helmet, liner, gloves, and jacket, that my mother—who has held a perpetual praying vigil the last three weeks for my safe return—will rush out the front door with tears in her eyes and hug my bug-splattered body. I expect my father will follow close behind, offer a strong but quick hug, then look around for someplace to put the bike before the neighbors see it. I slow the process to give them time to perform this ritual as I have envisioned it, but soon find myself standing alone in my T-shirt, so I walk around the side of the house to the sliding patio door and let myself in.

"I'm home!" I call out, and my words are quickly engulfed by the silent house.

"I'm home," I say, wandering from room to room. "I'm home safe, I'm alive and well, does anybody care?"

I pull my bags off the bike, take them downstairs to "my room," and change out of my riding pants into a pair of jeans. Out the backdoor, I see my father at the other end of the corral throwing hay to cattle. He sees me before I reach him and hollers out to me, "You made it!" He drops his pitchfork, climbs over the fence—still agile at seventy-three—strides toward me, and encloses me in a hug. He smells of sweat and cow manure, and tears well up in my eyes.

My father and I still disagree about most things, and he filled the first eighteen years of my life with his unspecified anger. The next eighteen years were filled with my anger at him. But somehow, without words, in the last few years my father and I have reached an accord. There's been no one illuminating moment of recognition and resolution, just a normal aging process between father and daughter. Apology, grace, and understanding happen in tiny gestures and brief moments.

"Your mother's uptown getting her hair done," he tells me, knowing that will be my first question, as it has been since I was old enough to speak.

"Oh."

"I need to finish feeding," he says. "I'll be done here in a few minutes."

"OK," I say and start back toward the house, but I'm still stuck on his words about my mother's whereabouts. I shuffle through the dirt back down to the house, feeling very much like the eight-year-old child whose mother went to the grocery store without her for the first time. I thought I had been traveling toward the state of Utah, I thought Salt Lake City was the end of my journey, but I wasn't quite right. On this entire trip, I've been doing exactly what the towheaded toddler was doing when her picture was snapped, searching frantically for the comfort of my mother's arms.

My mother's arms have been unconditionally open to me the entire forty-five years of my life. But twenty-five years ago, when I left the church she loves more than anything else of this world, I felt as if I had dropped a thin veil between us; nothing that could truly separate us, but something that would never again allow perfect unity as we had once known it.

From the darkness of the basement where I unpack my saddlebags, I hear the door slam above. I take the stairs two at a time and find her on the top step.

"You're home!" she shouts and pulls me into her arms. I feel the smooth dampness of her cheek next to mine.

"Your hair looks lovely," I tell her as we walk arm in arm into the kitchen. And, in fact, it does—gentle gray tufts frame her softly wrinkled, yet still beautiful, face.

"When did you get here?"

"About a half hour ago."

"Oh, I'm so glad you're home safe," she says, hugging me again.

"Yeah, me too."

"Are you hungry?"

"Yeah, I guess I am," I say, just realizing that I haven't eaten all day, never wanting to take the time to stop. She gets up and starts making us both a tuna sandwich.

"Mom?"

"Hm-hm?"

"You know I'm never going to join the Church again."

She turns and looks at me with an astonished look on her face. "Yes, of course I know that."

"And you're OK with that?"

Another astonished look. "Yes, of course."

The veil between us is utterly transparent from my mother's side. She's never felt it, never noticed it. She's never once talked to me about returning to the Church, never questioned that choice, my choice not to have children, or any other in my life.

The next day my mother and I drive into Salt Lake City. We wander the temple grounds as we always do whenever we go to the city together, both of us loving the pure beauty of the gardens. Arm in arm we walk around the temple in awe of its splendor, a building that she visits on a regular basis, a building I'm not allowed inside. Her face reveals a kind of peace and contentment I'm just beginning to understand.

"Have I been sealed to you?" I ask her, referring to the temple ritual that guarantees two people will be together in the next life.

"Of course," she says quietly.

# EPILOGUE

IN THE SPRING OF 2002, THE MORMON CHURCH PUT the finishing touches on the Nauvoo temple and held an open house for the general public, a common practice whenever the Church opens a new temple, before dedicating it and closing it off to all but those deemed worthy. The Nauvoo temple, however, drew uncommon crowds. The resurrection of the temple Joseph Smith had envisioned and helped build drew church members to Nauvoo from all over the world as if the prophet himself had been resurrected. My mother was among the crowd, clutching me by her side.

We had driven in a ridiculous fashion to get there—logging a couple of sixteen-hour days—so we could take a leisurely trip back to Utah via the Mormon Trail. As we entered Nauvoo from the south, as I had done before, my heart sank a little to see that the quiet little town I had encountered the previous fall was hopelessly buried beneath a noisy horde of Mormon tourists. My mother's vision, however, cut through the multitudes of faithful directly to the tree-lined streets and restored buildings of Joseph's city, and she burst into tears. I pulled the car to the side of the road within sight of the temple and joined her. Through the tears she stammered something about "Joseph" and "the beautiful city." She cried for a good, long time, and I didn't try to stop her tears or my own. That was one of the many things my trip along the Mormon Trail and my journey into my history had taught me—to accept those tears as a gift. My gut feeling is that this gift of easy tears goes back through the women of my family for many generations. I have spent my life trying to curb my propensity to cry, my free-flow of emotion, having been taught that such things are sure signs of weakness. But now I realize the opposite is true. The tears come from a deep place within me, a place formed by generations of women ancestors, a place that has much to teach me about myself. I would have been well served to welcome and pay attention to those spontaneous tears over the years instead of trying to stifle them.

My mother cried for Joseph, her prophet, upon seeing the place he built with his faithful followers. She cried for Joseph, the man, upon seeing the place where he walked and laughed and loved, upon seeing the place where he futilely sought refuge. She cried for Joseph's undeserved religious persecution; I cried for hers.

I've never witnessed a deeper love for a man than my mother's for Joseph Smith. I knew some of her tears that day in Nauvoo were caused by a feeling that she had somehow let him down during those years she was kept away from his church. From what I'd learned about Joseph during my journey, I think he had the capacity for compassion and understanding that would have let her off the hook for that, but I didn't say so. I knew the decisions she had made during those years still nagged at her, that she chided herself for being "weak," and at that time in Nauvoo I wanted her to shove those thoughts back down into the box labeled "unpleasant memories" and tape down the lid. I wanted our trip to Nauvoo, a place she had longed to see for most of her life, to be filled only with smiles and tears of joy.

A few months later, we sat at her kitchen table and I asked her why she made the choice to stay married after finding out it wasn't going to be the ideal Mormon marriage she wanted or anything remotely close. I asked her why she let my father keep her away from the church she loved so dearly. I'm not sure why I asked, knowing full well they were unfair questions, accusations really. On the cusp of her seventy-fifth birthday was not the time she should be asked to ponder such questions, now that she's made peace, such as it is, with her life. She should have told me to mind my own business, but she never would. The decisions she made during those years nag at me, as they do her, in an uncomfortable way, although I'm now at the age where I should be able to understand that, given her history and preparation, her beliefs and values, her family and religion, a different choice would have been inconceivable for a woman, a mother, of her generation and training. Yet I've faulted her for it. I suppose I'm a little angry with her for being sad so much of my life, a bit angry because I could not protect her from the pain of her own choices. I've made her difficult life more difficult with my insolence, and she shames me with her uncritical love, forgiving me over and over again.

MY MOTHER MOVED with reverence through the town where Joseph once lived, particularly the Carthage jail where he was held and eventually murdered. She dressed with great care the day we went through the temple, and I was struck by the difference between us that day. We both donned the white carpet-protective slippers over our dirty street shoes and walked through the temple arm in arm, led by an enthusiastic Mormon volunteer. But while I walked as an apostate, gawking at the temple's splendor and thinking that the rooms reminded me of fancy hotel ballrooms, my mother moved with a knowledge and confidence I seldom see in her. She carried that unique Mormon mix of exalted certainty and lowly meekness. She was in her element, among her people, sure of her place on this earth—and she was stunning. I walked by her side, humbled by her radiance.

As we left the temple, we were stopped on the nearest street corner by a "Christian" man handing out brochures disclaiming the evil cult of Mormonism. My mother's eyes filled with tears.

"Why do they have to do that?" she asked me with a choked voice and the lingering remnants of a century-and-a-half-old persecution. I know much of the outside world thinks Mormons are defensive about their religion, but given their history and the ongoing campaigns against them, I don't know how they could be otherwise.

"I don't know, Mom," I told her. "I don't know why they have to do that."


MY MOTHER SETTLED into the passenger seat with a look of peace and contentment as I drove her west along the Mormon Trail. I stole glances at her whenever I could, touched by her softness and by her unreserved trust in me. I did my best to challenge that trust by insisting on a picnic at Garden Grove in a strong, cold wind. I had planned it for so long—the two of us sitting on the grass in the very spot where her great-grandmother Maria roamed in her childhood years between

Nauvoo and Salt Lake City—and I was intent on the historic significance of it. So damn the cold spring winds; we were going to eat our smoked turkey sandwiches there in Garden Grove in spite of airborne potato chips and numb fingers. My mother indulged me by sticking her neck down into her zippered jacket, holding her can of Coke between her legs, sitting on her paper plate to keep it from blowing away, and eating her sandwich as quickly as humanly possible.

We entered Bridgewater, Iowa, in a steady, cool rain, which made it feel as if I had never left. I felt safe once again, sliding over the muddy roads in Gary's pickup truck to show my mother the small Mormon cemetery in the corner of a cow pasture. She struggled without complaint to bend her arthritic body low enough to climb through two tightly pulled strands of barbwire. I think Gary would have snipped those wires and come back to repair them later if he'd had a pair of wire cutters on him. He was kind with her, carefully taking her arm and helping her up the steep and slippery grade of the pasture. I was surprised to see a small fence—about two feet by four feet—had been built around those crumbling headstones, and I was deeply moved once again by the way the folks of Bridgewater, Iowa, care about my—and my mother's—history.

At Ash Hollow, I opened the car door on my mother's side for her to step out into the Nebraska sun and a take a walk to the top of the hill, but she hesitated. I saw in her face the overwhelming desire to please her daughter, but the desire was worn down by exhaustion. It broke my heart. On my motorcycle trip, it was here, alone on the crest of the hill at Ash Hollow, that the truths of myself and my journey had started to come into focus. I had looked forward to taking that walk with her hand in mine, to explain to her the reasons I could not return to the religion she loved more than her own life, to somehow find a way to reconcile the irreconcilable—her love for me with her love for the religion I continued to reject.

I saw at that moment—as if my eyes had suddenly matured from those of a child searching for its mother to those of a forty-five-year-old woman—the way rheumatoid arthritis had ravaged my mother's body. I had loved our walks together over the years and had insisted that she keep taking them with me under the pretense that it was good for her health. It might be, but the fact is I can't stand the thought of losing them. I need those walks just as surely as I needed my mother's comfort at age three.

The walk to the top of Ash Hollow was made long and arduous by her absence, and I realized then that it was time for me to start walking by her side instead of expecting she would walk by mine. This was made clear to me again in Sinks Canyon near Lander, where she did get out of the car and walk with me. I play it over again and again, that moment when she took a step back, not realizing the rock was behind her, that moment when the look of surprise and panic crossed her face as she fell awkwardly backward, striking the trail with her arm, hip, and knee. My stomach clutches now as I replay it in my mind. I suppose I started to move toward her, I suppose I started to speak, but it seems I was only capable of watching with horror. Her skin is paper-thin and tears like newsprint; it won't hold stitches and it never heals. As I watched the blood seep through the elbow of her jaunty purple-and-white-striped shirt, I felt as if my heart were bleeding all over the ground.

I'VE BEEN FEELING overly protective of my mother lately, bent on making the remainder of her life worry-free, at least as far as I'm concerned. It's an absurd notion; I'm incapable of living in a way that delivers it. I feel sometimes as if her main source of happiness comes from me, and I buckle under the burden of it. It forces me to try to live carefully so as not to cause her concern, but cautious living is not my strong suit. If it were in my power, I'd remove every bit of angst and worry from her final years and give her nothing but peace and beauty in its place, but alas, it is not.

My mother never stopped praying for me while I was on the motorcycle trip, and I'm sure she's still praying for me today. She prays for my safety, for my salvation, and most notably for my happiness. I think she worries that, by her example, she never taught me the pursuit of happiness or the expectation of joy. But I understand it now, and she'd be surprised to know that my happiness and joy come directly from what she did give me—although it remained buried until this journey demanded it and gently tugged it out of me—the practice of faith.

My mother has never stopped praying that I might find the same truth and beauty in Joseph's prophecy that she knows to be there. My place is not within the Mormon Church, that I now know with certainty. But my mother, along with her sisters and mother, and their mothers and grandmothers before them—through the quiet but persistent practice of Mormonism in a society that often considers them oppressed and brainwashed because of that practice—have taught me the essence of love and compassion, and most important, faith.

The journey along the trail and into my history changed me in ways that I'm still discovering. It sounds clichéd to say, "I found myself," but that is precisely what happened. I discovered that I possess a capacity for practicing faith as profound as that of my ancestors. From the outside, mine probably doesn't look the same as theirs. It might be unrecognizable even to my mother, who so closely associates the practice of her faith with the Mormon Church, but on the inside, it runs deep and strong and true, just like that of the women before me.

If asked if I believe in God, I would have to say yes, but I'm hesitant to call it that, hesitant to call it a "force" or a "higher power" or any of the euphemisms people have attempted to give it. My belief is not in the God of my childhood, is not in the God of the Mormon Church or the Catholic Church, or in the God of any Christian definition. That's where the practice of faith comes in. It allows me to stop trying to define God, stop trying to give God an image. It asks that I simply get comfortable with the mystery of God, the mystery of all life.

I'm still astounded by the practice of faith in a world filled with war and destruction, in a world where one species—my species—is driven by power and dominance over one another and over every other species, in a world where my species is quickly destroying its own habitat. In the face of this, my practice often falters. That's when I have to remind myself to stop searching so hard for it, that faith is not a "thing" you can hold tight to, it's more like a letting go, something you turn yourself over to.

I think my faith differs from that of my mother and my ancestors in one significant way: my practice of faith rests not in the promise of the heavens and the next life but in the earth and this life. I'm still struggling to understand it, and most times I can only try by becoming an observer of my own actions. Upon completing the motorcycle trip, I attempted to pick my life back up where I'd left it—in a modest house in the Sonoran Desert that I shared with my husband and three cats. But nothing was where I'd left it. Or more accurately, I was not where I'd left me.

As I wrote about my experience on the trail, I struggled to fit myself back into my own life, going through the daily motions as I had done for years. But the thoughts and feelings that had been dug out of me and dragged to the surface could not be shoved back in. Simply put, the contents of my consciousness had changed. I now lived each day in a way that put me at philosophical odds with the man I loved. Gradually, I became aware that staying demanded accommodations I could not offer with sincerity, and it put us at risk of damaging a friendship that had been strong for more than seventeen years. For many months, we refused to acknowledge what we both knew to be true—we were no longer good partners for each other. One evening I suggested to him that if we really loved each other as we claimed to do, then we should let each other go. Tears of relief flooded his eyes; we both knew immediately it was the right thing.

I was stunned by my own action and further stunned when this one monumental act seemed to trigger a series of losses in my life. The following year was filled with friends unexpectedly leaving town, many tears, and some doubt. But underneath the flurry of my life, if I sat quietly for a good, long while, something hummed reassuringly. When the last friend left town, I felt something settle. I instinctively knew the losses had subsided, and I consciously opted to trust something I am at a loss to name, knowing it will subtly guide me from this point forward. All I have to do is be aware of it, trust it, and refrain from demanding that it be analyzed and explained. The practice of faith.

In another significant way, my faith parallels that of my ancestors: it is steeped in and nurtured by the geography of Utah. It calls me home. I need the splendor of the Wasatch Mountains and the stillness of the Utah deserts. I need to dig in the same dirt that my ancestors dug; I need to walk the streets of the city they helped build. Utah is a peculiar place, but it's my place. Utah has always had a claim on me, and I've fought against it my entire life, thinking a return to Utah would mean a return to the Mormons. In a way, I guess I am returning to the Mormons—not to their church or their religion but to them, and that suits me. Fact is, I like Mormons, and I know an awful lot of them.

I'm also returning to my mother's arms. I tell myself that she'll need me as the years pass and her body continues to age. I'll be nearby to open jars and write grocery lists when the arthritis becomes too painful. I'll be there to carry baskets of laundry up the stairs when she's short of breath. I'll be where she can see me and talk to me and know that I'm safe so she won't have to worry about me. That's what I tell myself.

But the real truth is that I need her. I need her to walk with me through the gardens of the temple grounds with her arm looped through mine as she tells me the names of the flowers through as many seasons as we have left to us. I need her by my side in darkened movie theaters and on drives up Emigration Canyon. If it makes her smile, she might even get me to go to church with her once in a while. The reverent child who used to sit quietly in the back is long gone. But I'll be on my best be-havior and try, in my own bumbling way, to be even a fraction of the woman seen through her forgiving eyes.

# BIBLIOGRAPHY

I DID NOT SET OUT TO WRITE A HISTORICAL TEXT OF Mormonism or of the Mormon Trail, and if that's what one is looking for, there are far better sources than this book. The story I tell here is mine alone, but as far as it is determined by the men and women of Mormonism, I have attempted to fairly and honestly set down what I believe to be accurate.

The amount of literature covering Mormonism and the Mormon Trail is staggering. In addition, much of it is contradictory and unreliable; even the journals of the time period have often been written with a bent toward demonizing the Mormons or whitewashing the Mormons, depending upon the author's disposition. My own biases are duly noted and will be obvious in the reading of this book.

While I have waded into the sea of documents available to me, I have let others before me do the real work of researching and writing down Mormon history, while I stayed in the shallow end, for as Wallace Stegner put it while trying to do his own Mormon research, "The more one wades into this morass, the deeper he is mired and the farther from firm ground. There *is* no firm ground here." Because my intent was not to write history but instead to discover my own, I have relied upon those historians and writers I deem to be trustworthy and whose work seems to have withstood the test of time (though not without some controversy): Leonard J. Arrington, Fawn M. Brodie, Bernard DeVoto, and Wallace Stegner.

I made several attempts at trying to reach Church officials by phone to discuss this point or that, mostly in an effort to understand the Church's current official views on the status of women in the Church, and was always rebuffed with the utmost politeness. I did have access to the Church library and Church archives without question—as would any member of the general public who wanted to use them, as far as I could tell—and the folks who worked there went out of their way to help me find what I needed.

Because this is not a historical text, I have not attempted to cite bibliography by chapter and page. Throughout the book, I have extracted at times specific details and at times a general understanding of the time and place I was writing about from the following sources:

Arrington, Leonard J. & Davis Bitton. *The Mormon Experience*, 2nd ed. Chicago: University of Illinois Press, 1992.

Beecher, Maureen Ursenbach, ed. *The Personal Writings of Eliza Roxcy Snow.* Logan: Utah State University, 2000.

Brodie, Fawn M. *No Man Knows My History.* New York: Knopf, 1945.

Bushman, Claudia, ed. *Mormon Sisters.* Logan: Utah State University Press, 1997.

Carter, Kate, ed. *Heart Throbs of the West.* Salt Lake City: Daughters of Utah Pioneers, 1947.

Chatterley, Matthew L. *Wend Your Way.* Ames: Iowa State University Press, 2000.

Chittister, Joan. *In Search of Belief.* Liguori, MO: Liguoir: Triumph, 1999.

DeVoto, Bernard. *The Year of Decision, 1846.* New York: Truman Talley Books, 1943.

Godfrey, Kenneth W., Audrey M. Godfrey, and Jill Mulvay Derr, eds. *Women's Voices, An Untold History of the Latter-Day Saints, 1830–1900.* Salt Lake City: Deseret Book Co., 1982.

Hanks, Maxine, ed. *Women and Authority, Re-emerging Mormon Feminism.* Salt Lake City: Signature Books, 1992.

James, William. *The Varieties of Religious Experience.* New York: Touchstone, 1997.

Smart, Donna Toland, ed. *Mormon Midwife, the 1846–1888 Diaries of Patty Bartlett Sessions.* Logan: Utah State University Press, 1997.

Stanton, Elizabeth Cady. *Eighty Years & More.* New York: Schocken, 1971.

Stegner, Wallace. *The Gathering of Zion.* Lincoln: University of Nebraska Press, 1964.

The Church of Jesus Christ of Latter-day Saints Archives, Salt Lake City, Utah. Emma James Papers, Elizabeth Horrocks Jackson Kingsford Papers, Ella Campbell Papers, Letter of Elizabeth Sermon.

Ward, Maxine Carr, ed. *Winter Quarters, the 1846–1848 Life Writings of Mary Haskin Parker Richards.* Logan: Utah State University Press, 1996.

www.mormon.org. The official website of The Church of Jesus Christ of Latter-day Saints.

# ABOUT THE AUTHOR

Jana Richman recently left Tucson
and now lives in Salt Lake City.